# Fundamentals of Menu Planning

# Fundamentals of Menu Planning

**THIRD EDITION**

by

Paul J. McVety

Bradley J. Ware

&

Claudette Lévesque Ware

WILEY

John Wiley & Sons, Inc.

Copyright © 2009 by John Wiley & Sons, Inc. All rights reserved.

Published by John Wiley & Sons, Inc., Hoboken, New Jersey.

Published simultaneously in Canada.

For general information on our other products and services, or technical support, please contact our Customer Care Department within the United States at 800-762-2974, outside the United States at 317-572-3993 or fax 317-572-4002.

Wiley also publishes its books in a variety of electronic formats. Some content that appears in print may not be available in electronic books.

For more information about Wiley products, visit our Web site at http://www.wiley.com.

Library of Congress Cataloging-in-Publication Data

McVety, Paul J.
   Fundamentals of menu planning / by Paul J. McVety, Bradley J. Ware, & Claudette Lévesque Ware—3rd ed.
      p. cm.
   Includes bibliographical references and index.
   ISBN: 978-0-470-07267-7 (paper)
   1. Menus. 2. Food service. I. Ware, Bradley J. (Bradley John), 1953- II. Lévesque Ware, Claudette. III. Title.
   TX911.3.M45M38 2009
   642' .5—dc22                                           2007021310

Printed in the United States of America

10  9  8  7  6  5  4  3  2

# Contents

## Chapter 3  Nutrition and Menu Planning 37

## Chapter 4  Foodservice Menus 61

## Contents

# Preface

UNDERSTANDING the fundamentals of menu planning is essential to building a successful foodservice concept since the menu is ultimately the foundation upon which a foodservice operation builds both its reputation and profit. It is important to develop a workable, quality menu if your foodservice operation is to be profitable.

The menu is the focal point of any foodservice establishment. Therefore it is imperative that anyone entering the field has a solid background in all aspects of menu planning to succeed in a competitive environment. This is the primary reason why we wrote *Fundamentals of Menu Planning*. There are several menu planning books available that provide the reader with valuable information on managing the menu from a profitable standpoint but they do not necessarily cover all the topics that a student or professional needs to know in order to create a successful menu such as menu trends, the market, nutrition, the yield test, recipe costing, interpreting sales history, writing the menu, and merchandising the menu. Our goal with this book is to provide students, chefs, restaurateurs, and other foodservice professionals a comprehensive and up-to-date guide to all key aspects of menu planning. This text includes valuable resources for planning effective and successful menus, including concept development, design mechanics, menu pricing, market trends, and research.

Each chapter contains an introduction, learning objectives, highlighted key terms, review and discussion questions, and practice problems where appropriate.

We have extensively revised this *Third Edition* to address the issues and needs of today's foodservice industry by providing information on menu trends that have evolved since the second edition was published. This revision also contains new menus that represent a cross section of hotels and restaurant operations from across the country.

The content in this edition is divided into three parts. Part 1 focuses on the evolution of the menu and includes topics such as menu trends in the industry, performing market research and creating a market survey, nutrition and dietary guidelines, and menu planning. Part 2 examines the financial aspects of menu planning such as performing a yield test, creating and writing standardized recipes, and recipe costing. Part 3 covers writing, designing, and merchandising the menu. Topics such as selecting paper, type of printing, and color combination choices for menus are discussed, as well as principles of maintaining a balance, variety, composition of menu choices, descriptive copy, and truth-in-menu are discussed. This section also covers liquor and wine lists and descriptions of appetizers, soups, salads, sandwiches, entrées, specials, and desserts. Sales history and equipment analysis also appear in this third section since you need to establish the menu in order to earn a profit, interpret sales history and the effectiveness of menu engineering, and conduct an equipment analysis.

As instructors, we're constantly faced with the challenge of engaging our students in the subject matter. In addition to a thoroughly revised text, there are numerous tables and work forms to assist menu planners and additional pedagogical tools for teaching and learning. We are enthusiastic about this third edition of **Fundamentals of Menu Planning** and believe that it can serve as a practical and informative resource for both students and culinary professionals.

## New to this Third Edition

- Chapter 1 which has been renamed *Menu Trends in the Foodservice Industry* has been completely revised to reflect trends in menu development and analysis that have come into play since the last edition of this text.

- Chapter 2: *Market Survey* includes updated information, reflecting market survey trends that have recently emerged.

- Chapter 3: *Nutrition and Menu Planning* contains additional material on phytochemicals, antioxidants, dietary guidelines and recommendations, menu labeling laws, and examples of Food Pyramids, from around the world with their respective guidelines for dietary recommendations.

- An expanded collection of menus from various hotels and restaurants that are located throughout the country provide examples of à la carte, semi à la carte, prix fixe, brunch, special occasion, catering, institutional, and tea menus, to name a few.

- New menus have also been incorporated to illustrate balance, variety, composition, descriptive copy, and merchandising, considerations needed to develop a profitable menu.

- A more extensive appendix includes an expanded list of culinary terms and the most up to date versions of the National Restaurant Association's *A Practical Guide to the Nutritional Labeling Laws for the Restaurant Industry* and *Accuracy in Menus* guidelines.

- An increased number of practice problems have been incorporated, where appropriate, to reinforce student understanding of the key concepts presented.

## Additional Resources

- The ***Instructor's Manual*** (ISBN 978-0-470-25734-0) contains review exercises intended to be used as quizzes or as review exercises for each chapter. Problems that can be utilized as a take-home assignment or as an in-class activity, and suggested projects that may be modified or expanded by the instructor to best fit the abilities of students, are also presented. These projects, can also serve as individual or group in-class or take-home activities. Please contact your John Wiley & Sons representative for a copy of this resource.

- A ***Companion Website*** *(www.wiley.com/college/mcvety)* provides readers with additional resources, such as original menus from nationwide restaurants and relevant web links. In addition, downloadable electronic files are available to qualified instructors for the resources provided in the printed Instructor's Manual.

We are extremely excited about this new and improved ***Third Edition*** of ***Fundamentals of Menu Planning*** and feel that this revision continues to accommodate the needs of an extensive and diversified audience whose goal is to successfully design and implement an attractive and profitable menu.

## Acknowledgments

We would like to thank the following instructors for their insightful feedback during the course of their review of our revised ***Third Edition*** manuscript:

Jessica Backus-Foster, SUNY, Delhi
Eric Breckoff, J. Sargeant Reynolds Community College
Mary Rhiner, Kirkwood Community College
Diane Withrow, Cape Fear Community College

# Part 1

# EVOLUTION OF THE MENU

# Chapter 1

# NEW TRENDS IN THE FOODSERVICE INDUSTRY

PLANNING a profitable menu requires an extensive knowledge of food trends. This chapter explores each of the menu categories: appetizers, soups, salads, sandwiches, entrées, pastas and pizzas, accompaniments, desserts, and beverages, as well as current offerings in these classifications. The menu selections and their presentation are from some of the finest dining establishments in the United States.

## Objectives

- ❏ To introduce the student to current trends in the foodservice industry

- ❏ To delineate the various menu classifications and their offerings

- ❏ To provide the student with a collection of current industry menu items and their descriptive copy

# Foodservice Trends

THROUGHOUT the foodservice industry, chefs are utilizing indigenous ingredients from local farmers and purveyors. As early as the 1960s, Alice Waters, owner of Chez Panisse® in Berkeley, California, emphasized the importance of seasonality and the freshness of ingredients by promoting the purchase and use of products from local growers and purveyors. Today this trend has exploded throughout the foodservice industry in the United States, and chefs in fine dining restaurants, hotels, inns, and taverns are using local ingredients.

The menu of the Harraseeket Inn's Broad Arrow Tavern®, in Freeport, Maine, lists the local ingredients used in the menu items and from whom they are purchased. The lobster used in the lobster roll, for example, is purchased from Potts Harbour Lobster Co. located in Harpswell, while the beef and pork are supplied by Wolf's Neck Farm in Freeport.

At Green's Restaurant® in San Francisco, chef Annie Somerville supports local growers and purveyors and features products from the Green Gulch, Zen Center's Organic Farm in Marin, California. The chef uses Green Gulch beets, kale, lettuce, spinach, and fresh herbs and potatoes. The restaurant's Three Beet Salad and Spinach Salad contain only local ingredients.

Baby boomers throughout the country, with their sophisticated palates and culinary prowess, are demanding quality ingredients in meals offered at dining establishments that they frequent. This trend has been seen primarily in fine dining establishments where the price of items on the menu is inconsequential to guests. Fine dining restaurants, hotels, and spas throughout the United States have been diligent in answering these needs by acquiring the finest ingredients throughout the world. Restaurant Daniel® in New York City uses Muscovy duck in its Terrine of Muscovy Duck "à l'Orange." Chef Daniel Boulud also serves Caspian Sea Caviar and Roasted Colorado Loin of Lamb with Stewed Fennel.

At the Willard Intercontinental® in Washington, DC, the chefs prepare a Foie Gras accompanied by Port Wine Jelly and Black Winter Truffles. Entrées include Dover Sole, Chilean Sea Bass, and Maine Lobster, expensive choices that are offered at many white-tablecloth establishments across the country.

Another trend that is prevalent in the foodservice industry is a focus on healthy menu items that meet client demands. In the last few years, the number of spa resorts throughout the United States and abroad has increased substantially. These operations frequently offer their guests healthy menu items and in some cases provide a nutritional analysis of each menu offering.

At the Canyon Ranch Health Resort & Spa® in Tuscon, Arizona, chefs offer healthy breakfast menu choices, such as Peach Pear Smoothies with Protein Powder, Three Egg-White Omelets with a Vegetable Filling and Low-Fat Cheese, and Golden Flax Seed Breads (Fig. 1-1).

At the CuisinArt Resort & Spa® in Anguilla, chef Daniel Orr and chef de cuisine Christopher Heath create delicious organic and hydroponic salads made with ingredients from their own gardens. The resort also features black-eyed peas, Caribbean callaloo, Chinese longbeans, peppers, pumpkins, and soybeans. The resort's gardens and orchards produce avocados, guavas, limes, oranges, and star fruit, plus other healthy accompaniments. Perhaps the most popular entrée at this legendary spa is the Basil-Marinated Spiny Lobster. Other entrées include fish from local waters, steaks, poultry, pastas, and pizza.

Although most popular on upscale dining menus, healthy food items are also seen on other foodservice industry segment menus. Dinner houses such as Applebee's Neighborhood Grill & Bar®, T.G.I. Friday's®, and Uno Chicago Grill®, just to name a few, are also answering requests for healthy offerings. Applebee's Neighborhood Grill & Bar® formed a partnership with Weight Watchers International Inc., a few years ago and introduced a select number of food items that carry the Weight Watchers' logo on the menu, such as the Grilled Tilapia with Mango Salsa, and a Tango Chicken Sandwich. T.G.I. Friday's® has developed a variety of Atkins low-carbohydrate menu items, including a Tuscan Spinach Dip, a Grilled Buffalo Chicken Salad, and Shrimp Key West.

Even quick-service or fast food industry restaurants now offer healthy alternatives for the more health-conscious segment of the population. Taco Bell® allows customers to order a number of entrées "free style," where the traditional cheese and sauce can be replaced with fiesta salsa. The Beef Crunchy Taco, Bean Burrito, and Chicken Fiesta Burrito are some of these items. McDonald's® Chef, Garden, Grilled Chicken Caesar, and McSalad Shaker salads, as well as the Fruit'n Yogurt Parfait with or without granola, also accommodate the health-conscious consumer.

# Appetizers

Appetizers are the prelude to the meal. They are generally spicy and are served with either wine or a cocktail. Appetizers can be either hot or cold. Customers expect a variety of appetizer offerings on the menu that appeal to many tastes. Appetizers might include beef, fish or seafood, poultry, vegetables, and fruit choices. Throughout the food industry today, appetizers have a global flare.

**Figure 1-1. Breakfast Menu**

# Breakfast

## Balanced Selection

| | Calories | Fat grams | Fiber grams |
|---|---|---|---|
| Three Egg-White Omelet | 115 | 5 | 1 |
| With vegetable filling & low-fat cheese | | | |
| ▲ Golden Flax Seed Bread | 125 | 2 | 2 |
| ▲ Fresh Fruit Plate | 120 | tr | 6 |

### The perfect combination of great taste and good nutrition

• Generous amounts of vegetables and fruits
• Variety of fiber-rich foods such as whole grains and beans
• Foods high in protein at each meal
• Small amounts of healthy fats such as olive oil, nuts and flax seeds
• Delicious flavors in moderate, satisfying portions

## Juices

• ▲ Cranberry Juice Nectar   55/tr/0
• ▲ Grape Juice   55/0/0
• ▲ Grapefruit Juice   50/tr/tr
• ▲ Apple Juice   70/tr/0
• ▲ Orange Juice   55/tr/tr
• ▲ Tomato Juice   20/tr/tr
• ▲ Pomegranate Juice   65/tr/tr

*The serving size of all juices is 4 oz.*

## Fruits

• ▲ Cantaloupe (1/4)   50/tr/2
• ▲ Honeydew (1/8)   60/tr/tr
• ▲ Grapefruit (1/2)   40/tr/tr
• ▲ Banana (1/2)   60/tr/2
• ▲ Stewed Prunes (3)   100/tr/2

## Entrees

WHOLE-WHEAT PANCAKES (3)   345/8/4
    Choice of blueberry, apple or mango,
    served with maple syrup

MESQUITE FLOUR PANCAKES (3)   335/7/4
    With maple syrup

FRENCH TOAST   350/9/3
    With maple syrup & walnuts

LOX AND BAGEL   245/6/2
    With low-fat cream cheese

HOT STEEL-CUT OATS   160/3/8

ALPINE MUESLI   275/9/6

CAJUN POACHED EGG**   230/11/2
    Served in a bowl with spicy tomato andouille sauce
    and sprouted multi-grain toast

THREE EGG-WHITE OMELET   45/tr/tr
    With 1 whole egg & 2 egg whites   105/5/tr
    With vegetable filling   15/tr/1
    & low-fat cheese   55/5/tr

SCRAMBLED, POACHED OR HARD-BOILED EGG**
75/5/0

## Accompaniments

Breakfast Sausage Link (1)   70/3/tr
▲ Peach Pear Smoothie   190/tr/5
    With protein powder   *
Low-Fat Cottage Cheese   40/1/0
Nonfat Yogurt
    Plain   65/0/tr
    Fruit   85/0/tr
Low-Fat Cream Cheese   45/4/0
Almond Butter Delight   65/4/tr
    A blend of almond butter, nonfat ricotta,
    vanilla & honey
▲ Fruit Preserves   30/tr/1
▲ Apple Butter   50/tr/1

## Breads

Fresh Muffin of the Day   *
Fresh Gluten-Free Muffin of the Day   *
Zucchini Bread   100/3/1
Banana Bread   125/5/1
▲ Golden Flax Seed Bread   125/2/2
▲ Sprouted Multi-Grain Bread   90/tr/1
▲ Rice Bread (gluten-free)   165/5/2
▲ Bagels (1/2)
    Plain   160/1/2
    Honey Grain   165/1/2
    Pumpernickel   165/1/3

Calories/Fat Grams/Fiber Grams   tr = trace (less than 1 gram)   ■ Contains a trace of alcohol   ▲ Vegan (contains no animal products)   • Spicy
* Please ask your server for today's selection, its calorie count, fat grams and fiber grams
Please let your server know your time restrictions. If you have food allergies and are interested in an ingredient list, please ask your server.

**NO SALT ON THE TABLE?**
OUR CHEFS DO USE A MODERATE AMOUNT OF SALT WHEN PREPARING OUR RECIPES TO ENHANCE THE FLAVOR OF THE FOOD. IF YOU WOULD LIKE A LITTLE MORE, ASK YOUR SERVER FOR A SALT SHAKER.

**Courtesy of Canyon Ranch Health Resort, Tucson, AZ**

At NAHA® in Chicago, chef/owner Carrie Nahabedian has created a number of appetizers that reflect a universal theme. The lounge menu features the NAHA Mezze, which consists of Hummus Babaganoush, Pita Bread Crisps, Armenian String Cheese, Kalamata Olives, Mediterranean Greek Salad, Feta Cheese Turnovers, and Spiced Beef. The dinner menu has selections such as Tartare of Hawaiian Yellowfin Tuna, Door County Golden Whitefish Caviar, and Cured Tasmanian Ocean Trout with a Mosaic of Niçoise Garnishes, Aigrelette Sauce, and Toasted Brioche. The Cannelloni of Delicate Squash is made with Hedgehog Mushrooms, "Melted" Leeks, Italian Frisee and Chives, and Apple Cider Brown Butter.

Dinner houses and family-style restaurants are also serving appetizers with a global theme. Applebee's Neighborhood Grill & Bar® serves Thai Chicken Pizza and T.G.I. Friday's® prepares Zen Chicken Pot Stickers, which are fire-grilled dumplings stuffed with minced chicken and vegetables sprinkled with pico de gallo and served with a sweet and tangy Szechwan dipping sauce. At Ruby Tuesday®, Crispy Buffalo Wontons are served with bleu cheese dressing and crunchy celery sticks for dipping.

Perkins Restaurant & Bakery®, a popular family restaurant, serves Santa Fe Mini Chimis, crispy flour tortillas stuffed with smoked chicken, black beans, corn, jalapeño Jack cheese, red peppers, and spinach with ranch dressing. Chili's Grill & Bar® has also created appetizers with an Asian influence. Selections include: Southwestern Eggrolls made with smoked chicken, black beans, corn, jalapeño Jack cheese, red peppers, and spinach wrapped inside a crispy flour tortilla with an avocado ranch dipping sauce. The Boneless Shanghai Wings, which are crispy breaded chicken breasts topped with sweet and spicy ginger-citrus sauce and sesame seeds, are served with a spicy-cool wasabi-ranch dressing for dipping.

# Soups

Soups are generally presented after the appetizers on a menu. They are offered hot or cold, and are classified as clear or unthickened, thick, and specialty. Clear soups encompass bouillons, broths, consommés, and vegetable soups. Thick soups consist of bisques, chowders, creams, potages, and purées. Specialty soups are linked to national or regional cuisines, such as French onion, gumbo creole, gazpacho, or vichyssoise. Restaurants throughout the industry are serving traditional soups that are hearty and are representative of comfort foods. Customers are also demanding healthy, tasty, and creative soups.

At Antoine's® in New Orleans, the menu lists eight soups that are classical, varied, and unique. They include Gumbo Créole, Bisque de crevisses cordial, Consommé chaud au vermicelle, Vichyssoise, Bisque de crevettes, Potage alligateur au sherry, Consommé froid en tasse, and Soupe à l'oignon gratinée. Each of the soups may be purchased by the cup or the bowl.

The chefs at Canyon Ranch Health Resort® have created soups that have a nutritional flare. Caribbean Plantain, Miso, Chicken Noodle, and Gazpacho are some of these creations. Each of these soups is hearty and made with fresh vegetables, herbs, and spices.

"Old-fashioned," "traditional," and "large portions" are words that best describe the soups at Uno Chicago Grill®. The French Onion, Broccoli and Cheddar, Mrs. O'Leary's Clam Chowder, Veggie Soup, Mom's Old Fashioned Tomato Soup, Windy City Chili, and Chicken and White Bean Soup are all a meal in a bowl.

# Salads

SALADS are also prepared hot or cold and may be served as an accompaniment or as a main course or entrée on the menu. Sometimes a salad is served in lieu of an appetizer or soup and is called a first-course salad. Generally first-course salads include poultry, fish and seafood, specialty meats, and fruits or vegetables. In fine dining establishments the first-course salad is usually light and simple, consisting of mixed greens with a light vinaigrette. Main-course or entrée salads are usually served cold. Caesar Salad with Gulf Shrimp, Duck Salad with Asian Vegetables, or a Fruit Salad with Cheeses and Specialty Meats are all popular options. At fine dining restaurants, the first-course salad has remained simple and light in preparation and presentation. Many of these establishments serve a salad of baby greens with a light vinaigrette, enhanced with goat cheese, Bosc pears, and candied pecans, or a garden salad of fresh vegetables. The main function of these salads is to cleanse the palate.

Entrée salads are showing up on restaurant menus as healthy alternatives for customers who prefer a lighter fare. At the Waldorf=Astoria® in New York City, the chefs at Oscar's® serve a variety of nutritious low-carbohydrate salads at lunchtime. These include the Julius Caesar, Orange-Basil Shrimp Salad, and the Seared Yellow Fin Tuna Niçoise. Other main-course salads are the Spicy Chicken Asian Salad, Spinach Cobb Salad, Warm Goat Cheese Tart, and the South of the Border Salad.

Chefs at Commander's Palace® in Las Vegas prepare creative salads with a twist, such as the Creole Seasoned Gulf Shrimp Salad of grilled jumbo shrimp, romaine lettuce, an anchovy-garlic emulsion, garlic-roasted French bread croutons, marinated anchovies, and shaved Three Sisters Farmstead Serena cheese. The Commander's Blue Crab Cobb Salad with crisp greens, Gruyère cheese, brioche croutons, apple-smoked bacon, tomato, chopped egg, dressing, and fresh Louisiana jumbo lump crabmeat is also a very popular item.

Restaurant chains are now preparing main-course salads with an Asian influence using healthy ingredients. Houlihan's®, at various locations, offers nutritious salads, such as the Rare Asian Tuna Salad and the Oriental Grilled Chicken.

Burger King® has the Tendergrill™ Garden Salad of grilled chicken breast, fresh lettuce, grape tomatoes, baby carrots, red onions, cucumbers, and Parmesan cheese, garnished with Parmesan toast and a choice of dressing.

# Sandwiches

LUNCHEON patrons may choose hot or cold sandwiches in lieu of an entrée. Sandwiches of beef, fish or seafood, poultry, vegetables, and fruits are all popular. They can be as simple as a hamburger with cheese or as sophisticated as the Maine Lobster Roll made with Fresh Lobster meat on a brioche with mixed salad greens, and a rémoulade sauce, which is served at the Oak Room in the Fairmont Copley Plaza® in Boston.

Despite the variety of creative sandwiches offered today, the most popular sandwich is still the hamburger. Restaurants serve variations on "the burger" utilizing high-end ingredients to entice patrons. Ruby Tuesday® prepares over 20 different types of hamburgers using ground beef, ground turkey, range-fed bison, and lean chicken breast. Such offerings include the Black and Blue Burger, the Mushroom Swiss Turkey Burger, the Bison Bacon Cheeseburger, and the Hickory Chicken Burger. Emeril's® luncheon menu at the Walt Disney World® Resort in Orlando, Florida, serves a Kobe hamburger with homemade sea salt and vinegar chips, shaved iceberg lettuce, tomatoes, and pickles. In Monterey, California, the Blue Moon® restaurant's lunchtime menu includes an American Kobe® Burger with sautéed mushrooms, onions, and hot mustard aioli on a toasted onion roll with garlic fries.

Foodservice operations are also introducing creative grilled and toasted sandwiches on their menus. Panera Bread® has created a number of sandwiches on a variety of freshly baked breads and rolls that use high-quality meats, cheeses, and vegetables. Two of the many creative Panera® signature sandwiches are the Fontega Chicken Panini® with red onions, mozzarella cheese, tomatoes, chopped basil, chipotle mayonnaise, grilled hot on a rosemary and onion focaccia, and the Pepperblue Steak® of tender, slow-roasted steak filets with a gorgonzola toasted red pepper sauce, lettuce, tomatoes, and onions, between two slices of freshly toasted ciabatta bread. Patrons who prefer a meatless sandwich can select the Garden Veggie or the Tuna Salad.

The upscale Laurel Grill & Bar®, in Boston serves a variety of unique grilled sandwiches, including the Smoked Turkey and Bacon Sandwich with iceberg lettuce, tomatoes, and tarragon whole-grain mustard sauce on grilled sourdough, and the Warm Roast Beef Sandwich with smoked mozzarella, romaine, and ancho chili raisin chutney on toasted French bread.

Throughout the country, sandwich wraps are also appearing on luncheon menus. The FloodTide Restaurant® at the Inn At Mystic® in Connecticut incorporates Asian ingredients into a chicken wrap using spiced curry, raisins, mangos, cherry peppers, smoked gouda, and mixed lettuce. The Canyon Ranch Health Resort® features a Chicken Pesto Wrap on the luncheon menu that has roasted bell peppers and romaine lettuce wrapped in a whole-wheat tortilla, with a side of salad.

In the limited-service segment of the industry, Arby's® restaurants have a variety of low-carb wraps on their menu, such as the Roast Turkey Ranch and Bacon Wrap with cheddar cheese, red onions, fresh tomatoes, and green leaf lettuce rolled in a low-carb tortilla. A Chicken Club Wrap prepared with shredded cheddar cheese, pepper bacon, fresh tomato, green leaf lettuce, and honey mustard sauce on a low-carb wheat tortilla is also a popular health-conscious choice.

# Entrées

## Meats

Entrées make up the largest category on the menu and are usually further divided into subcategories that include both hot and cold items. Hot entrées include meat, poultry, and fish and seafood. Cold entrées generally consist of main course salads or cold plates. Meats are the most popular entrée subcategory on the menu, consisting of beef, lamb, pork, and veal. Meats are expensive to purchase and should be cross-utilized throughout the menu in the appetizer, salad, and entrée sections. They should also be prepared in a variety of ways, such as braising, broiling, grilling, roasting, sautéing, and smoking.

Steakhouses are more popular than ever and clearly reflect the American affinity for beef. The upscale Gibsons Steakhouse® in Chicago offers a variety of steaks and chops, including Filet Mignon, Bone-In Sirloin, Big Porterhouse, Porterhouse Steak, Small Bone-In Sirloin, London Broil, New York Sirloin, Small New York Sirloin, Sliced Sirloin with Red Wine Sauce, Veal Chop, Double Lamb Chop, Spicy Pork Chops with Apple Sauce, One Spicy Pork Chop with Apple Sauce, and Chopped Steak and Baby Back Ribs.

The Capital Grille® in Orlando, Florida, also features a variety of steaks on the menu. There is the Dry Aged Sirloin Steak, Dry Aged Porterhouse Steak, Dry Aged Steak au Poivre with Courvoisier Cream, a Filet Mignon, a Delmonico Steak, the Kona Crusted Dry Aged Sirloin Steak with Caramelized Shallot Butter, a Porcini Rubbed Delmonico with 8-Year Aged Balsamic, and a Sliced Filet Mignon with Cippolini Onions and Wild Mushrooms (Fig. 1-2).

Steaks are also popular items at restaurants that cater to families. The Cheesecake Factory® features steaks that have a global appeal, such as Crispy Spicy Beef with green beans, shiitake mushrooms, onions, carrots, and sesame seeds in a sweet-spicy sauce served with white rice. A Hibachi Steak made of sliced hanger steak and sautéed shiitake mushrooms over onions, bean sprouts, and a soy steak sauce served with tempura asparagus and wasabi mashed potatoes is a popular choice. For those who prefer "classical" cuisine, the restaurant prepares a Steak Diane that includes medallions of beef steak covered with black peppercorns and a rich mushroom wine sauce served with mashed potatoes and slow-grilled onions.

Executive chefs are also offering high-end specialty meats to meet customer demands. Takashi Yagahashi, the executive chef at the Wynn Las Vegas®, showcases Braised Kurobuta Short Ribs at his dining room at Okada. At the Hyatt Regency Resort and Spa® in Scottsdale, Arizona, Chef de Cuisine William Bradley features Braised Kobe Beef Short Ribs. The Oak Room® in Boston serves a 10- or 14-ounce American Kobe® Beef Steak with a choice of sauces, such as Béarnaise, Mint Jelly, Sweet Onion Chutney, Wild Mushroom Sauce, Horseradish Sauce or Merlot Demi Glace.

# Pork

Pork ribs are one of the most common subcategories within the meat section on restaurant menus. Applebee's Neighborhood Bar & Grill® has Baby

**Figure 1-2. Dinner Menu**

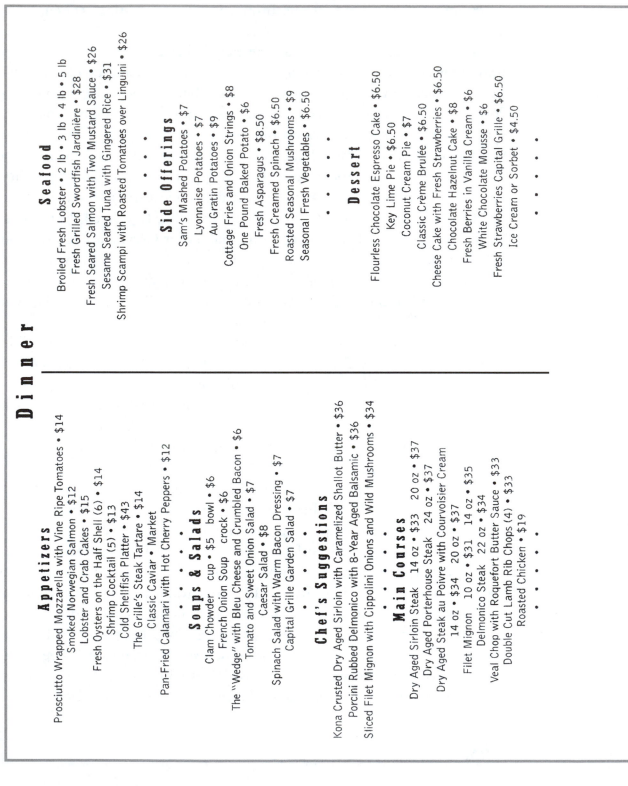

# Dinner

## Appetizers

Prosciutto Wrapped Mozzarella with Vine Ripe Tomatoes • $14
Smoked Norwegian Salmon • $12
Lobster and Crab Cakes • $15
Fresh Oysters on the Half Shell (6) • $14
Shrimp Cocktail (5) • $13
Cold Shellfish Platter • $43
The Grille's Steak Tartare • $14
Classic Caviar • Market
Pan-Fried Calamari with Hot Cherry Peppers • $12

## Soups & Salads

Clam Chowder    cup • $5    bowl • $6
French Onion Soup    crock • $6
The "Wedge" with Bleu Cheese and Crumbled Bacon • $6
Tomato and Sweet Onion Salad • $7
Caesar Salad • $8
Spinach Salad with Warm Bacon Dressing • $7
Capital Grille Garden Salad • $7

## Chef's Suggestions

Kona Crusted Dry Aged Sirloin with Caramelized Shallot Butter • $36
Porcini Rubbed Delmonico with 8-Year Aged Balsamic • $36
Sliced Filet Mignon with Cippolini Onions and Wild Mushrooms • $34

## Main Courses

Dry Aged Sirloin Steak    14 oz • $33    20 oz • $37
Dry Aged Porterhouse Steak    24 oz • $37
Dry Aged Steak au Poivre with Courvoisier Cream
    14 oz • $34    20 oz • $37
Filet Mignon    10 oz • $31    14 oz • $35
Delmonico Steak    22 oz • $34
Veal Chop with Roquefort Butter Sauce • $33
Double Cut Lamb Rib Chops (4) • $33
Roasted Chicken • $19

## Seafood

Broiled Fresh Lobster • 2 lb • 3 lb • 4 lb • 5 lb
Fresh Grilled Swordfish Jardinière • $28
Fresh Seared Salmon with Two Mustard Sauce • $26
Sesame Seared Tuna with Gingered Rice • $31
Shrimp Scampi with Roasted Tomatoes over Linguini • $26

## Side Offerings

Sam's Mashed Potatoes • $7
Lyonnaise Potatoes • $7
Au Gratin Potatoes • $9
Cottage Fries and Onion Strings • $8
One Pound Baked Potato • $6
Fresh Asparagus • $8.50
Fresh Creamed Spinach • $6.50
Roasted Seasonal Mushrooms • $9
Seasonal Fresh Vegetables • $6.50

## Dessert

Flourless Chocolate Espresso Cake • $6.50
Key Lime Pie • $6.50
Coconut Cream Pie • $7
Classic Crème Brulée • $6.50
Cheese Cake with Fresh Strawberries • $6.50
Chocolate Hazelnut Cake • $8
Fresh Berries in Vanilla Cream • $6
White Chocolate Mousse • $6
Fresh Strawberries Capital Grille • $6.50
Ice Cream or Sorbet • $4.50

Courtesy of The Capital Grille, Orlando, FL

Back Ribs with French fries, cole slaw, and baked beans, while Longhorn Steakhouse®'s luncheon menu serves Baby Back Ribs with jalapeño cole slaw and seasoned French fries. Chili's® serves its famous double-basted Baby Back Ribs, and Outback Steakhouse® has Ribs On The Barbie; mouthwatering Baby Back Ribs served with Aussie chips and warm cinnamon apples.

Comfort foods are yet another popular trend appearing on restaurant menus. The Cheesecake Factory® offers Shepherd's Pie and Meatloaf, while Bob Evans® serves Country-Fried Steak, Slowly Roasted Chicken Pot Pie, an Open-Faced Roast Beef Sandwich, and Chicken-N-Noodles. Fine dining restaurants such as Stephanie's on Newbury® in Boston offers Shepherd's Pie, Meatloaf, Ground Sirloin Burger, and a Cuban Sandwich on the luncheon menu.

At Restaurant Daniel® in New York City, Executive Chef Jean-François Bruel and Chef de Cuisine Eddy Leroux prepare comfort foods with a "classical" theme. The Duo of Dry Aged Beef consisting of Ribs with Bone Marrow Crusted Tardivo Radicchio and Seared Rib Eye with Creamy Celery and Red Wine-Torpedo Shallot Marmalade, are such examples.

Oscar's® at the Waldorf=Astoria® features a number of daily luncheon comfort foods specials as well. On Tuesday, Meatloaf, Braised Chard, and Fried Macaroni and Cheese are featured. On Wednesday, there's Yankee Pot Roast, Horseradish Mashed Potatoes, and Roasted Winter Vegetables, and on Sunday, the Braised Lamb Shank is served with Lemon, Garlic, and Herb White Bean Purée.

# Poultry

The poultry subcategory on the menu generally includes chicken, duck, pheasant, and quail. Poultry is extremely versatile and can be prepared in a number of interesting ways: baked, barbecued, braised, fried, grilled, and roasted. Chicken, like meat, can be cross-utilized throughout the menu with little effort. Poultry has gained popularity in recent years as a healthy alternative to red meat, and chefs are serving poultry on their menus more than ever before.

Today family restaurants and fine dining establishments are featuring poultry items prepared in a variety of imaginative ways. Bugaboo Creek Steak House®cross-utilizes chicken throughout its dinner menu. Chicken is used in the BBQ Chicken Nachos, Grilled Chicken Salad, Split-Roasted Chicken, and the Cariboo Chicken.

At Smokey Bones Barbeque & Grill® chicken is prepared with a culinary flare on the luncheon menu. A Grilled Chicken and Black Bean Quesadilla with cheese, tomatoes, and green onions wrapped in a honey wheat tortilla serves as an appetizer. Entrée salads include the Chopped BBQ Chicken Salad and the Grilled Chicken Cobb Salad. Customers may also add Herb Grilled Chicken Breast to any salad for an additional charge. A Sliced Smoked Turkey Sandwich with hot Swiss cheese, a Grilled Chicken Flatbread Sandwich, a Grilled Chicken Club Sandwich, as well as an Herb Grilled Chicken Breast with peppercorn bacon, and Swiss cheese on a toasted French roll are also available. Entrées at Smokey Bones include BBQ platters, such as the Sliced Smoked Breast and the BBQ & Chicken. For the more adventurous patron, the Portobello Chicken, which is an herb-grilled chicken breast served over a Portobello mushroom stuffed with Feta cheese and spinach artichoke dip, and garnished with fresh diced fruit, is available.

Poultry is also prepared in many upscale establishments, such as the Bombay Club® in New Orleans, where a number of unique appetizers are offered, including the Roasted Duck, Asparagus, and Brie Empanadas drizzled with sweet soy sauce and tomato oil, and the Port-Soaked Lamb Chops that are grilled and served on a bed of wild mushrooms and leeks garnished with toasted hazelnuts and black mission fig reduction. In the entrée section, poultry items are well represented with a Duck Duet—a leg of Duck Confit and pepper-seared boneless breast with sweet potato beignets and a Calvados and Vermont maple syrup duck reduction; and the Chicken and Mushroom Saltimbocca served with chive mashed potatoes.

The luncheon menu at NAHA® in Chicago has chicken, duck, and quail in the entrée section, offering patrons an array of choices. Popular choices include: the Split Roasted Young Chicken served with Organic Farm Egg and Wood-Grilled Winter Kale with a "Ragout" Applewood Slab Bacon, Red Pearl Onions, Oven-Cured Tomatoes and Sweet Garlic; and the Blossom Honey "Lacquered" Aged Moulard Duck Breast, with Glazed Young Carrots and Turnips, Broccoli Rabe, and Port. The Roast Quail "Hunter's Style" with Wild Boar Bacon is presented with Smoked Bulb Onions and Oyster Mushrooms, Fingerling Potatoes, Braised Tomatoes, and Tarragon.

## Fish and Seafood

Fish and seafood are abundantly flavorful and are offered on most menus. The fish and seafood section includes freshwater and saltwater fish. Flatfish, roundfish, crustaceans, and mollusks are all popular categories. They are an excellent source of vitamins, minerals, and protein, and their fat content is relatively low. Many nutritionists suggest that even fish with a high fatty content is a healthy and beneficial choice. Salmon, tuna, and mackerel are rich in omega-3 fatty acids.

Fish and seafood can be extremely expensive as well as highly perishable, and should be cross-utilized on the menu. They can be prepared in a variety of ways, including baked, broiled, fried, grilled, poached, sautéed, and smoked. Patrons in all segments of the foodservice industry are becoming more sophisticated and are willing to try fish that go beyond the traditional offerings of haddock, salmon, shrimp, and tuna. Shaw's Crab House® in Chicago offers a complete sushi bar and a variety of shucked oysters from around the country: Deer Creek oysters from Puget Sound, in Washington State, and Watch Hill oysters from Watch Hill, Rhode Island. Customers can also select less common varieties of fish, including Grilled Ecuadorian Mahi Mahi, Sautéed Lake Erie Yellow Perch, and Sautéed Bay of Fundy Sea Scallops.

Today, health-conscious diners are demanding more baked, grilled, and roasted fish and seafood items rather than deep-fried or sautéed selections. Red Lobster®, at numerous locations, gives patrons the option of selecting catfish, tilapia, and trout broiled, fried, grilled, or blackened. Legal Sea Foods®, at most of its locations, offers fish and seafood that is brushed with herb vinaigrette or Cajun spices and grilled over a hot fire. Arctic Char, Swordfish, Bluefish, Sea Scallops, and Skewered Shrimp are also available.

Diners are also demanding that restaurant chefs prepare more flavorful fish and seafood items. Menus that specialize in fish and seafood are incorporating glazes, vinaigrettes, tomato sauces, oil instead of butter, and a number of unique crusts. Shaws Crab House® in Chicago offers a selection of tasty and healthy items: highlights include Sautéed Alaskan Halibut with Roasted Vegetables and a Citrus Glaze; Grilled Gulf Yellowfin Tuna with Crispy Noodles, Caramelized Soybeans, Peanuts, and a Ginger Soy Vinaigrette; and a Sautéed Maine Boat Cod that is coated in a Horseradish Crust and served with Green Beans and Herb Lemon Butter. They also serve a sautéed George's Bank Haddock with a Parmesan Crust accompanied by Sautéed Spinach and a Lemon Butter. Fulton's Crab House® at Walt Disney World® Resort in Orlando, Florida, also offers healthy alternatives on its dinner menu. Columbia Salmon charcoal grilled with a fire-roasted tomato sauce pesto, and julienne vegetables; and a charcoal-grilled White Hapu'upu'u, with a spicy peach glaze, balsamic reduction, and sautéed baby vegetables are two of these menu items.

## Pastas and Pizzas

Pasta and pizza are generally presented as entrées on restaurant menus. In many cases they are strategically placed on the menu in their own section. Pastas and pizzas are very popular with customers. As they are relatively inexpensive to make in terms of food cost, they are therefore very profitable. Pasta can be baked or boiled, and pizza is usually baked or grilled.

Restaurants are becoming increasingly creative with pastas. At Bertucci's Brick oven ristorante®, the pastas are prepared from original Italian recipes, using fresh herbs, spices, chicken, seafood, and vegetables. Each pasta dish is prepared to order and tossed with al dente pasta. Two of the many pasta offerings include: the Rigatoni Abruzzi on al dente pasta with Roasted Peppers, Sweet Italian Sausage in a Mildly Spicy Tomato Sauce; and a Four Cheese Ravioli that is a Home-Style Ravioli overstuffed with a blend of Ricotta, Parmesan, Romano, and Fontina, topped with Tomato Sauce and Fresh Basil.

Café 1401® at the Willard Intercontinental® in Washington, D.C., also serves a variety of distinctive pastas on its luncheon menu. A Penne tossed in a Tarragon Cream Sauce with Strips of Smoked Chicken, Julienne of Bell Peppers and Garden Peas, dusted with Parmesan Cheese, is a tasty and creative item, as is the Maccherini Rigate with Oxtail Braised in Barolo Wine. Pasta classics include: Spaghetti served with a choice of Bolognese, Tomato, Carbonera, Alfredo, or Aglio E Olio Sauce, and Spinach and Pecorino Cheese Ravioli tossed in Pesto Sauce with fresh Tomato and Black Olive.

Many restaurant chains are currently offering customers the option of creating their own pasta. At Bertucci's brick oven ristorante®, patrons can select Rigatoni, Linguini, or Trenette, with either Pomodoro or Bolognese Sauce, accompanied by four Polpette (meatballs). Bertucci's also has traditional favorites, such as Lasagna al Forno and Lobster Ravioli.

The preparation of pizza has also changed dramatically in recent years. Restaurants have created a variety of doughs in an effort to make their pizza stand out among the competition. Uno Chicago Grill® has a Flatbread Pizza crust made with an organic flour. The Oregano Pizza Bistro & Patio®, in Scottsdale, Arizona, serves a pizza crust made with cornmeal and beer. Bellini's Ristorante Italiano® in North Conway, New Hampshire, accommodates customers with certain allergies with gluten-free pizza for one. Pizza Hut® also has a wide variety of signature crusts: Cheesy Bites Pizza, Pan Pizza, Hand-Tossed Style Pizza, Thin'N Crispy®, Stuffed Crust Pizza, 4 for All® Pizza, and the Full House XL Pizza™.

Traditional pizzas, such as the pepperoni or sausage, are still popular on many restaurant menus, but customers have a number of creative pizzas to select from as well. Wolfgang Puck at Spago® in Beverly Hills has a number of pizza selections that are not your ordinary classic offerings. The restaurant serves a Pizza with Smoked Salmon & Salmon Caviar and a Sautéed Shrimp and Pesto with Roasted Peppers, Garlic Rapini, Goat Cheese and Basil. It also offers a pizza with Garlic Chicken & Baby Artichokes with Sweet Onions, Tomatoes, Roasted Eggplant, and Parsley.

At Bellini's Ristorante Italiano®, the brick-oven pizzas are unique because the flour and tomatoes used are imported from Italy. The restaurant serves traditional pizza, such as Pizza Margarita and Pepperoni, but it showcases a Pizza Mushroom Pesto, which is made of fresh basil sauce with puréed pine nuts and Romano cheese topped with Mushrooms and Mozzarella, and a Pizza Tuscan, which has sausage, potato, olive oil, and fresh oregano.

Pizza customers are looking for variety, and many chains are answering their requests with creative ideas. Some restaurant chains are allowing customers the opportunity to create their own pizzas. At Olive Garden Italian Restaurant®, diners can make their own pizza using pepperoni, bell peppers, Italian sausage, black olives, mushrooms, artichokes, onions, and Romano tomatoes. Some Cicis® locations offer an all-you-can eat menu of pizza, pasta, and salad. At select Uno Chicago Grill® restaurants, patrons can select an individual or regular serving of deep-dish pizza with various fillings and toppings, including: anchovies, broccoli, cheese, chicken, eggplant, green peppers, Kalamata olives, mushrooms, onions, pepperoni, pesto, roasted red peppers, roasted vegetables, sausage, and tomato sauce.

## Accompaniments

ACCOMPANIMENTS consist of pasta, potato, rice, and vegetable selections. For the most part, they are inexpensive and can be prepared in a number of ways: broiled, grilled, roasted, sautéed, and steamed. Accompaniments are often featured on the à la carte menu to increase the average check. In some high-end specialty restaurants that specialize in steaks, a listing of accompaniments or extras is commonplace. Maxwell and Dunne's Steakhouse® on Long Island, New York, has a variety of potatoes, and vegetables on the dinner menu. These include roasted garlic mashed potatoes, sweet potato fries, crispy fried onion rings, steamed asparagus, and sautéed broccoli rabe. At some locations, Ruth's Chris Steak House® serves au gratin potatoes, steak fries, shoestring, Lyonnaise, and cottage. Vegetables include broiled tomatoes, fresh broccoli or cauliflower au gratin, and fresh spinach either creamed or au gratin, and fresh asparagus with Hollandaise or au gratin.

Accompaniments are also featured at numerous restaurants with the entrées as an intricate part of the plate. In the Marsh Tavern® at the Equinox Resort & Spa®, in Manchester, Vermont, a number of dinner entrées incorporate the accoutrements in a unique fashion. The Flat Iron Steak is prepared with Parsnip and Potato Purée, Honey Glazed Carrots, Asparagus, Roasted Garlic Jus, and Peppercorn Crème Fraîche; while the Charbroiled

Double Cut Pork Chop is served with Pecan Cheddar Polenta with Red Cabbage and Apples, and a Dried Cherry Sauce. At the Mansion on Turtle Creek® in Dallas, Texas, the frequently changing dinner menu might offer such creative entrées such as Chilean Sea Bass with Walnut Crust; Roasted Garlic Shrimp on Creamy Potato Blinis with Spicy Grilled Zucchini Salad; Texas Steak Diane with Queso Fresco Potatoes, Grilled Asparagus & Chorizo Avocado Nacho; or Roasted Pheasant on Butternut Squash Purée with Oregon White Truffle Gravy, Winter Braised Cabbage & Gnocchi Meunière.

## Desserts

DESSERTS are extremely versatile and inexpensive to prepare. Selections include cakes, custards, pies, puddings, tarts, and soufflés. Desserts are very profitable and should be strategically placed on the menu to maximize sales. They are also an integral part of the overall dining experience, because dessert offerings frequently leave the last impression.

Decadent desserts are being offered on menus throughout the foodservice industry. The Cosmopolitan® café in San Francisco serves a number of "over-the-top" desserts, including: Molten Center Chocolate Bread Pudding, Espresso Crème Anglaise, and Whipped Mascarpone; Warm Peach Tarte Tatin with Caramel Sauce; and Cinnamon Gelato. It also has a Chocolate Trio Dark Chocolate Bundt Cake, Milk Chocolate Crème Brûlée, and White Chocolate-Espresso Parfaits.

At Charlie Palmer's Aureole NY®, the chefs make a number of incredible desserts that include: Anjou Pear and Pumpkin Cobbler with Tahitian vanilla ice cream, brown butter, and pear emulsion; Grilled Pineapple Upside-Down Cake with coconut rum gelato; Cocoa Meringue and Chocolate Napoleon molten cassis truffle, with red currant ice cream; and fresh Raspberries or Strawberries with sweet cream crème fraîche or crème Chantilly.

Dinner houses are serving phenomenal desserts as well. Ruby Tuesday's® serves an Ice Cream Pie that is a monstrous wedge of vanilla ice cream pie with Butterfinger® chunks, a layer of chocolate ice cream and fudge in a chocolate-crumb crust topped with chocolate sauce. Diners may also choose the Strawberry Tallcake, composed of three layers of light and airy sponge cake and strawberry mousse. The dessert is then drenched in strawberry sauce, topped with vanilla Blue Bell Ice Cream®, and finished with a cloud of whipped cream. Some Chili's® serve a Molten Chocolate Cake made of warm chocolate cake with a chocolate fudge filling topped with vanilla ice cream under a crunchy chocolate shell. They also have a Chocolate Chip Paradise Pie that consists of a warm, chewy bar layered with chocolate chips, walnuts, and coconut, topped with vanilla ice cream and drizzled with hot fudge and caramel.

Dessert menus are now much more elaborate and multifaceted than ever before. Pastry chef Timothy Dahl at NAHA® in Chicago has divided his dessert menu into four categories: Signature Desserts, Cheese Course, Dessert Wines, and After Dinner Spirits (Fig. 1-3). At the Waldorf=Astoria's Peacock Alley®, pastry chef Nancy Olson has created a number of intricate desserts that range from a lemon soufflé, to a tasting of ice creams and sorbets that include rum raisin, chocolate praline, banana, and blood orange. Olson serves a selection of artisanal cheeses as well.

# Beverages

BEVERAGES are by far the most profitable items on any menu. The beverage classification consists of wines, beers, mixed drinks, after-dinner drinks, and nonalcoholic beverages. In recent years, bottled water, martinis, margaritas, frozen drinks, and teas have also gained popularity due to customer demands.

Bottled water is currently featured in quick-service, dinner houses, and upscale restaurants. Burger King® and Taco Bell® sell Aqufina® water, and Applebee's Neighborhood Grill & Bar has Poland Spring® bottled water. At high-end restaurants, bottled water is usually sold by the liter bottle and is served chilled. At Oliver's® in the Mayflower Park Hotel® in Seattle, Washington, alcohol-free refreshers include San Pellegrino® Sparkling Water and Panna® Still Water. Ken Frank, chef/owner at La Toque, in Rutherford, California, offers a five-course prix fixe dinner that comes with a bottle of either San Pellegrino® or Evian®.

Martinis, margaritas, and frozen drinks, prepared and presented with an artistic flair, are the rage on beverage menus. Dave & Buster's® serves a number of signature martinis, such as: the Classic Cosmopolitan made with Absolut Citron, Grand Marnier, and a splash of Cranberry Juice; the Big Apple, made with Smirnoff Green Apple Twist, Pucker Sour Apple, and Lime Juice: and the Tuscon Orange, which includes Stoli Ohranj, Blood Orange Syrup, Orange Juice, and Soda Water with a Lemon Twist. Several T.G.I. Friday's® locations offer classic concoctions, such as: Tom Collins,

**Figure 1-3. A Dessert Menu**

# NAHA

## desserts

Chestnut "Financier" Cake, Bittersweet Chocolate Ice Cream, Bourbon Gelée and *Manuka* Smoked Sea Salt

....

Espresso Panna Cotta,
"Cara Cara" Oranges Caramel Citrus and Coconut Sorbet

....

NAHA Sundae of Caramelized "Lady Anne" Apples and Butterscotch,
Pecan Praline, Vanilla Bean Ice Cream and "Shagbark" Hickory Nut Shortbread

**11**

## cheese course

***Robiola Langhe*** Three Milk Cheese from Italy,
***Pont L'Eveque*** French Cow's Milk Cheese from Normandy,
***Petit Basque*** Sheep's Milk Cheese from Pyrénées and
***Fromage Des Vignerons*** Fresh Cow's Milk "Epoisses" Cheese from Burgundy

**16**

## Timothy Dahl-Pastry Chef

## dessert wines

| | | | | |
|---|---|---|---|---|
| 04 | Inniskillin Icewine | Vidal Oak Aged | VQA Niagara | 16gl |
| 04 | Boutari | Muscat of Samos | Samos, Greece | 8gl |
| 01 | Chateau Bel Air | Saint-Croix-Du-Mont | France | 10gl |

## after dinner spirits

| | | |
|---|---|---|
| Ramos Pinto | Collector Vintage Character | 10 |
| Hardy's | XO Cognac | 24 |
| Francois Voyer Napoleon | Grande Champagne | 15 |
| Poggio Basso | Grappa Nebbiola | 20 |

Courtesy of NAHA, Chicago, IL

Gimlets, Manhattans, Cape Codders, and Sea Breezes. They also feature a number of margaritas: the Ultimate Margarita, which is a blend of José Cuervo Gold with Triple-Citrus Margarita Mix of Lemon, Lime and Orange flavors, garnished with Fresh slices of Lime and Orange; and the Ultimate Strawberry or Raspberry Margarita. A very popular frozen drink is the Ultimate Mudslide, made of a blend of Kahlua, Vodka, Bailey's Irish Cream, and Ice Cream.

## Tea Menus

TEA menus are found mainly in hotels and at high-end restaurants and are traditionally used for "teas." The Cocktail Terrace® at the Waldorf=Astoria® in New York City, offers a variety of teas. The "Champagne Tea" includes tea sandwiches, scones, pastries, and the house brut, while the "Classic Afternoon Tea" consists of tea sandwiches, scones, and assorted pastries. The "Light Tea" includes scones and pastries.

NAHA®, a high-end restaurant in Chicago, offers an extensive selection of teas and herbal infusions. The menu is divided into four distinct categories: Performance Tea (Midnight Jasmine Bloom and Under Garden); Reserve Tea (Royal Ceylon Platinum Tips, and Imperial Royal Snowflake); Vintage Tea (1978 Vintage Pu-erh, and 2000 Vintage Pu-erh); and the Herbal Infusions (Lemon Grass Wild Rose and South of France Rooibos).

## For Review and Discussion

1. Discuss three trends that are currently influencing salad offerings on the menu.

2. Name the three subclassifications of entrées, and discuss the trends occurring in each of these.

3. List three pizza and pasta trends, and discuss why they are popular with diners.

4. What is the importance of cross-utilization of meat, fish, and seafood?

5. Explain the value of promoting desserts and alcoholic beverages on the menu.

# Chapter 2

# MARKET SURVEY

Foodservice operators must perform a market survey to acquire information about a particular location and the types of residents who live there, so they can establish a foodservice operational concept that will meet the needs of their target market. The **market survey** is a detailed study of the people, the community, and the physical location of the foodservice establishment. This chapter discusses the elements that must be analyzed in a market survey.

## Objectives

❏ To determine what a market survey is

❏ To identify how a restaurant owner should use a market survey

❏ To illustrate the steps one needs to take in order to complete a market survey

# Preliminary Steps

THERE are two basic steps in preparing a market survey. The first step is to establish the style and the type of foodservice operation or concept, and the second is to determine the community's need for such a business establishment. This planning should be done before any money is invested.

The foodservice planner needs to address many issues, such as

- **Style of menu**
- **Type of clientele**
- **Type of cuisine**
- **Style of atmosphere**
- **Style of interior decor**
- **Expense of food, labor, and overhead**
- **Desired profit**
- **Amount of capital to be invested**
- **Regulations for operating on a daily basis**
- **Architect**
- **Lawyer**
- **Accountant**
- **Chef**
- **Staff**

Information must be carefully collected and analyzed when one is preparing a market survey. The market survey indicates whether the community possesses the factors necessary to support an investor's foodservice operation.

The second step is to determine the community's needs or demands for such a foodservice operation. Most corporations, foodservice chains, and hotels complete step two, which is the key element in lowering the risk of failure.

# Areas of Analysis

A MARKET survey provides a detailed analysis of the customer, the community, and the physical location of the foodservice operation.

# Customer

The customer is one of the most important elements of a foodservice operation. It is the customer who ultimately determines the operation's success or failure. The customer(s) is also known as the market. Key factors to consider about customers include:

- **Desired market**
- **Market classifications**
- **Gender**
- **Age**
- **Disposable income**
- **Food preferences**
- **Social habits**
- **Education**
- **Religious orientation**
- **Ethnicity**
- **Occupation**
- **Arrival patterns**
- **Preferred days for dining out**

# Desired Market

The owner must decide on the desired market/customer(s) that the foodservice concept is to attract. It is important to establish the market early in the business plan so that every aspect of this plan answers the wants and needs of the targeted customer. The greater the owner's knowledge and understanding of the customer, the better the service provided because the operation will satisfy the needs of customers that existing establishments currently do not meet. The ultimate goal of any marketing plan is to provide an excellent dining experience that satisfies the customer. Satisfied customers are the key to a longer and more profitable existence.

# Market Classifications

Individuals in the United States are classified in particular generation categories based on the year in which they were born. People born between 1946 and 1964 are known as Baby Boomers, those born between 1965 and

1978 are called Gen Xers, and individuals born between 1979 and 1994 are referred to as Gen Y. People within each of these generations have unique yet common needs and desires. Frequently they have similar opinions and points of view due to having lived during the same period of time and having had similar experiences. Although the gap or difference of opinions is narrow within a particular generation, the gap between various generations is much wider. At times different generations view the world in dramatically different ways. In order to be successful, it is important to recognize the innate differences of these target markets.

## Gender

A knowledge of the gender of patrons who will frequent the foodservice establishment is another important consideration when preparing a business plan. Gender influences many decisions within the business plan, including: the type of layout for the foodservice operation, the size of the chairs, the interior design color scheme, and the type of cuisine and portion size of food items to be served. These factors assist the owner in determining the marketing and merchandising methods needed to generate sales.

## Age

Knowing the age of the target market helps to determine several factors. As people age, their desires and dietary and emotional needs change. Each age group—Baby Boomers, Gen X, and Gen Y—has a different point of view on dining preferences. These include:

The type of cuisine and food selection

Price

Portion size

Nutrition and nutritional requirements

Style of atmosphere

Lighting level in the dining room, rest rooms, and so on

Texture of the functional and decorative materials used

Style of entertainment

Accessibility of the operation and movement within it

Type and intensity of background music

Size of lettering on the menu

Service style

Layout and design of the foodservice operation

## Disposable Income

Disposable income is the amount of income that remains after taxes and personal bills have been paid. Disposable income is also called entertainment, fun, or luxury money. The greater the income a market has, the greater the amount of disposable income available for dining. To estimate a market's disposable income, research the demographic information of the targeted community, and review the information under the category "Household Income." Disposable income typically reflects a household's income bracket.

Information on disposable income is helpful in forecasting the annual sales for the financial statements of a business plan. An owner who wishes to open a full-service fine dining restaurant with a check average of $75 per person must know that there is an adequate number of households with enough disposable income to support this check average. If 1 percent of a community of 25,000 households (equal to 250 households) has an annual disposable income of $8,000 and the remaining households have less disposable income, these numbers may not support a $75-check-average, fine dining concept. Several other factors in addition to disposable income must also be researched and interpreted prior to making a final decision on the check average and foodservice concept.

## Food Preferences

Knowing the foods and/or cuisines that a target market prefers is also imperative in achieving success. By collecting menus from several foodservice operations that have similar concepts and looking for items listed on the majority of these menus, it is possible to deduce that these items sell well. If five out of seven menus list French onion soup, it may be a good idea to include French onion soup as one of the hot soups. When Caesar's salad appears on every menu, this is a great indicator that customers enjoy Caesar's salad and will purchase this item. Another helpful resource of information concerning the salability of items is food and beverage purveyors. These individuals can be reliable in attesting to the food items/ingredients that are best sellers. If beef outsells poultry, consider placing more beef dishes on the menu. Use this same concept with all the other categories on the menu.

# Social Habits

An understanding of how the market socializes helps to determine the type and style of entertainment that should be offered.

# Education

People who have a higher level of education tend to be more receptive to new ideas and to trying something new. Over their life spans, they also earn more money and have a higher level of disposable income to dine out more often. Knowing the targeted market's educational background also allows for the use of more appropriate language in designing the descriptive copy of items on the menu. The staff's level of education, however, dictates the type and training method(s) that must be provided.

# Religious Orientation

Some religious cultures have laws that restrict the consumption of particular food items and the method of preparation of others. Knowing customers' religious backgrounds can help to build sales. If it is known that a large number of patrons are Catholic, for example, offering a fish special on Fridays during Lent will augment sales.

# Ethnicity

It is impractical to open an Italian specialty restaurant in a community that is heavily populated by people of Chinese descent, as in all probability the rate of success will not be very high. Recognizing a market's ethnic background and offering some favorite authentic national dishes is a good way to add variety to the menu. Chefs may also use fusion cooking—the blending of different ethnic dishes together—to create a more interesting menu.

# Occupation

A knowledge of the target market's type of employment can assist in the planning of dishes on the menu and their portion size. Customers who work in occupations that require more physical activity, such as construction, will burn more calories on the job and require heartier portion sizes. Guests who expend less physical effort on the job burn less calories and may prefer food items that contain fewer calories, fats, and sugar in smaller portions.

The allotted time that the targeted market has for lunch is another factor to consider. Most customers are in a hurry to eat lunch, whether they have 30 minutes or 1 hour to do so. Insight about occupation provides information that should be reflected in menu offerings that require limited preparation time and allow for quick service.

## Arrival Patterns

The term **arrival patterns** refers to the hours at which groups of customers dine out. Knowing arrival patterns allows for appropriate and adequate dining room setup and timely turnover time that allows for increased covers and greater sales. A knowledge of the number of single people, couples, and parties of three or more and the time of day at which these various groups dine allows the maître d' to maximize dining room seating capacity. Families with young children, for example, tend to dine out from 4:30 P.M. to 7:00 P.M.; large groups without children frequent dining establishments from 7:00 P.M. to 9:00 P.M.; and couples often dine between 8:00 P.M. and 11:00 P.M. The proper arrangement of tables and chairs in the dining room to accommodate each of these groups usually results in a higher turnover rate and increased sales.

## Preferred Days for Dining Out

Knowing which business days are popular and which are slower helps to establish the need for merchandising and marketing programs. Fridays, Saturdays, and Sundays are very popular days for dining out, because people are often paid on Thursday or Friday and have greater disposable income and more time to go out. Monday is usually the slowest day of the week, because little, if any, disposable income is left over from the weekend and time for dining out is limited.

The key factors discussed are but a sampling of information that should be acquired on the target market. The greater the understanding of the market/customer, the easier it is to satisfy customer demands. Customers expect an enjoyable experience when they dine at a restaurant. Owners should go one step further and provide them with a *great* dining experience.

# The Community

The geographic region, district, city, or town from which the majority of the foodservice operation's customers come is known as the **community**. Elements to study within the community include

- **Growth rate**
- **Availability of liquor licenses**
- **Existence of competition**
- **Public services provided**
- **Requirements of the state Board of Health**
- **Number of families**
- **Potential for advertising**

## ❧ Growth Rate

If a community has a declining population, it is wise to discover the reason for the decline and to think twice about building or operating an establishment there. For example, it would be a mistake to build in a location where the unemployment rate is high. High unemployment means that businesses are closing and that people are moving elsewhere to find work. Other reasons not to choose a location include a high crime rate, high rents, and high taxes. An investor must take into consideration the amount of time it takes to collect data and to analyze the market survey which is approximately six months to two years. It then takes another six to nine months to build the operation.

## ❧ Availability of Liquor Licenses

Alcoholic beverages are one of the most profitable commodities that the foodservice industry has to sell. Obtaining a liquor license in some communities is a very expensive and difficult task. Each state and community has its own laws and procedures.

Foodservice investors usually start the process of obtaining a liquor license by completing the proper application. The investor is then placed on a waiting list. Once there is an opening for a license, the investor is called to go before a committee that regulates the license. The committee interviews the candidate and approves or denies the issuance of the license. Most communities, depending on state law, grant a limited number of licenses. The supply is low and the demand is high, thereby making the value and sometimes the cost of licenses high.

Another method of obtaining a liquor license is to buy a foodservice operation that already has a liquor license that can be transferred to the new owner. The transfer of the license must be approved by the committee that regulates liquor licenses. All liquor licenses have to be renewed on an annual basis and may be revoked at any time if the investor breaks the law. It is important to check with local and state government agencies about liquor liability and costs.

## Existence of Competition

The market survey must take into consideration two basic types of competition: direct and indirect. **Direct competition** includes foodservice operations that are directly related (similar) to an operation. They offer similar cuisine, décor, check average, capacity, and turnover rate. For example, if the investor wants to operate a steak house, the survey should indicate how many other steak houses there are in the community and which ones would be considered direct competition.

**Indirect competition** consists of foodservice operations that are not similar to that of the investor but who are competing for the same customers. Location near indirect competition can be beneficial. Competition analysis should be done to determine if the community can support another operation.

## Public Services Provided

To help calculate overhead expenses, the investor needs to know which public services are covered by tax dollars and which services will cost additional monies. Police and fire protection are usually provided, but the availability and cost of other types of services vary from one community to another.

## Requirements of the State Board of Health

The Board of Health serves to protect the public from circumstances that may place the public's health in danger. When the Board of Health inspects a foodservice operation, it is performing a public service for the community. If there is evidence of food contamination in a restaurant, the Board of Health may cite the operator or even shut down the operation.

Before any money is invested in a project, the Board of Health and the local fire department must examine the restaurant's blueprints. Both departments can save an owner time and money by indicating where there are violations in the project. Each community and state has different laws pertaining to health and fire codes, and it is important to be aware of these laws.

### ❧ Number of Families

The number of families in a community usually indicates whether the community has a stable and/or a growing population. When there are many families with children in a community, there is usually a large school system. The school system can be a good source for an effective merchandising program. If the investor's market is families, a favorite dessert contest might provide a great promotional program. The students in grades four, five, and six might draw posters of their favorite desserts and give the desserts names. The foodservice operator could choose the winner at the restaurant and give prizes to all who participate.

### ❧ Potential for Advertising

One of the key elements to a successful advertising program is communicating on the customers' level. If the investor is trying to attract business executives, an ad in the *Wall Street Journal* would be appropriate, although this ad would not be effective in attracting a different type of clientele. The amount of exposure or circulation that each advertising method provides is important. Analyze the Community's Newspapers, Radio Stations, Periodicals, and Television Stations. Enough money should be set aside in the budget to run an effective advertising campaign. Planning ahead for advertising can allow for promotions throughout the year.

## The Location

One of the first steps in choosing a location is to determine future needs. Planning ahead is vital when choosing a location. The needs of a foodservice operator who wants to establish a chain of operations differ from those of an individual who wants to open a single operation. Knowing what one wants and needs before looking for a location helps to eliminate much wasted time and frustration. An excellent location alone does not guarantee a foodservice operation's success, nor does a poor location necessarily determine failure. When selecting a location, an investor should first analyze the population of the state, city, and suburban communities. Population trends may shift drastically in a city if it is dependent on a particular industry for financial survival. When a factory or a company closes, the people in that city or community must travel elsewhere for work. The foodservice operation that depends on these customers could also be closing its doors. It is important to note the rate at which a state, city, or suburban community is growing. Refer to Figure 2-1 for other considerations in analyzing the feasibility of a location for a foodservice operation.

# Figure 2-1. Checklist for Analyzing the Location of a Foodservice Operation

(1) Zoning
    Current zoning of site
    Use permits needed
    Height restrictions
    Front line setback
    Side yard requirements
    Back yard requirements
    Restrictions on signs
    Parking requirements
    Other restrictions

(2) Area characteristics
    Type of neighborhood
    Type of businesses
    Growth pattern
    Proposed construction
    Other available sites
    Zoning of adjacent sites

(3) Competition
    Number of food facilities in drawing
        area of site
    Number of seats
    Type of menu offered
    Method of service
    Check averages
    Number of cocktail lounges
    Quality of drinks
    Bar service available at tables
    Annual sales

(4) Physical characteristics
    Type of topsoil
    Type of subsoil
    Depth of water table
    Presence of rocks
    Load-bearing capacity
    Direction of slopes
    Surface drainage
    Percolation test results
    Natural landscaping
    Other features

(5) Size and shape (including sketch)
    Length
    Width
    Total square feet
    Square footage needed for building
    Square footage needed for parking
    Space for other requirements

(6) Costs
    Cost per front foot
    Cost per square foot
    Total cost of site
    Cost of comparable sites nearby
    Costs for land improvements
    Real estate taxes
    Other taxes

(7) Utilities
    Location, cost, and size or capacity of
        Storm sewer

        Sanitary sewer
        Gas lines
        Water lines
        Electricity
        Steam

(8) Streets
    Basic patterns
    Width or lanes
    Paved
    Curbs and gutters
    Sidewalks
    Lighting
    Public transportation
    Grades
    Hazards

(9) Positional characteristics
    Distance and driving time to
        Central business district
        Industrial centers
        Shopping centers
        Residential areas
        Recreational areas
        Sporting events
        Educational facilities
        Special attractions
        Other activity generators

(10) Traffic information
    Distance to nearest intersection
    Traffic characteristics
    Traffic counts
        Site street

        Adjacent streets

    Anticipated changes

(11) Visibility
    Distances of sight from
        Left
        Right
        Across
        Obstructions
        Location of signs

(12) Services
    Quality of police protection
    Quality of fire protection
    Location of hydrant
    Availability of trash pickup
    Availability of garbage pickup
    Other services required

(13) General recommendations
    Suitability
    Desirability
    Other recommendations

Distance          Driving
                  Time

Day    Time    Count

From E.A. Kazarian, *Foodservice Facilities Planning, 3rd ed.*, New York: John Wiley & Sons © 1989

# Other Things to Consider

## ❧ Zoning

There are three major types of zones: residential, industrial, and commercial. Each zone has zoning ordinances that must be obeyed. One cannot freely erect any type of building in a residential zone. This zoning restricts business developments for the safety of the residents who live in the zone. Industrial zones are established for large-volume companies while commercial zones accommodate small-volume companies. It is important to check with the Zoning Board to find out the types of restrictions on the land on which you plan to build, because compliance with the Zoning Board regulations is mandatory. Zoning laws change as the population changes in a community.

## ❧ Area Characteristics

The type of neighborhood in which an establishment is located will have a great effect on business. If the neighborhood has a high crime rate, if pollution is evident, or if the neighborhood opposes development it will be difficult to succeed.

## ❧ Physical Characteristics

Analyzing the land (soil) provides insight regarding the needs and the cost of development. For landscaping purposes, topsoil should be analyzed for nutrient and mineral content. The direction in which the land slopes, is a consideration for proper drainage. Large rocks and trees might have to be cleared, which adds to the cost of the project.

A **percolation test** should be done on the land to estimate the time it takes for water to be absorbed into the soil for proper drainage. A percolation test is done by placing small holes throughout the lot below the frost line (6 to 10 feet), filling them with water, and timing how long it takes the soil to absorb the water. If it takes more than 20 minutes, the land usually will not pass the percolation test and the investor will not be allowed to obtain a building permit, because the land is deemed unsafe for building. The percolation test also indicates the type of soil, rock, and clay that are under the topsoil. Typically today many restaurants are leased, so the percolation test is more a concern for the landlord. This is not something that has to be done unless you are buying the restaurant and the land it occupies.

## ❧ Size, Shape, and Costs

The Department of Health and the Zoning Board must review renovation or new construction blueprints. These blueprints must be printed by a registered architect. Both organizations will want to make sure that the building materials used and total square footage meet their regulations. The architect must also see that all materials purchased are of an acceptable quality.

## Streets and Traffic Information

Street patterns, such as one-way streets, should be noted. Foodservice operations located on one-way streets usually do not have as much traffic as operations located on two-way streets. Drivers have better access to an operation if it is on a two-way street. The width of the street and the width of the driveway are important as well. Because delivery trucks must easily enter and exit the establishment.

Intersections always slow down potential customers. When stopped at an intersection for the traffic light or a stop sign, people have time to look around and notice businesses. The slower the speed limit, the greater the opportunity to observe an operation. Traffic counts of how many cars pass the location of an establishment can be obtained through the city transportation office. The greater the number of cars that pass by, the greater the potential for customers.

## Sales Generators

Civic centers, theaters, and shopping malls can generate sales.

## Visibility

The visibility of a foodservice operation can reduce or increase the cost of advertising. A property that has high visibility saves on advertising dollars, while one located in a city and hidden by a building requires more advertising to let people know where it is located.

## Parking

Adequate parking is necessary to attract customers. The parking area must be designed to accommodate:

- **Customers**
- **Employees**
- **Lights**
- **Dumpsters**
- **Delivery trucks**
- **Landscaping**

## Snow and Trash Removal

Removal of snow and trash is expensive. It is prudent to check local rates and methods of removal.

## ❧ Obtaining Information for the Market Survey

The information for completing a market survey should be collected from these sources:

- **National Restaurant Association**
- **Chamber of Commerce**
- **Better Business Bureau**
- **Small Business Association (SBA)**
- **Public library**
- **Economic Development Department of city or state**
- **City Hall**
- **Tourist Information Bureau**
- **U.S. Census Bureau**
- **Banking and financing corporations**
- **Real estate agencies**
- **Surveys you conduct**
- **Internet, state Web sites of Economic Development Agencies**

# For Review and Discussion

1. Define **market survey**.

2. Give three elements about a community that should be evaluated prior to building a foodservice operation.

3. What is disposable income?

4. List two methods of obtaining a liquor license.

5. What is the purpose of a percolation test?

# Chapter 3

# NUTRITION AND MENU PLANNING

THIS chapter examines the role of nutrients in foods and their relationship to health. Methods to improve the nutrient quality of food items offered in the foodservice industry are introduced, as is the planning of nutritious diets.

 *Objectives*

❏ To provide the student information on the basics of nutrition

❏ To discuss the relationship of nutrition to health

❏ To illustrate how menus can be nutritious and still profitable to the foodservice operation

# Nutrition Basics

NUTRITION is the study of how food is used by the body. Food is composed of nutrients, which are chemical compounds needed for survival. Some of these are essential nutrients, which cannot be made in the body and must be supplied by food or supplements. Examples of essential nutrients are minerals (such as iron and calcium), vitamins, and certain amino acids that combine to form protein. Without a source of these essential nutrients, good health cannot be maintained. Other nutrients are equally important for survival, but these essential nutrients can be synthesized in the body if the raw materials are available. Examples of these types of nutrients include the fatty substance lecithin and the nonessential amino acids.

The six major nutrient groups are:

1. **Proteins**

2. **Carbohydrates**

3. **Fats**

4. **Vitamins**

5. **Minerals**

6. **Water**

*Proteins* provide calories, synthesize new body tissue during growth, and replace worn-out cells. Proteins also form hormones, enzymes, and antibodies that are required to perform numerous bodily processes and to maintain immunity to diseases.

*Carbohydrates* include sugars, starches, and fiber. Carbohydrates are the most important energy source for the body, particularly the nervous system. Dietary fiber, which consists mostly of indigestible carbohydrates, helps to regulate the movement of food through the digestive tract.

*Fats* are a very concentrated energy source, which provide more than twice as many calories as an equal amount of protein or carbohydrate. Some fats are *saturated*, which means that their chemical structure contains the maximum number of hydrogen atoms (i.e., they are saturated with hydrogen). These fats are solid and tend to be found in animal products. Fats that contain fewer hydrogen atoms than required in their chemical structure and are liquid at room temperature are called *unsaturated fats*. Chemical structures known as double bonds replace the missing hydrogen atoms in these fats. If a fat has one double bond, it is a *monounsaturated fat*. If it has two or more double bonds, it is a *polyunsaturated fat*. Commonly used monounsaturated fats include olive oil and corn, soybean, and sunflower oils. Unsaturated fats can be turned into solid, saturated fat by a process called *hydrogenation*. Unsaturated fats that have been hydrogenated, and therefore made more saturated, convey many of the same health risks as fats that are naturally saturated.

*Vitamins* are chemical compounds that are involved in various metabolic reactions in the body (Table 3-1). They are divided into two groups:

1. *Fat-soluble vitamins:* Vitamins A, D, E, and K

2. *Water-soluble vitamins:* B vitamins and vitamin C

*Minerals* are crystalline chemical elements that comprise about 4 percent of a person's weight. Like vitamins, they perform various functions (Table 3-2). Calcium, phosphorous, sodium, potassium, magnesium, sulfur, and chlorine are considered macronutrients, because they are present in the body in relatively large amounts. The micronutrients, or trace minerals, are so named because of the extremely minute quantities found in the body. These micronutrients include iron, zinc, selenium, manganese, copper, iodine, and fluorine, to name a few. Altogether, there are 22 minerals known to be required.

*Water*, often taken for granted, is perhaps the most vital nutrient. While a person can survive for weeks or months without the other essential nutrients, a complete deprivation of water would cause death within a few days. Water dissolves and transports nutrients into, throughout, and from the body. It also regulates body temperature, lubricates joints, is involved in chemical reactions, and helps cells retain their shape.

### Table 3-1. Vitamins

| VITAMIN (CHEMICAL NAME) FOOD SOURCES | FUNCTIONS | DEFICIENCY SYMPTOMS |
|---|---|---|
| Vitamin A (retinol, carotene) liver, butter, carrots, pumpkin | Enables eyes to adjust to changes in light; maintains cells of skin, eyes, intestines, and lungs | Night blindness; keratinization (formation of thick, dry layer of cells on skin and eyes) |
| Vitamin D (ergocalciferol, cholecalciferol) fortified milk, fish livers | Enhances calcium and phosphorus absorption | Rickets in children; osteomalacia in adults |
| Vitamin E (alpha-tocopherol) vegetable oils | Acts as an antioxidant, protecting substances damaged by exposure to oxygen | Rare, but may cause hemolytic anemia in premature infants |
| Vitamin K (phylloquinone menaquinone) dark green leafy vegetables, liver | Essential for blood clotting | Rare, causes hemorrhaging |

*(Continues)*

**Table 3-1. (Continued)**

| VITAMIN (CHEMICAL NAME) FOOD SOURCES | FUNCTIONS | DEFICIENCY SYMPTOMS |
|---|---|---|
| Vitamin B1 (thiamin)<br>pork, whole grains | Part of coenzyme thiamin pyrophosphate, which is needed for metabolism of carbohydrates and fat | Beriberi, which results in appetite loss, nausea, vomiting, impaired heart function |
| Vitamin B2 (riboflavin)<br>milk, green vegetables, cheese | Part of coenzymes flavin mononucleotide and flavin adenine dinucleotide, which aid in the release of energy from fat, protein, and carbohydrate | Ariboflavinosis, with symptoms of cracked and dry skin around nose and mouth |
| Vitamin B3 (niacin)<br>milk, whole grains, nuts | Part of nicotinamide adenine dinucleotide and nicotinamide adenine dinucleotide phosphate, which are needed for energy release in cells | Pellagra, causing dermatitis, diarrhea, and dementia |
| Vitamin B6 (pyridoxine)<br>liver, bananas, wheat bran | Vital for amino acid synthesis and breakdown | Abnormal protein metabolism, poor growth, convulsions, anemia, decreased antibody formation |
| Vitamin B12 (cobalamin)<br>almost all animal products none in plant products) | Aids in formation of nucleic acids; needed for proper red blood cells development | Pernicious anemia, which causes megaloblastic anemia and spinal cord degeneration |
| Folic acid<br>dark green, leafy vegetables | Needed for cell growth and reproduction and amino acid metabolism | Megaloblastic anemia, which is characterized by abnormally large red blood cells that have failed to mature properly |
| Biotin<br>egg yolk, liver, nuts | Part of enzyme system acetyl coenzyme A, which is necessary for producing energy from glucose and forming fatty acids, amino acids, nucleic acids, and glycogen | Very unlikely, but could cause dermatitis, fatigue, loss of appetite |
| Pantothenic acid<br>liver, eggs, peas, peanuts | Part of coenzyme A, which is involved in releasing energy from carbohydrates, fat, and protein; also part of enzyme needed for fatty acid synthesis | Unlikely; causes fatigue, headaches, muscles cramps, poor coordination |
| Vitamin C (ascorbic acid)<br>citrus fruits, broccoli, strawberries | Needed for formation of collagen, which binds cells together and maintains elasticity and strength of blood vessels | Scurvy, with symptoms of bleeding and swollen gums, poor wound healing |

## Table 3-2.  Minerals

| MINERAL/FOOD SOURCE | FUNCTIONS | DEFICIENCY SYMPTOMS |
| --- | --- | --- |
| Calcium<br>    milk, soybeans | Forms bones and teeth; essential for blood clotting; involved with nerve stimulation, muscle contraction, and good muscle tone | Osteoporosis, causing bones to become brittle and break easily; most likely to occur in postmenopausal women |
| Phosphorus<br>    meat, poultry, carbonated drinks | Combines with calcium to form bones and teeth; part of nucleic acids; part of substances that store and release energy | Unlikely, but can cause weakness, appetite loss, bone pain |
| Sodium<br>    table salt, cured meats, processed foods | Dissolved in water outside cells where it maintains osmotic balance and regulates water balance; aids in transmitting nerve impulses | Very unlikely; causes cardiac arrest, convulsions |
| Potassium<br>    oranges, bananas, winter squash | Dissolved in water inside cells to maintain osmotic balance and regulate water balance; aids in transmitting nerve impulses | Irregular heart beat |
| Magnesium<br>    milk, whole grains, nuts | Needed to conduct nerve impulses; catalyst in many energy transfer and release reactions | Nerve tremors, convulsions, behavioral disturbances |
| Sulfur<br>    Eggs, cabbage, meat | Component of several amino acids and vitamins | Extremely unlikely |
| Chlorine<br>    table salt, meat, milk, eggs | Part of hydrochloric acid in stomach, which aids in digestion and absorption; when bound to sodium or potassium, involved in maintaining water balance in cells | Loss of appetite, poor growth, weakness |
| Iron<br>    liver, nuts, meat, spinach | Part of hemoglobin which carries oxygen in the blood; part of myoglobin which transfers oxygen from hemoglobin to muscle cells | Anemia which causes low hemoglobin levels and fatigue |
| Zinc<br>    meat, fish, milk | Needed for collagen formation; component of insulin | Impaired growth, wound healing, sexual dysfunction, taste dysfunction |
| Selenium<br>    meat, seafood, wheat | Antioxidant | Not observed in humans |
| Manganese<br>    cereal, legumes | Needed for bone development | No deficiency observed in humans; in deficient animals, it causes slowed growth, deformities, and interferes with reproduction |

*(Continues)*

**Table 3-2. (Continued)**

| MINERAL/FOOD SOURCE | FUNCTIONS | DEFICIENCY SYMPTOMS |
|---|---|---|
| Copper<br>  nuts, dried beans, liver | Needed for hemoglobin and connective tissue formation | Anemia |
| Iodine<br>  saltwater fish and shellfish, iodized salt | Part of thyroid hormones that regulate basal metabolism | Goiter |
| Fluorine<br>  fluoridated water, sardines, tea | Strengthens bones and teeth | Teeth less resistant to decay |

# Phytochemicals

Phytochemicals are nonnutrient compounds made by plants. There are more than 1,000 known phytochemicals. Recent studies suggest that a diet rich in fruits, vegetables, dry beans, and grains may reduce the risk of heart disease and hypertension. Many phytochemicals also have antioxidant properties that may also reduce the risk of some cancers, such as breast, colon, ovarian, and prostate cancer. Table 3-3 provides examples of phytochemicals, how they work, and their food source. Five to nine servings daily of fruits and vegetables, along with legumes, whole grains, nuts, and seeds are recommended.

**Table 3-3. Major Phytochemicals**

| PHYTOCHEMICALS | HEALTH BENEFITS | FOOD SOURCES |
|---|---|---|
| Capsaicinoids | Curtail the risk of cancer | Chili peppers |
| Flavonoids | Prevent blood clots, reduce tumor growths, lessen the risk of heart disease | Berries, herbs, tea, vegetables, wine |
| Isoflavones (phytoestrogens) | Prevent bone loss reduce the risk of cancer and heart disease | Barley, chickpeas, flaxseed, soybeans, soy milk, tofu |
| Isothiocyanates | Protect against breast and prostate cancer | Bok choy, Broccoli, Brussels sprouts, cabbage, cauliflower, collard greens, kale, rutabagas, turnips |

**Table 3-3. (Continued)**

| PHYTOCHEMICALS | HEALTH BENEFITS | FOOD SOURCES |
| --- | --- | --- |
| Monoterpenes | Inhibit cancer development, stimulate cell development | Citrus peels, kale, essential oils |
| Organosulfur compounds | Benefit the immune system, reduce the production of cholesterol in the liver | Chives, garlic, leeks, onions, shallots |
| Phytosterols | Diminish the risk of cancer | Legumes, nuts, seeds, vegetable oils |
| Sponins | Aid the immune system, reduces the risk of cancer | Beans, cereals, ginseng, herbs, licorice root, soy beans |
| Sterois | Reduce cholesterol | Vegetable oils |

# Guidelines and Recommendations for Meeting Nutrient Needs

NUTRITIONISTS and health professionals concur that in order to receive an adequate supply of nutrients, it is important to consume a variety of foods. The Recommended Dietary Allowance (RDA) was developed by the Food and Nutrition Board of the National Research Council—National Academy of Sciences and is intended to be a generous recommendation that should meet the nutrient needs of practically all healthy persons. The RDA is grouped by age and sex, and also makes recommendations for pregnant and lactating females. Recommendations for calorie intake and a range of estimated safe and adequate levels for additional vitamins and minerals are also included in the RDA. A new set of standards, known as the Dietary Reference Intakes (DRI), is also gaining in popularity. The DRI standards have established dietary nutrient intakes for healthy individuals based on age and gender. The United States Department of Agriculture (USDA) has developed dietary guidelines that are specific for the American general population.

# USDA Dietary Guidelines for Americans 2005

## ❧ Adequate Nutrients within Calorie Needs

Consume a variety of nutrient-dense foods and beverages within and among the basic food groups while choosing foods that limit the intake of saturated and *trans* fats, cholesterol, added sugars, salt, and alcohol.

Meet recommended intakes within energy needs by adopting a balanced eating pattern, such as the U.S. Department of Agriculture (USDA) Food Guide or the Dietary Approaches to Stop Hypertension (DASH) Eating Plan.

## ❧ Weight Management

To maintain body weight in a healthy range, balance calories from foods and beverages with calories expended.

To prevent gradual weight gain over time, make small decreases in food and beverage calories and increase physical activity.

## ❧ Physical Activity

Engage in regular physical activity and reduce sedentary activities to promote health, psychological well-being, and a healthy body weight.

To reduce the risk of chronic disease in adulthood: Engage in at least 30 minutes of moderate-intensity physical activity, above usual activity, at work or home on most days of the week.

For most people, greater health benefits can be obtained by engaging in physical activity of more vigorous intensity or longer duration.

To help manage body weight and prevent gradual, unhealthy body weight gain in adulthood: Engage in approximately 60 minutes of moderate- to vigorous-intensity activity on most days of the week while not exceeding caloric intake requirements.

To sustain weight loss in adulthood: Participate in at least 60 to 90 minutes of daily moderate-intensity physical activity while not exceeding caloric intake requirements. Some people may need to consult with a healthcare provider before participating in this level of activity.

Achieve physical fitness by including cardiovascular conditioning, stretching exercises for flexibility, and resistance exercises or calisthenics for muscle strength and endurance.

## ❧ Food Groups to Encourage

Consume a sufficient amount of fruits and vegetables while staying within energy needs. Two cups of fruit and 2½ cups of vegetables per day are recommended for a reference 2,000-calorie intake, with higher or lower amounts depending on the calorie level.

Choose a variety of fruits and vegetables each day. In particular, select from all five vegetable subgroups (dark green, orange, legumes, starchy vegetables, and other vegetables) several times a week.

Consume 3 or more ounce-equivalents of whole-grain products per day, with the rest of the recommended grains coming from enriched or whole-grain products. In general, at least half the grains should come from whole grains.

Consume 3 cups per day of fat-free or low-fat milk or equivalent milk products.

## ❧ Fats

Consume less than 10 percent of calories from saturated fatty acids and less than 300 mg/day of cholesterol, and keep *trans* fatty acid consumption as low as possible.

Keep total fat intake between 20 to 35 percent of calories, with most fats coming from sources of polyunsaturated and monounsaturated fatty acids, such as fish, nuts, and vegetable oils.

When selecting and preparing meat, poultry, dry beans, and milk or milk products, make choices that are lean, low-fat, or fat-free.

Limit intake of fats and oils high in saturated and/or *trans* fatty acids, and choose products low in such fats and oils.

## ❧ Carbohydrates

Choose fiber-rich fruits, vegetables, and whole grains often.

Choose and prepare foods and beverages with little added sugars or caloric sweeteners, such as amounts suggested by the USDA Food Guide and the DASH Eating Plan.

Reduce the incidence of dental caries by practicing good oral hygiene and consuming sugar- and starch-containing foods and beverages less frequently.

## ❧ Sodium and Potassium

Consume less than 2,300 mg (approximately 1 teaspoon of salt) of sodium per day.

Choose and prepare foods with little salt. At the same time, consume potassium-rich foods, such as fruits and vegetables.

### ❧ Alcoholic Beverages

Those who choose to drink alcoholic beverages should do so sensibly and in moderation—defined as the consumption of up to one drink per day for women and up to two drinks per day for men.

Alcoholic beverages should not be consumed by some individuals, including those who cannot restrict their alcohol intake, women of child-bearing age who may become pregnant, pregnant and lactating women, children and adolescents, individuals taking medications that can interact with alcohol, and those with specific medical conditions.

Alcoholic beverages should be avoided by individuals engaging in activities that require attention, skill, or coordination, such as driving or operating machinery.

### ❧ Food Safety

To avoid microbial foodborne illness:

Clean hands, food contact surfaces, and fruits and vegetables. Meat and poultry should not be washed or rinsed.

Separate raw, cooked, and ready-to-eat foods while shopping, preparing, or storing foods.

Cook foods to a safe temperature to kill microorganisms.

Chill (refrigerate) perishable food promptly and defrost foods properly.

Avoid raw (unpasteurized) milk or any products made from unpasteurized milk, raw or partially cooked eggs or foods containing raw eggs, raw or undercooked meat and poultry, unpasteurized juices, and raw sprouts.

*Note: The* Dietary Guidelines for Americans 2005 *contains additional recommendations for specific populations. The full document is available at* www.healthierus.gov/dietaryguidelines. *Courtesy of U.S. Department of Agriculture.*

# Food Pyramids

## MyPyramid

In 2005 the USDA introduced MyPyramid, which proved to be vastly different from the traditional Food Guide Pyramid. This new version has a variety of models (12 in all) that are based on caloric need and physical activity.

**Figure 3-1. MyPyramid**

**Figure 3-1. MyPyramid (Continued)**

| GRAINS<br>Make half your grains whole | VEGETABLES<br>Vary your veggies | FRUITS<br>Focus on fruits | MILK<br>Get your calcium-rich foods | MEAT & BEANS<br>Go lean with protein |
|---|---|---|---|---|
| Eat at least 3 oz. of whole-grain cereals, breads, crackers, rice, or pasta every day<br><br>1 oz. is about 1 slice of bread, about 1 cup of breakfast cereal, or ½ cup of cooked rice, cereal, or pasta | Eat more dark-green veggies like broccoli, spinach, and other dark leafy greens<br><br>Eat more orange vegetables like carrots and sweetpotatoes<br><br>Eat more dry beans and peas like pinto beans, kidney beans, and lentils | Eat a variety of fruit<br><br>Choose fresh, frozen, canned, or dried fruit<br><br>Go easy on fruit juices | Go low-fat or fat-free when you choose milk, yogurt, and other milk products<br><br>If you don't or can't consume milk, choose lactose-free products or other calcium sources such as fortified foods and beverages | Choose low-fat or lean meats and poultry<br><br>Bake it, broil it, or grill it<br><br>Vary your protein routine — choose more fish, beans, peas, nuts, and seeds |

For a 2,000-calorie diet, you need the amounts below from each food group. To find the amounts that are right for you, go to MyPyramid.gov.

| Eat 6 oz. every day | Eat 2½ cups every day | Eat 2 cups every day | Get 3 cups every day;<br>for kids aged 2 to 8, it's 2 | Eat 5½ oz. every day |

**Find your balance between food and physical activity**

- Be sure to stay within your daily calorie needs.
- Be physically active for at least 30 minutes most days of the week.
- About 60 minutes a day of physical activity may be needed to prevent weight gain.
- For sustaining weight loss, at least 60 to 90 minutes a day of physical activity may be required.
- Children and teenagers should be physically active for 60 minutes every day, or most days.

**Know the limits on fats, sugars, and salt (sodium)**

- Make most of your fat sources from fish, nuts, and vegetable oils.
- Limit solid fats like butter, margarine, shortening, and lard, as well as foods that contain these.
- Check the Nutrition Facts label to keep saturated fats, *trans* fats, and sodium low.
- Choose food and beverages low in added sugars. Added sugars contribute calories with few, if any, nutrients.

**MyPyramid.gov**
STEPS TO A HEALTHIER YOU

USDA
U.S. Department of Agriculture
Center for Nutrition Policy and Promotion
April 2005
CNPP-15

USDA is an equal opportunity provider and employer.

Courtesy of U.S. Department of Agriculture

As illustrated in Figure 3-1, the MyPyramid has six vertical colored bands that represent each of the food groups. Orange represents grains, green is for vegetables, red for fruits, yellow for oil, blue for dairy, and purple for meat, bones, fish, and nuts. The width at the base of the band indicates the size of the portion that should be consumed. Brown rice, steamed spinach, apples, skim milk, and grilled salmon can be enjoyed in large quantities as they have little or no solid fats. Foods such cakes and ice cream, which are high in solid fats, sugar, or sweeteners, should be consumed in moderation, and are therefore represented by thinner bands.

From the bottom to the top of the pyramid, each food group category constricts to indicate moderation in portion size. The action figure ascending the stairs symbolizes the overall importance of daily activity and its direct relationship to weight loss and maintaining weight loss.

## Other Food Guide Pyramids

In 2000 the Oldways Preservation and Exchange Trust developed a number of food pyramids that further accommodate cultural and ethnic food choices, such as Asian (Fig. 3-2), Latin American (Fig. 3-3), Mediterranean (Fig. 3-4), and Vegetarian (Fig. 3-5) cuisines. Each includes a list of common foods and beverage recommendations.

## Nutrition Labeling

The U.S. Recommended Daily Allowance developed by the Food and Drug Administration (FDA) was based on the 1968 revision of the Recommended Dietary Allowances. This was the first labeling system for the listing of nutrient levels on food labels. In 1990 the Nutrition Labeling and Education Act and regulations set by the FDA and the USDA established that by the year 1994, all packaged foods would be required to carry labels listing a food's nutritional content. (See Appendix F for more information on labeling.)

**Figure 3-2. Traditional Healthy Asian Diet Pyramid and Daily Beverage Recommendations**

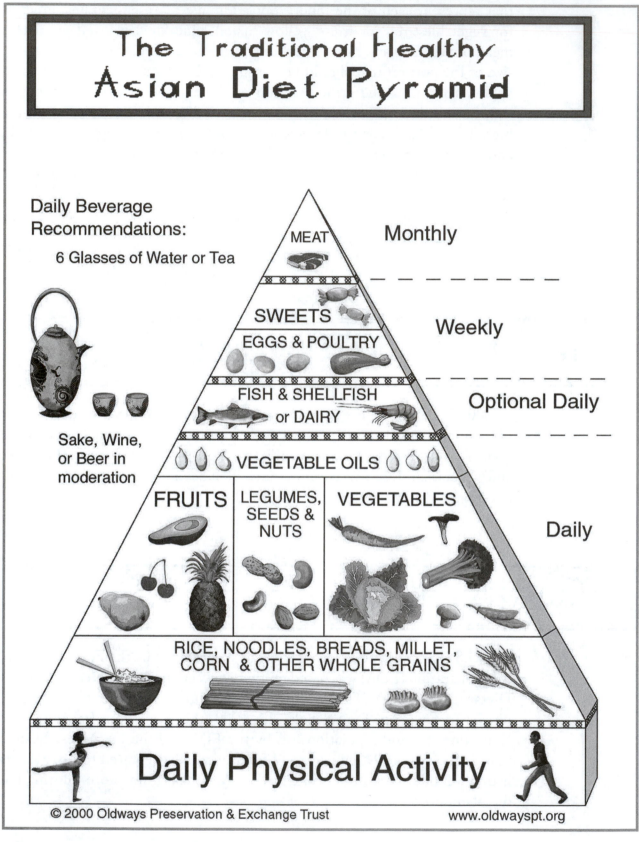

The Traditional Healthy Asian Diet Pyramid

Daily Beverage Recommendations:

6 Glasses of Water or Tea

Sake, Wine, or Beer in moderation

MEAT — Monthly

SWEETS
EGGS & POULTRY — Weekly

FISH & SHELLFISH or DAIRY — Optional Daily

VEGETABLE OILS

FRUITS | LEGUMES, SEEDS & NUTS | VEGETABLES — Daily

RICE, NOODLES, BREADS, MILLET, CORN & OTHER WHOLE GRAINS

Daily Physical Activity

© 2000 Oldways Preservation & Exchange Trust          www.oldwayspt.org

**Figure 3-3. Traditional Healthy Latin American Diet Pyramid and Daily Beverage Recommendations**

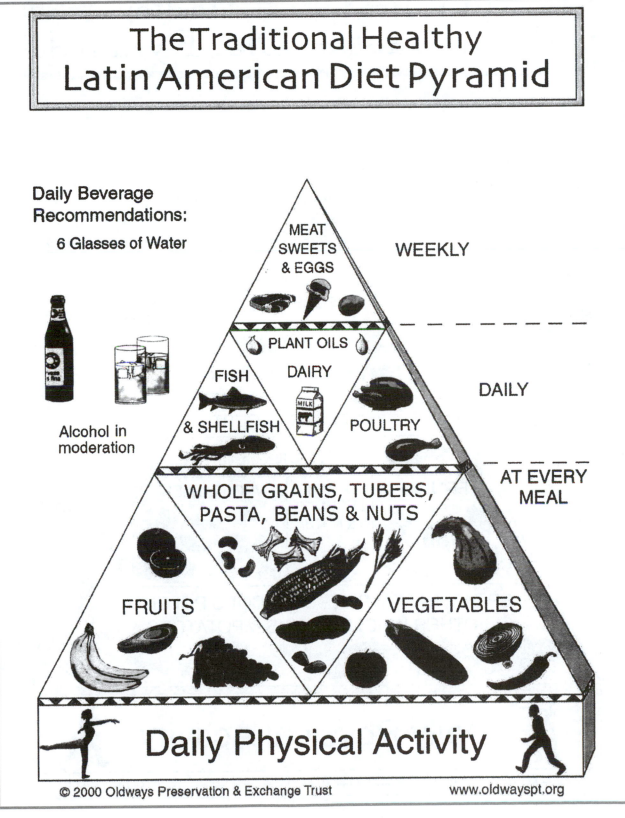

© 2000 Oldways Preservation & Exchange Trust        www.oldwayspt.org

**Figure 3-4. Traditional Healthy Mediterranean Diet Pyramid and Daily Beverage Recommendations**

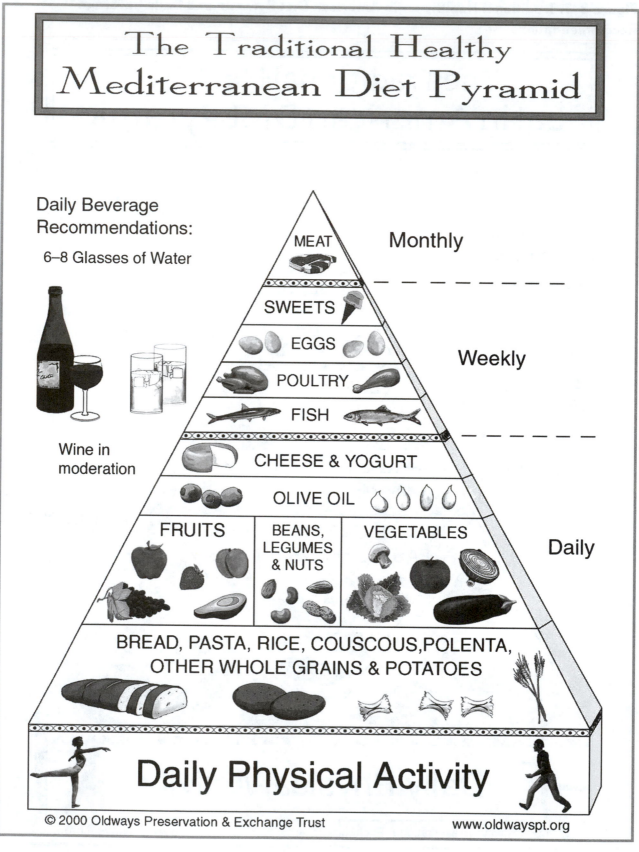

# The Traditional Healthy Mediterranean Diet Pyramid

Daily Beverage Recommendations:

6–8 Glasses of Water

Wine in moderation

MEAT — Monthly

SWEETS

EGGS

POULTRY — Weekly

FISH

CHEESE & YOGURT

OLIVE OIL

FRUITS | BEANS, LEGUMES & NUTS | VEGETABLES — Daily

BREAD, PASTA, RICE, COUSCOUS, POLENTA, OTHER WHOLE GRAINS & POTATOES

## Daily Physical Activity

www.oldwayspt.org

**Figure 3-5. Traditional Healthy Vegetarian Diet and Daily Beverage Recommendations**

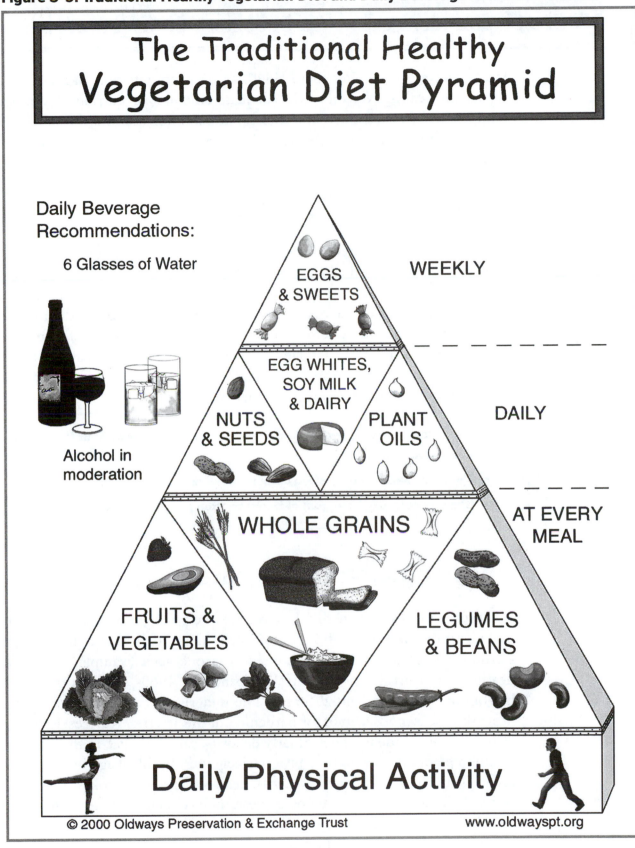

# The Traditional Healthy Vegetarian Diet Pyramid

Daily Beverage Recommendations:

6 Glasses of Water

Alcohol in moderation

EGGS & SWEETS — WEEKLY

EGG WHITES, SOY MILK & DAIRY

NUTS & SEEDS — PLANT OILS — DAILY

WHOLE GRAINS — AT EVERY MEAL

FRUITS & VEGETABLES — LEGUMES & BEANS

Daily Physical Activity

© 2000 Oldways Preservation & Exchange Trust — www.oldwayspt.org

# Relationship of Nutrition to Health

AMERICANS are becoming increasingly aware that nutrition has a strong impact on health. Not only will adequate amounts of nutrients promote good health by preventing deficiencies, but good nutrition may also help in the prevention of chronic diseases and in increasing longevity.

## Preventing Deficiencies

Fortunately in the United States, our abundant food supply makes it possible for most individuals to be well nourished. However, obtaining enough of certain nutrients may still be a problem for some groups of people. Females of reproductive age often receive too little iron in their diets, making iron-deficiency anemia the most common nutrient deficiency in this country. In addition, females are frequently victims of osteoporosis, which develops after menopause, usually after years of a chronically low calcium intake. Other vulnerable groups include:

- **The elderly, whose physical and economic restrictions may limit their ability to eat a nutritious diet**
- **The poor, because they often cannot afford an adequate diet**
- **Chronic eaters, whose goal of thinness often precludes eating nutritiously**

## Avoiding Chronic Diseases

Many chronic diseases in this country are the result of a combination of overnutrition and the advances of technology that make life easier. Cardiovascular disease (or heart disease) is one such example. Although deaths from heart disease have declined since the 1960s, it is still the number-one killer in the United States. The underlying condition that causes heart disease is *atherosclerosis*, or hardening of the arteries. Atherosclerosis is characterized by the presence of fatty deposits, called *plaques*, in the arteries. As these plaques develop, they progressively increase blockage in the arteries, causing chest pain (*angina pectoris*), heart attacks, and strokes. Extensive research has identified high blood cholesterol levels, cigarette smoking, high blood pressure, obesity, and physical inactivity as some of the major contributors to the development of atherosclerosis.

The risk of heart disease is increased when blood cholesterol levels are above 200 mg per 100 ml of blood. In addition to an awareness of total blood cholesterol, it is important to know the amounts of "good" (high-density lipoproteins[HDL]) and "bad" (low-density lipoproteins[LDL]) cholesterol in the blood. A high proportion of LDL cholesterol increases risk of cardio-vascular disease whereas a high proportion of HDL lowers the risk. To lower blood cholesterol, the National Cholesterol Education Program recommends a diet that contains less than 300 milligrams of cholesterol per day and promotes the reduction of fat intake to no more than 30 percent of calories consumed and saturated fat to less than 10 percent of energy. Of this allowance, less than one-third should be saturated fat. Recent research also suggests that other dietary changes also may lower the risk of cardiovascular disease. These include the consumption of highly unsaturated fatty acids (omega-3 fatty acids) found in salmon and other fatty fish, dietary fiber (particularly oat bran and pectin), and monounsaturated fats such as olive oil.

Some forms of cancer have been linked to diet. Numerous research studies suggest that a high-fiber diet can prevent colon cancer. The consumption of generous amounts of foods containing vitamin E and beta-carotene (the orange pigment in vegetables that is converted to vitamin A) may reduce the risk of lung cancer. A high-fat intake, however, has been implicated as a risk factor for breast, colon, and prostate cancers. The National Cancer Institute has released dietary guidelines designed to reduce the incidence of cancer and cancer-related deaths. These recommendations include raising fiber to 20 to 30 grams daily, eating more fruits and vegetables, and lowering fat and alcohol consumption.

A medical problem that plagues approximately 25 percent of adult Americans is *high blood pressure*, or *hypertension*. Called the silent killer, because it usually has no symptoms, high blood pressure can cause strokes, heart attacks, and kidney failure. A high sodium intake is frequently linked with high blood pressure, and diet therapy often includes sodium restriction. Most Americans consume far more sodium than they need. Some foods naturally contain a large amount of sodium, but the vast majority of salt and other sodium-containing ingredients are added for flavor in processed foods. The American Heart Association recommends a maximum of 3,000 milligrams sodium per day. Individuals who consume processed foods and/or frequently dine in restaurants and other foodservice establishments can easily exceed this recommendation.

Another problem that afflicts approximately one-fourth of adults in the United States and contributes to a myriad of problems is obesity. Obesity may cause heart disease, diabetes, high blood pressure, and even cancer. There are numerous reasons for obesity, which may be physiological and/or environmental. A sedentary lifestyle combined with high caloric intake most certainly contributes to the development of obesity in many individuals.

When people are persuaded to consume calorie-laden meals and snacks by a bombardment of advertisements and to limit physical activity using the conveniences provided by modern technology, calorie intake increases while calorie expenditure decreases, resulting in obesity. A good treatment plan to control weight includes a lower-calorie, nutritionally balanced diet, a change in eating habits, and a reasonable amount of physical activity.

# Diabetes Type 1 and 2

DIABETES *mellitus*, commonly known as diabetes, is a disease in which the body cannot make insulin or effectively utilize insulin. Diabetes can lead to blindness, cardiovascular disease, kidney disease, and premature death. Currently over 20 million children and adults in the U.S. suffer from diabetes. There are 2 types of diabetes, Type 1 and Type 2.

*Type 1 diabetes*, previously called insulin-dependent diabetes mellitus (IDDM), is the more dangerous type and occurs when the body is not able to make insulin. Type 1 diabetes is less common than Type 2 diabetes, occurring in only 10 to 20 percent of all diabetes cases diagnosed. Type 1 diabetes strikes children and young adults, but can be controlled through diet and exercise.

*Type 2 diabetes* accounts for 80 to 90 percent of all cases. Previously, referred to as non–insulin-dependent diabetes or adult-onset diabetes, Type 2 diabetes is usually seen in adults. Type 2 diabetes occurs when the body does not produce an adequate amount of insulin or the cells disregard the insulin produced. African Americans, Latinos, and Native Americans tend to be more susceptible to Type 2 diabetes than others in the population. Children and adolescents who are overweight or obese are also sometimes diagnosed with this serious illness.

# Nutritional Implications for Menu Planning

WHEN planning a menu for a foodservice operation, it is important to consider nutrient needs. Although some people still are unconcerned about nutrition, an ever-growing number of Americans want the opportunity to select nutritious foods.

Foodservice operations that offer nutritious foods help to heighten an awareness of nutrition. A nutrient breakdown of menu items, printed general nutrition information on the menu, and a health-oriented newsletter are just a few vehicles that can increase interest in healthful eating. Staff members who possess some knowledge about nutrition are also invaluable as they are able to answer guests' questions about the foods they are serving. Foodservice personnel can be educated about nutrition through seminars and by encouraging employees to take courses on this subject.

# Ingredients and Preparation

THE ingredients and methods of preparation a foodservice operation uses have a vast effect on the food's nutrient content. It is desirable to maximize the amount of vitamins, minerals, and fiber and to minimize calories, fat, cholesterol, sodium, and sugar.

Vitamins are very fragile substances that can be destroyed by exposure to acid, alkali, heat, light, and air. The enzymes naturally present in foods can also destroy vitamins. Water-soluble vitamins may be lost when they leach into the cooking water and the water is discarded. Frozen fruits and vegetables are generally higher in vitamins than their fresh or canned counterparts, because they usually are frozen immediately after harvesting and have undergone minimal processing. Fresh foods, however, may travel great distances to the market, and it may be days or even weeks before they are sold "fresh." During this lag time, a large percentage of vitamins may be lost, as time deterioration affects product quality. Canned foods experience harsher processing conditions and might not be eaten for months or years after harvesting.

Tailoring a foodservice operation's cooking methods to minimize vitamin loss can be achieved by adhering to eight guidelines:

1. **Avoid overcooking food.**
2. **Steam, stir-fry, or microwave foods instead of boiling. If cooking in water cannot be avoided, use as little as possible and reuse that water in a soup or stock gravy.**
3. **Keep food wrapped to prevent oxidation.**
4. **If appropriate, keep foods cool to decrease the activity of enzymes.**
5. **Do not add baking soda to green vegetables to give them a bright green color.**
6. **Store foods in the dark or in opaque containers.**

7. **Cut foods into medium-size pieces for cooking. Large pieces usually cook too slowly, and very small pieces promote oxidation and loss of vitamins into the cooking water.**

8. **Avoid holding food at serving temperature for a prolonged period, as on a steam table. This procedure not only increases vitamin loss, but also affects texture and increases the risk of food poisoning.**

As compared to vitamins, minerals are relatively indestructible, although they can be lost in the cooking water and drippings from roasted or broiled meats. Precautions such as reusing the cooking water and the defatted drippings can help retain the mineral content.

The fiber content of a meal is also very important. Using high-fiber ingredients and not removing the peel from some fruits and vegetables contributes to adding fiber. Serving whole-grain breads and rolls, incorporating legumes into the menu, and using unpeeled potatoes in soups and stews are just a few other ways to increase a meal's fiber level.

The fat content of a food usually can be lowered with little change in flavor. Simply decreasing the amount of butter, margarine, or oil for sautéing can greatly reduce fat and therefore calorie content. Lower-fat ingredients, such as fish, skinless poultry, lean meats, and low-fat milk products, can have the same effect. Broiling, steaming, or poaching foods also produces a final product that is lower in fat than fried foods.

Instead of using the traditional fat and flour roux for thickening, flour can be mixed with a cold liquid and heated until thickened, omitting fat completely. Chilling stocks and soups, then removing the fat that has hardened on top is also an effective way to decrease fat calories. When fat levels are lowered in a food, cholesterol is often reduced at the same time.

One of the most common high-cholesterol ingredients used in many foods is egg yolk. It is often possible to substitute two egg whites for one whole egg or to use a cholesterol-free egg substitute. Decreasing saturated fat in foods and raising the proportion of unsaturated fat may help to reduce blood cholesterol levels. Use liquid oils instead of solid fats. Avoid most animal fats as well as highly saturated vegetable fats, such as coconut and palm oils.

Salt is another expendable item in most recipes because herbs and spices may be substituted to enhance the lost flavor. Cooking with fresh or frozen ingredients is preferable because most canned foods contain high levels of sodium.

Replacing rich, sugary desserts with fresh fruits and lighter, low-fat choices on a menu will help patrons lower their sugar and calorie intake. While dessert is often an opportunity to indulge, a delicious fruit sorbet or light soufflé can be satisfying without a high-sugar and high-calorie intake.

**Figure 3-6. Luncheon Menu**

# Lunch

## Balanced Selection

|  | Calories | Fat grams | Fiber grams |
| --- | --- | --- | --- |
| Spinach Salad with Strawberry Vinaigrette | 120 | 5 | 2 |
| Sole Francaise | 420 | 13 | 5 |
| Pecan Tartlet | 170 | 7 | 1 |

*The perfect combination of great taste and good nutrition*

- Generous amounts of vegetables and fruits
- Variety of fiber-rich foods such as whole grains and beans
- Foods high in protein at each meal
- Small amounts of healthy fats such as olive oil, nuts and flax seeds
- Delicious flavors in moderate, satisfying portions

## Soups & Salads

- Caribbean Plantain Soup    55/tr/2
- ▲ Miso Soup    40/1/tr
- Chicken Noodle Soup    115/2/2
- ▲ Gazpacho    45/tr/2
- Spinach Salad with Strawberry Champagne Vinaigrette    120/5/2

## Entrees

**▲● ASIAN COLD NOODLE SALAD    260/8/5**
Carrots, edamame and red bell peppers tossed with an Asian coconut dressing, served over spaghetti

**BLUE PLATE SPECIAL    425/12/5**
Turkey meatloaf served with mashed potatoes, gravy and sautéed green beans

**SOLE FRANCAISE    420/13/5**
Sole breaded with flour and dipped in a egg and parmesan cheese mixture and sautéed until golden brown served with sautéed rapini and spaghetti topped with marinara sauce

**PIZZA WITH CARAMELIZED ONIONS    315/11/5**
On a multi-grain crust with Canyon Ranch Pizza sauce, topped with mozzarella cheese and caramelized onions

**CHICKEN PESTO WRAP    340/10/3**
Chicken, roasted red bell peppers, pesto and romaine lettuce wrapped in a whole-wheat tortilla and served with the side salad of the day

**BUILD YOUR OWN SANDWICH    \***
With your choice of assorted breads, vegetables, roast turkey, roast beef, tuna salad, Swiss cheese and cheddar cheese

**▲ VEGETARIAN BEAN CHILI    175/2/7**

**VEGETARIAN BURGER    325/5/8**
Grilled veggie burger, lettuce, tomato and red onion on a soft sprouted multi-grain roll, served with the side salad of the day

**▲ FRESH STEAMED VEGETABLE BASKET    80/tr/7**

## Accompaniments

- ▲ Marinated Tofu    70/5/1
- Chicken (1 ounce)    45/1/0
- Fruit Smoothie with protein powder    *
- Nonfat Cottage Cheese    35/tr/0
- Nonfat Plain Yogurt    55/0/tr
- ▲ Baked Sweet Potato    160/tr/5
- ▲ Baked Potato    170/tr/3
- ▲ Seasoned Brown Rice    90/tr/tr
- ▲ Hummus with Lavosh    160/5/4

## Desserts

- ▲ Fresh Fruit Plate    120/tr/6
- ▲ Fruit Sorbet    75/tr/tr
- Canyon Ranch Homemade Ice Cream    100/4/tr
- With nonfat fudge sauce    190/4/tr
- Chocolate Chip Cookies (2)    170/6/1
- Cookie of the Day    *
- Pecan Tartlet    170/7/1

Calories/Fat Grams/Fiber Grams    tr = trace (less than 1 gram)    ■ Contains a trace of alcohol    ▲ Vegan (contains no animal products)    • Spicy
\* Please ask your server for today's selection, its calorie count, fat grams and fiber grams

**SALMON FROM A FARM?**
We are now serving a high quality, certified organic farm-raised salmon from Chile. The practices of organic aquaculture are consistent with our high standards for serving clean and wholesome food: no hormones or antibiotics, sustainable environmental practices, and feed with high quality ingredients.

Courtesy of Canyon Ranch Health Resort, Tucson, AZ

Reducing the amount of sugar in a recipe often requires experimentation. Adding chopped fruit, extra spices, and extracts can compensate for the loss of sweetness. Canyon Ranch Health Resort® in Tucson, Arizona, offers a number of nutritious items on its luncheon menu (Fig. 3.6).

# For Review and Discussion

1. Name the six groups of nutrients that provide a nutritious diet.
2. Explain MyPyramid.
3. Which groups of people are likely to be deficient in nutrients, and why?
4. List five contributors to the development of atherosclerosis.
5. Which dietary changes can help prevent heart disease?
6. Discuss how a foodservice operation might want to offer more nutritious foods to its customers.

## ACKNOWLEDGMENT

Thanks to Jennifer Schlitzer, M.S., R.D., for her contributions to this chapter.

# Chapter 4

# FOODSERVICE MENUS

A MENU is a list of food and beverage items. To plan a profitable menu, a foodservice professional must first identify the style of menu to be used: *à la carte*, *semi à la carte*, or *prix fixe*. This chapter explores the characteristics of a variety of foodservice menus including breakfast, brunch, luncheon, dinner, tasting, special occasion, ethnic, specialty, catering, room service, institutional, wine, dessert, tea, and lounge.

## Objectives

❏ To define the three styles of menus: à la carte, semi à la carte, and prix fixe

❏ To present in detail the important elements of the various food-service menus discussed in this chapter

❏ To define three types of service: American, French, and Russian

# Menu Styles

In the foodservice industry, there are three styles of menus: à la carte, semi à la carte, and prix fixe.

On the **à la carte menu**, as shown in Figure 4-1, everything on the menu is priced separately, from appetizers to desserts.

On the **semi à la carte menu**, as shown in Figure 4-2, appetizers, soups, and desserts usually are priced separately. The entrée traditionally includes a salad, potato, vegetable, and sometimes a beverage. This style of menu is the most popular today.

The **prix-fixe menu**, as shown in Figure 4-3, offers a complete meal at a set price.

# Breakfast Menus

Most breakfast menus contain both à la carte and semi à la carte sections. The à la carte section offers juices, fruits, cereals, eggs, meats, pancakes, French toasts, waffles, bakery goods, side dishes, and beverages. The semi à la carte section offers a wide variety of combinations (e.g., two eggs any style with bacon or sausage served with toast; or three pancakes with syrup and bacon or sausage served with home fries). The prices of food items on a breakfast menu range from low to moderate due to the fact that most people do not expect to pay much for breakfast. However, in high-end restaurants and large hotels, the cost can be considerably higher. Most breakfast items generally are cooked to order, requiring the chefs or breakfast chefs to be quick and well organized. Breakfast service for the most part is *American service*. A waitstaff person takes the order and brings it to the table, and a dining room attendant later clears the table. The menu in Figure 4-4 is a combination à la carte and prix-fixe menu. The prix-fixe section includes three courses: appetizers, entrées, and desserts. Most of the items, such as the appetizers, egg dishes, steak, trout, and crêpes, are served hot.

# Brunch Menus

A BRUNCH menu consists of both breakfast and luncheon items, and is generally served in hotels and high-end restaurants from 10:00 A.M. until 3:00 P.M. The brunch menu can be quite elaborate. Brunch menus offer items such as juices, fruit, appetizers, soups, sandwiches, breakfast items (eggs, French toasts, bacon, etc.), pastries, breads, and desserts. The La Isla® menu in Figure 4-5 offers an extensive listing of low- to moderate-priced items, such as thirst quenchers, coffee, appetizers, soups, salads, sandwiches, eggs, omelets, pancakes, French toasts, and a number of accompaniments. This style of menu is both à la carte and semi à la carte. Many items are served individually, but the eggs and omelets are served with the traditional accompaniments.

# Luncheon Menus

A LUNCHEON menu can be à la carte or semi à la carte (Fig. 4-6). À la carte items include appetizers, salads, cold and hot sandwiches, entrées, desserts, and beverages. The semi à la carte section lists entrées served with salad, vegetables, potato, or rice. Many luncheon menus offer daily specials, such as soups, sandwiches, or pastas, that are prepared in a variety of ways. Entrée specials might include Baked Salmon on Monday, and Chicken Pot Pie on Tuesday. Specials are presented in a variety of ways: on a blackboard at the entrance of the restaurant; inside the menu as a clip-on; or verbally by the servers. For the most part luncheon items are not as expensive as the dinner menu listings because the portion sizes are smaller. Prices on the luncheon menu depend on the menu item, the type of operation, and the location of the establishment. Prices can range from low to high. Luncheon items are generally baked, barbecued, braised, broiled, fried, grilled, poached, roasted, sautéed, simmered, smoked, and steamed so a fully equipped kitchen is essential. Luncheon items such as appetizers, soups, entrées, and desserts are frequently made from scratch and require preparation by someone who has a solid culinary foundation. Luncheon service is most frequently American service, which is quick and efficient. Most patrons have limited time for lunch, and they expect fast service as well as good food.

**Figure 4-1. À la Carte Menu**

# Sonsie

## spring asparagus starters

Asparagus & Leek Salad w/Bacon Wrapped Oysters … Smokey Crème Fraiche 12.00

Batter Fried Asparagus w/Fava Beans, Tomato & Fresh Mozzarella 11.00

Garden Chopped Salad w/Sheep's Milk Camembert & Grilled Asparagus 12.00

Walnut Crust Shrimp w/White Asparagus, Brown Butter & Lemon 13.00

Kobe Beef Steak & Egg w/Asparagus … Truffle Aroma 15.00

## appetizers

Iced Malepeque Oysters w/Assorted Condiments 2.25 ea*

Tuna Sashimi w/Tempura Purple Nori Rolls … Spring Blossoms 15.00*

Flash Fried Calamari w/Yellow Tomato Sauce & Crispy Hot Cherry Peppers 10.75

Steamed Black Mussels w/Corona Beer, Chile & Lime Butter 12.00

oVietnamese Vegetable Spring Rolls 9.00

Ginger Carrot Bisque w/Curry Popcorn & Coconut Cream 7.75

Red Leaf Salad w/Cucumber & Tomatoes 7.50 w/Warm Crispy Goat Cheese 9.50

Eggless Caesar Salad w/Parmesan Croutons 8.50

## pasta

Angel Hair w/Veal Meatballs, Plum Tomatoes & Shaved Pecorino 14.75

Mushroom Tofu Ravioli w/Miso Bouillon … Organic Spinach 15.00

Sweet Potato Stuffed Gnocchi w/Chicken, Country Ham & Crumbled Goat Cheese 15.50

Corn Fettuccini w/Grilled Chipotle Shrimp … Sweet Pea Guacamole 16.00

Black Spaghetti w/Scallops, Mussels, Garlic & Mint 16.00

oMee Krob: Thai Crispy Noodles…Spicy, Spicy, Spicy! 16.00

## from the brick oven

Brick Oven Focaccia w/Whole Roasted Garlic & Assorted Olives 9.00

Pizza w/Fresh Tomatoes, Mozzarella & Basil Pesto 9.75 w/Sopressata 11.00

Goat Cheese Pizza w/Sweet Roasted Peppers & Calamata Olives 11.00

Pizza w/Grilled Mushrooms, Caramelized Onions & Brie 11.00

White Cheese Pizza w/Soft Ricotta, Sliced Garlic & Prosciutto 10.75

Spring Onion Pizza w/Wood Smoked Bacon & Farmer's Cheese 10.75

Pizza "Burger" w/Cheddar Cheese & Fixings 11.00

Chicken & Jack Cheese Pizza w/Guacamole, Salsa & Sour Cream 12.00

**Courtesy of Sonsie, Boston, MA**

**Figure 4-1.  À la Carte Menu (Continued)**

# Sonsie

## main dishes

Grilled Salmon w/Tarragon Mayonnaise, Beets & Crab Fritters 24.00

Baked Lemon Sole w/Artichokes & Olive Tapenade 22.00

Crisp Fried Golden Trout w/Crayfish Tails ... Tabasco Remoulade 23.00

Shelled Lobster w/Spring Vegetable Ragout & Saffron 34.00

Tonight's Market Fish *priced nightly*

Baked Ricotta Flan w/Grilled Asparagus, White Beans & Yellow Tomato 15.00

Maple Glazed Roast Chicken w/Buttermilk Whipped Potatoes ... Pecan Spinach 18.00

Grilled Pork Tenderloin w/Wild Mushroom Morel Cream & Sweet Braised Onion 20.00

Charcoal Duck Breast & Roasted Leg w/Strawberry Rhubarb Coulis 21.50*

Grilled Loin Lamb Chops w/Blue Cheese & Bacon Tomato Stack ...Fingerling Potatoes 28.00*

16oz. Grilled Sirloin Steak 32.50*

Classic Steak Au Poive 34.00*

## sides

Simple Mashed Potatoes 4.00

Hot & Spicy French Fries 4.00

Individual Baked Potato Gratin 5.00

Spinach w/Garlic & Extra Virgin Olive Oil 4.00

My Favorite Stir Fry Green Beans 4.00

Sugar Snap Peas Au Beurre 4.00

Grilled Portobello Caps w/Parsley & Lemon 6.00

Deep Fried Smoked Onion Rings 4.00

Potato & Vegetable Sampler 15.00

## sweets

Lemon Brûlée Tart w/Lemon Sorbet & Fresh Raspberries 8.00

Roasted Rhubarb Pavlova ... Candied Ginger Ice Cream 8.00

Fresh Strawberry Trifle w/Vanilla Custard & Crisp Filo 8.00

Espresso Ice Cream Profiteroles w/Caramel & Nutella 8.00

Rich Dark Chocolate Hazelnut Gateau w/Frangelico Chantilly 8.00

Warm Chocolate Bread Pudding w/Soft Whipped Cream ... Chocolate Drizzle 8.00

Chocolate Malt Sandwich Cookies 4.75

Seasonal Cheese Plate w/Guava Paste & Toasted Whole Almonds 12.00

* These items are served raw, undercooked or may be cooked to your specifications.
Consuming raw or undercooked shellfish, seafood, poultry,
eggs or meat may increase risk of food borne illness
oContains fish sauce
Please ask your server for specifics about ingredients and cooking preparations.
An 18% gratuity will be added to parties of six or more.

Artwork by Martabel Wasserman, Age 17, Providence RI

**Chef Bill Poirier**

Courtesy of Sonsie, Boston, MA

**Figure 4-2. Semi à la Carte Menu**

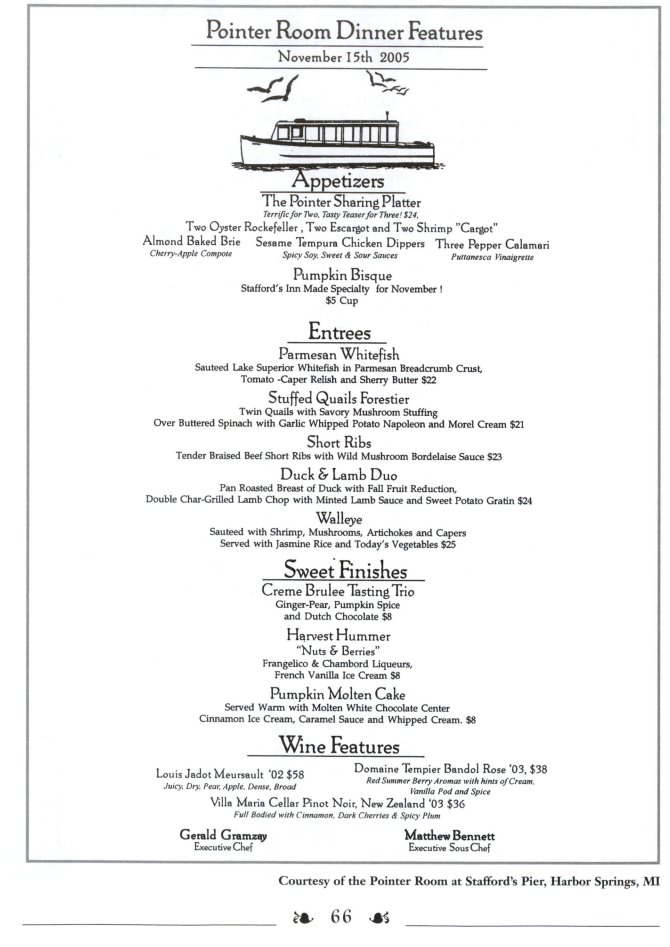

# Pointer Room Dinner Features
## November 15th 2005

## Appetizers

### The Pointer Sharing Platter
*Terrific for Two, Tasty Teaser for Three! $24,*
Two Oyster Rockefeller , Two Escargot and Two Shrimp "Cargot"

**Almond Baked Brie**
*Cherry-Apple Compote*

**Sesame Tempura Chicken Dippers**
*Spicy Soy, Sweet & Sour Sauces*

**Three Pepper Calamari**
*Puttanesca Vinaigrette*

### Pumpkin Bisque
Stafford's Inn Made Specialty  for November !
$5 Cup

## Entrees

### Parmesan Whitefish
Sauteed Lake Superior Whitefish in Parmesan Breadcrumb Crust,
Tomato -Caper Relish and Sherry Butter $22

### Stuffed Quails Forestier
Twin Quails with Savory Mushroom Stuffing
Over Buttered Spinach with Garlic Whipped Potato Napoleon and Morel Cream $21

### Short Ribs
Tender Braised Beef Short Ribs with Wild Mushroom Bordelaise Sauce $23

### Duck & Lamb Duo
Pan Roasted Breast of Duck with Fall Fruit Reduction,
Double Char-Grilled Lamb Chop with Minted Lamb Sauce and Sweet Potato Gratin $24

### Walleye
Sauteed with Shrimp, Mushrooms, Artichokes and Capers
Served with Jasmine Rice and Today's Vegetables $25

## Sweet Finishes

### Creme Brulee Tasting Trio
Ginger-Pear, Pumpkin Spice
and Dutch Chocolate $8

### Harvest Hummer
"Nuts & Berries"
Frangelico & Chambord Liqueurs,
French Vanilla Ice Cream $8

### Pumpkin Molten Cake
Served Warm with Molten White Chocolate Center
Cinnamon Ice Cream, Caramel Sauce and Whipped Cream. $8

## Wine Features

**Louis Jadot Meursault '02 $58**
*Juicy, Dry, Pear, Apple, Dense, Broad*

**Domaine Tempier Bandol Rose '03, $38**
*Red Summer Berry Aromas with hints of Cream,*
*Vanilla Pod and Spice*

**Villa Maria Cellar Pinot Noir, New Zealand '03 $36**
*Full Bodied with Cinnamon, Dark Cherries & Spicy Plum*

**Gerald Gramzay**
Executive Chef

**Matthew Bennett**
Executive Sous Chef

**Courtesy of the Pointer Room at Stafford's Pier, Harbor Springs, MI**

**Figure 4-3. Prix-fixe Menu**

## *Valentine's Dinner*
### *Saturday, February 11, 2006*

## APPETIZERS

Curried Sweet Potato Soup
With Coconut Cream and Candied Pecans

Medley of Atlantic Oysters
Crème Fraîche and Caviar, Champagne Gelee, traditional Cocktail Sauce

Stage Neck Inn Lobster Bisque

Gulf Shrimp Cocktail

Duck Confit Spring Roll
Pickled Ginger Slaw and Ponzu

## SALADS

Caesar Salad with Grape Tomatoes, Kalamata Olives, and Asiago Crisp

Iceberg Wedge
With Creamy Bleu Cheese and Warm Crumbled Bacon

Garden Salad

Grilled Fennel and Mesclun
With Pomegranate Seeds and Pistachios with Raspberry Walnut Vinaigrette

## ENTRÉES

Roast Rack of Lamb
With Dijon Rosemary Crust, Mint Demi-glace, and Pommes Anna

1 ½ lb. Boiled Lobster
Herbed Red Potatoes

1 ½ lb. Baked Stuffed Lobster
Herbed Red Potatoes

Chinese Five-Spice Rubbed Duck
Ginger Plum Reduction, Green Tea Jasmine Rice

Tenderloin of Beef Wellington
Tarragon Demi-glace, Duxelle of Mushrooms, Mousse Truffée Pâté

Cedar-smoked Salmon
Soy Balsamic Orange Glaze, Warm Wild Rice, Swiss Chard, and Chevre Cheese Salad

Pan-seared Medallions of Venison
Currant Demi-glace, Sweet Potato Custard

**Courtesy of Stage Neck Inn, York Harbor, ME**

## Figure 4-4. Breakfast Menu

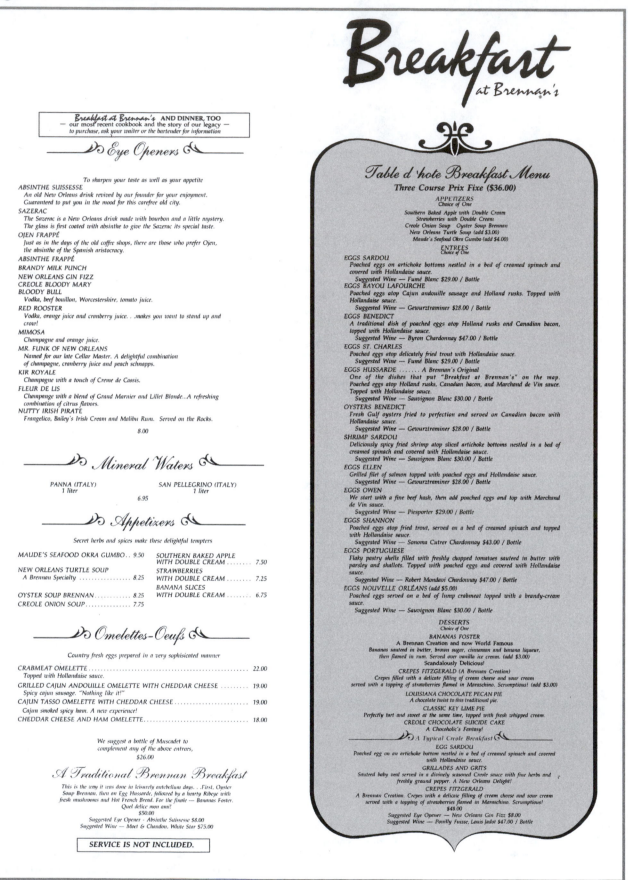

**Figure 4-4. Breakfast Menu**

*Breakfast at Brennan's* **AND DINNER, TOO**
— our most recent cookbook and the story of our legacy —
to purchase, ask your waiter or the bartender for information

### Eye Openers

*To sharpen your taste as well as your appetite*

**ABSINTHE SUISSESSE**
An old New Orleans drink revived by our founder for your enjoyment. Guaranteed to put you in the mood for this carefree old city.

**SAZERAC**
The Sazerac is a New Orleans drink made with bourbon and a little mystery. The glass is first coated with absinthe to give the Sazerac its special taste.

**OJEN FRAPPÉ**
Just as in the days of the old coffee shops, there are those who prefer Ojen, the absinthe of the Spanish aristocracy.

**ABSINTHE FRAPPÉ**

**BRANDY MILK PUNCH**

**NEW ORLEANS GIN FIZZ**

**CREOLE BLOODY MARY**

**BLOODY BULL**
Vodka, beef bouillon, Worcestershire, tomato juice.

**RED ROOSTER**
Vodka, orange juice and cranberry juice. . .makes you want to stand up and crow!

**MIMOSA**
Champagne and orange juice.

**MR. FUNK OF NEW ORLEANS**
Named for our late Cellar Master. A delightful combination of champagne, cranberry juice and peach schnapps.

**KIR ROYALE**
Champagne with a touch of Creme de Cassis.

**FLEUR DE LIS**
Champange with a blend of Grand Marnier and Lillet Blonde...A refreshing combination of citrus flavors.

**NUTTY IRISH PIRATE**
Frangelico, Bailey's Irish Cream and Malibu Rum. Served on the Rocks.

8.00

### Mineral Waters

PANNA (ITALY)
1 liter

SAN PELLEGRINO (ITALY)
1 liter

6.95

### Appetizers

*Secret herbs and spices make these delightful tempters*

| | | | |
|---|---|---|---|
| MAUDE'S SEAFOOD OKRA GUMBO . . 9.50 | SOUTHERN BAKED APPLE WITH DOUBLE CREAM . . . . . . . . 7.50 |
| NEW ORLEANS TURTLE SOUP | STRAWBERRIES |
| A Brennan Specialty . . . . . . . . . . . . . . . . 8.25 | WITH DOUBLE CREAM . . . . . . . . 7.25 |
| | BANANA SLICES |
| OYSTER SOUP BRENNAN . . . . . . . . . . . 8.25 | WITH DOUBLE CREAM . . . . . . . . 6.75 |
| CREOLE ONION SOUP . . . . . . . . . . . . . . 7.75 | |

### Omelettes-Oeufs

*Country fresh eggs prepared in a very sophisticated manner*

CRABMEAT OMELETTE . . . . . . . . . . . . . . . . . . . . . . . . . . . . . . . . . . . . 22.00
Topped with Hollandaise sauce.

GRILLED CAJUN ANDOUILLE OMELETTE WITH CHEDDAR CHEESE . . . . . . . . . 19.00
Spicy cajun sausage. "Nothing like it!"

CAJUN TASSO OMELETTE WITH CHEDDAR CHEESE . . . . . . . . . . . . . . . . . . . . . . . 19.00
Cajun smoked spicy ham. A new experience!

CHEDDAR CHEESE AND HAM OMELETTE . . . . . . . . . . . . . . . . . . . . 18.00

We suggest a bottle of Muscadet to
complement any of the above entrees,
$26.00

### A Traditional Brennan Breakfast

This is the way it was done in leisurely antebellum days. . .First, Oyster Soup Brennan, then an Egg Hussarde, followed by a hearty Ribeye with fresh mushrooms and Hot French Bread. For the finale — Bananas Foster. Quel delice mon ami!
$50.00
Suggested Eye Opener - Absinthe Suissesse $8.00
Suggested Wine — Moet & Chandon, White Star $75.00

**SERVICE IS NOT INCLUDED.**

---

# Breakfast
*at Brennan's*

### Table d'hote Breakfast Menu
**Three Course Prix Fixe ($36.00)**

**APPETIZERS**
*Choice of One*
Southern Baked Apple with Double Cream
Strawberries with Double Cream
Creole Onion Soup   Oyster Soup Brennan
New Orleans Turtle Soup (add $3.00)
Maude's Seafood Okra Gumbo (add $4.00)

**ENTREES**
*Choice of One*

**EGGS SARDOU**
Poached eggs on artichoke bottoms nestled in a bed of creamed spinach and covered with Hollandaise sauce.
Suggested Wine — Fumé Blanc $29.00 / Bottle

**EGGS BAYOU LAFOURCHE**
Poached eggs atop Cajun andouille sausage and Holland rusks. Topped with Hollandaise sauce.
Suggested Wine — Gewurztraminer $28.00 / Bottle

**EGGS BENEDICT**
A traditional dish of poached eggs atop Holland rusks and Canadian bacon, topped with Hollandaise sauce.
Suggested Wine — Byron Chardonnay $47.00 / Bottle

**EGGS ST. CHARLES**
Poached eggs atop delicately fried trout with Hollandaise sauce.
Suggested Wine — Fumé Blanc $29.00 / Bottle

**EGGS HUSSARDE . . . . . . . A Brennan's Original**
One of the dishes that put "Breakfast at Brennan's" on the map. Poached eggs atop Holland rusks, Canadian bacon, and Marchand de Vin sauce. Topped with Hollandaise sauce.
Suggested Wine — Sauvignon Blanc $30.00 / Bottle

**OYSTERS BENEDICT**
Fresh Gulf oysters fried to perfection and served on Canadian bacon with Hollandaise sauce.
Suggested Wine — Gewurztraminer $28.00 / Bottle

**SHRIMP SARDOU**
Deliciously spicy fried shrimp atop sliced artichoke bottoms nestled in a bed of creamed spinach and covered with Hollandaise sauce.
Suggested Wine — Sauvignon Blanc $30.00 / Bottle

**EGGS ELLEN**
Grilled filet of salmon topped with poached eggs and Hollandaise sauce.
Suggested Wine — Gewurztraminer $28.00 / Bottle

**EGGS OWEN**
We start with a fine beef hash, then add poached eggs and top with Marchand de Vin sauce.
Suggested Wine — Piesporter $29.00 / Bottle

**EGGS SHANNON**
Poached eggs atop fried trout, served on a bed of creamed spinach and topped with Hollandaise sauce.
Suggested Wine — Sonoma Cutrer Chardonnay $43.00 / Bottle

**EGGS PORTUGUESE**
Flaky pastry shells filled with freshly chopped tomatoes sauteed in butter with parsley and shallots. Topped with poached eggs and covered with Hollandaise sauce.
Suggested Wine — Robert Mondavi Chardonnay $47.00 / Bottle

**EGGS NOUVELLE ORLÉANS (add $5.00)**
Poached eggs served on a bed of lump crabmeat topped with a brandy-cream sauce.
Suggested Wine — Sauvignon Blanc $30.00 / Bottle

**DESSERTS**
*Choice of One*

**BANANAS FOSTER**
A Brennan Creation and now World Famous
Bananas sauteed in butter, brown sugar, cinnamon and banana liqueur, then flamed in rum. Served over vanilla ice cream. (add $3.00)
Scandalously Delicious!

**CREPES FITZGERALD** (A Brennan Creation)
Crepes filled with a delicate filling of cream cheese and sour cream served with a topping of strawberries flamed in Maraschino. Scrumptious! (add $3.00)

**LOUISIANA CHOCOLATE PECAN PIE**
A chocolate twist to this traditional pie.

**CLASSIC KEY LIME PIE**
Perfectly tart and sweet at the same time, topped with fresh whipped cream.

**CREOLE CHOCOLATE SUICIDE CAKE**
A Chocoholic's Fantasy!

### A Typical Creole Breakfast

**EGG SARDOU**
Poached egg on an artichoke bottom nestled in a bed of creamed spinach and covered with Hollandaise sauce.

**GRILLADES AND GRITS**
Sauteed baby veal served in a divinely seasoned Creole sauce with fine herbs and freshly ground pepper. A New Orleans Delight!

**CREPES FITZGERALD**
A Brennan Creation. Crepes with a delicate filling of cream cheese and sour cream served with a topping of strawberries flamed in Maraschino. Scrumptious!
$48.00
Suggested Eye Opener — New Orleans Gin Fizz $8.00
Suggested Wine — Pouilly Fuisse, Louis Jadot $47.00 / Bottle

**Figure 4-4. Breakfast Menu (Continued)**

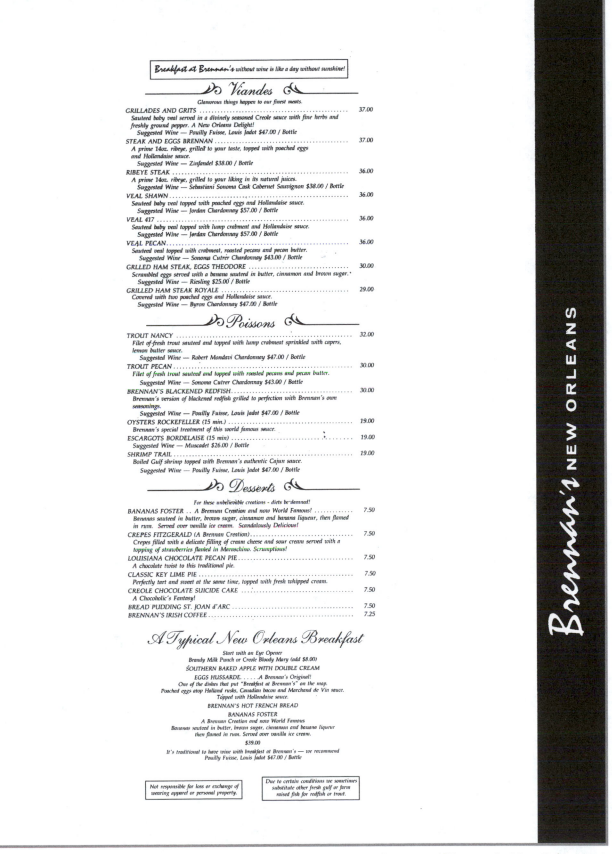

*Breakfast at Brennan's without wine is like a day without sunshine!*

## Viandes

*Glamorous things happen to our finest meats.*

**GRILLADES AND GRITS** .................................................. 37.00
*Sauteed baby veal served in a divinely seasoned Creole sauce with fine herbs and freshly ground pepper. A New Orleans Delight!*
*Suggested Wine — Pouilly Fuisse, Louis Jadot $47.00 / Bottle*

**STEAK AND EGGS BRENNAN** ........................................... 37.00
*A prime 14oz. ribeye, grilled to your taste, topped with poached eggs and Hollandaise sauce.*
*Suggested Wine — Zinfandel $38.00 / Bottle*

**RIBEYE STEAK** ........................................................ 36.00
*A prime 14oz. ribeye, grilled to your liking in its natural juices.*
*Suggested Wine — Sebastiani Sonoma Cask Cabernet Sauvignon $38.00 / Bottle*

**VEAL SHAWN** ......................................................... 36.00
*Sauteed baby veal topped with poached eggs and Hollandaise sauce.*
*Suggested Wine — Jordan Chardonnay $57.00 / Bottle*

**VEAL 417** ............................................................. 36.00
*Sauteed baby veal topped with lump crabmeat and Hollandaise sauce.*
*Suggested Wine — Jordan Chardonnay $57.00 / Bottle*

**VEAL PECAN** .......................................................... 36.00
*Sauteed veal topped with crabmeat, roasted pecans and pecan butter.*
*Suggested Wine — Sonoma Cutrer Chardonnay $43.00 / Bottle*

**GRLLED HAM STEAK, EGGS THEODORE** ............................... 30.00
*Scrambled eggs served with a banana sauteed in butter, cinnamon and brown sugar.*
*Suggested Wine — Riesling $25.00 / Bottle*

**GRILLED HAM STEAK ROYALE** ........................................ 29.00
*Covered with two poached eggs and Hollandaise sauce.*
*Suggested Wine — Byron Chardonnay $47.00 / Bottle*

## Poissons

**TROUT NANCY** ........................................................ 32.00
*Filet of fresh trout sauteed and topped with lump crabmeat sprinkled with capers, lemon butter sauce.*
*Suggested Wine — Robert Mondavi Chardonnay $47.00 / Bottle*

**TROUT PECAN** ........................................................ 30.00
*Filet of fresh trout sauteed and topped with roasted pecans and pecan butter.*
*Suggested Wine — Sonoma Cutrer Chardonnay $43.00 / Bottle*

**BRENNAN'S BLACKENED REDFISH** ..................................... 30.00
*Brennan's version of blackened redfish grilled to perfection with Brennan's own seasonings.*
*Suggested Wine — Pouilly Fuisse, Louis Jadot $47.00 / Bottle*

**OYSTERS ROCKEFELLER (15 min.)** ..................................... 19.00
*Brennan's special treatment of this world famous sauce.*

**ESCARGOTS BORDELAISE (15 min)** ..................................... 19.00
*Suggested Wine — Muscadet $26.00 / Bottle*

**SHRIMP TRAIL** ........................................................ 19.00
*Boiled Gulf shrimp topped with Brennan's authentic Cajun sauce.*
*Suggested Wine — Pouilly Fuisse, Louis Jadot $47.00 / Bottle*

## Desserts

*For these unbelievable creations - diets be damned!*

**BANANAS FOSTER .. A Brennan Creation and now World Famous!** ...... 7.50
*Bananas sauteed in butter, brown sugar, cinnamon and banana liqueur, then flamed in rum. Served over vanilla ice cream. Scandalously Delicious!*

**CREPES FITZGERALD (A Brennan Creation)** ........................... 7.50
*Crepes filled with a delicate filling of cream cheese and sour cream served with a topping of strawberries flamed in Maraschino. Scrumptious!*

**LOUISIANA CHOCOLATE PECAN PIE** .................................... 7.50
*A chocolate twist to this traditional pie.*

**CLASSIC KEY LIME PIE** ............................................... 7.50
*Perfectly tart and sweet at the same time, topped with fresh whipped cream.*

**CREOLE CHOCOLATE SUICIDE CAKE** .................................... 7.50
*A Chocoholic's Fantasy!*

**BREAD PUDDING ST. JOAN d'ARC** ..................................... 7.50

**BRENNAN'S IRISH COFFEE** ............................................ 7.25

### A Typical New Orleans Breakfast

*Start with an Eye Opener*
*Brandy Milk Punch or Creole Bloody Mary (add $8.00)*
SOUTHERN BAKED APPLE WITH DOUBLE CREAM

EGGS HUSSARDE . . . . . A Brennan's Original!
*One of the dishes that put "Breakfast at Brennan's" on the map.*
*Poached eggs atop Holland rusks, Canadian bacon and Marchand de Vin sauce.*
*Topped with Hollandaise sauce.*

BRENNAN'S HOT FRENCH BREAD

BANANAS FOSTER
*A Brennan Creation and now World Famous*
*Bananas sauteed in butter, brown sugar, cinnamon and banana liqueur*
*then flamed in rum. Served over vanilla ice cream.*

$39.00

*It's traditional to have wine with breakfast at Brennan's — we recommend*
*Pouilly Fuisse, Louis Jadot $47.00 / Bottle*

*Not responsible for loss or exchange of wearing apparel or personal property.*

*Due to certain conditions we sometimes substitute other fresh gulf or farm raised fish for redfish or trout.*

**Brennan's NEW ORLEANS**

Courtesy of Brennan's, New Orleans, LA

**Figure 4-5. Brunch Menu**

## LA ISLA SUNDAY BRUNCH
Open for Sunday Brunch 10am to 3pm

### HUEVOS ~ EGGS

**Churrasco a Caballo con Arroz y Frijoles Negros ~ Steak and Eggs** — 12.00
grilled skirt steak served with fried eggs, rice and black beans

**La Isla Huevos Rancheros** — 7.00
two eggs poached in a spicy tomato sauce atop a fried tortilla shell served on a bed of black beans and rice

**Sandwich de Huevo, Tocineta y Queso ~ Bacon, Egg and Cheese Sandwich** — 4.00

**Dos Huevos al Gusto ~ Two Eggs Any Style** — 5.00
served with homefries and toast

### TORTILLAS ~ GOURMET OMELETTES
omelettes served with home fries and toast

**Tortilla de Camarones y Queso de Cabra ~ Spicy Shrimp and Goat Cheese Omelette** — 9.00
sautéed shrimp in spicy creole sauce topped with goat cheese

**Tortilla de Cebolla, Chorizo y Manchego ~ Chorizo Omelette** — 7.00
onion, chorizo and manchego cheese omelette

**Tortilla de Platano Maduro, Espinaca y Queso Blanco ~ Plantain and Spinach Omelette** — 7.00
yellow plantain, white cheese and spinach omelette

**Five Vegetable Egg White Omelette** — 7.00
a fluffy omelette filled with spinach, tomato, mushroom, onion and peppers

### PANCAKES
we serve 100% vermont maple syrup

**Buttermilk Pancakes** — 6.00
**Blueberry Mango Pancakes** — 7.00

### FRENCH TOAST

**La Isla Stuffed French Toast** — 7.00
thick slices of egg bread dipped in an egg batter with almond and corn flake coating stuffed with strawberry and guava cream cheese

**French Toast** — 5.00
egg bread dipped in cinnamon egg batter, topped with toasted almonds and powdered sugar

### ON THE LIGHTER SIDE

**Avena ~ Oatmeal** — 4.00
100% rolled oats cooked in skim milk
with bananas — 5.00

### ACOMPAÑANTES ~ SIDES

**Tocineta ~ Bacon** — 3.00
**Chorizo ~ Spanish Sausage** — 3.50
**Jamon ~ Ham** — 3.00
**Pan Cubano o Pan de Trigo ~ Cuban Toast or Wheat Toast** — 1.50
**Papas de la Casa ~ Homefries** — 3.00
**Maduros ~ Sweet Plantains** — 4.00
**Arroz Blanco ~ White Rice** — small 2.50   large 3.50
**Frijoles Negros ~ Black Beans** — small 2.00   medium 3.00   large 4.00
**Frutas ~ Fruit** — 4.00
seasonal fresh fruit cup

---

## LA ISLA SUNDAY BRUNCH
Open for Sunday Brunch 10am to 3pm

### SALADITOS ~ APPETIZERS

**Empanada ~ Turnover** — 3.00
a delicious crescent-shaped pastry turnover filled with chicken or beef

**Papa Rellena ~ Stuffed Potato** — 3.00
mashed potato stuffed with ground meat, crispy outside and soft inside

**Croquetas de Jamon o Pollo ~ Ham or Chicken Croquettes** — 1.50
homemade filling consisting of ground chicken or ham, breaded and fried

### ENSALADAS ~ SALADS

**La Isla House Salad** — 6.00
field green salad with balsamic vinaigrette
with chicken — 7.00
with shrimp (6) — 9.00

**Ensalada de Espinaca y Remolacha Asada ~ Spinach and Roasted Beet Salad** — 8.00
spinach tossed with mango, avocado, maytag blue cheese, oranges, red onion in a champagne vinaigrette with toasted macadamia nuts served over roasted beets
with chicken — 9.50

### SANDWICHES

**Sandwich Cubano ~ Cuban Sandwich** — 6.00
roasted pork, ham, swiss cheese and pickle topped with a garlic mojo

**Jamon y Queso ~ Ham and Cheese** — 4.00

**Grilled Chicken Media Noche** — 5.00
grilled chicken breast topped with tomato, avocado and mixed field greens on toasted Cuban bread

**Pan con Bistec ~ Steak Sandwich** — 7.00
a grilled steak topped with lettuce, tomato, onions and crispy potato sticks

### COMFORT FOOD

**Ropa Vieja ~ Braised Shredded Flank Steak** — 9.00
served with white rice and black beans

**Sopa de Pollo ~ Chicken Soup** — small 3.00   large 4.00

**Sopa del Dia ~ Chef's Soup du Jour**
cup or bowl

### THIRST QUENCHERS

**Jugo de Naranja Natural ~ Fresh-Squeezed Orange Juice** — 3.00

**Tropical Milkshakes ~ all flavors listed** — 3.00   additional flavors add 1.00
made with milk or just blended with ice — 5.00
coco (coconut) ~ guanabana (sour sop) guayaba (guava) ~ mango ~ mamey ~ leche malteada (malted milk) ~ papaya (banana) ~ trigo (wheat)

**Morir Soñando ~ Orange Cream Frappe** — 4.00
fresh orange juice, evaporated milk and sugar

**Snapple** — 1.50
iced tea, peach iced tea, diet iced tea, orangeade, grapeade, kiwi & mango

**Sodas** — 1.50

**Goya Nectars** — 1.50
mango, peach, guava, soursop and pear

### CAFE ~ COFFEE
decaf available

**Espresso** — 1.25
**Cappucino** — 3.00
**Te ~ Tea** — 1.25
**Cafe con Leche ~ Cuban Coffee** — small 1.50   large 2.50
**Cafe Malecon ~ Iced Spanish-Style Coffee** — 2.50

**Figure 4-6. Luncheon Menu**

# Greens Restaurant

February 22, 2006

### APPETIZERS

**Mesquite Grilled Asparagus** with shaved Midnight Moon goat cheese, watercress and meyer lemon shallot vinaigrette.   9.50

**Three Beet Salad** - Golden, chioggia and red beets with haricots vert, fennel, treviso radicchio, watercress, Roquefort and champagne vinaigrette.   9.75

**Spinach Salad** - Savoy spinach and Knoll Farms chicory with Mt. Vikos feta, kalamata olives, croutons, red onions, garlic, mint, sherry vinegar and hot olive oil.   9.50

**Greens Caesar** - Romaine hearts with garlic croutons, parmesan and creamy black pepper dressing.   9.25

**Caldo Thalpeño** – Mexican chic pea soup with crisp corn tortillas, crème fraiche and cilantro.
    Cup   5.50        Bowl    6.50

**Black Bean Chili** with Vella dry jack and crème fraiche.
    Cup   5.50        Bowl    6.50

### ENTREES

**Indian Curry** - Carrots, butternut squash, cauliflower, turnips, peppers, fingerling potatoes, broccoli and snap peas stewed with tomatoes, coconut milk, lemongrass, ginger, chilies and cilantro. Served with pistachio basmati rice and winter fruit chutney.   12.75

**Mediterranean Sampler** - Filo turnover with fromage blanc, leeks and thyme; French lentil salad with lemon, mint and ricotta salata; cucumbers with yogurt and mint; hummous; grilled pita bread; spicy tomato jam.   13.75

**Grilled Portobello and Crimini Mushroom Sandwich** on Acme bread with spring onions, taleggio and asiago. Served with garden lettuces, piquillo peppers, pine nuts and sherry vinaigrette.   12.50

**Asian Tofu Sandwich** - Grilled tofu in spicy peanut sauce with pickled carrots, jicama and cilantro on Acme petite baguette. Served with little gems, tat soi, grilled shiitake mushrooms, watermelon radish and sesame ginger vinaigrette.   9.75

**Pasta e Fagioli** - Caserecce and Italian butter beans with roasted tomatoes and garlic, grilled onions, Knoll Farms chard, gaeta olives, basil and parmesan.   12.00

**Mesquite Grilled Brochettes** of mushrooms, peppers, yellow finn potatoes, red onions, garnet yams, fennel, cherry tomatoes and marinated tofu with chipotle vinaigrette. Served with pumpkin seed brown rice and Mexican cabbage slaw.   12.50

*Signed copies of Everyday Greens and Fields of Greens are available.*
*Speak with your server for details.*

*Greens was established by the San Francisco Zen Center in 1979.*
*We support local growers and purveyors and feature the produce of Green Gulch,*
*Zen Center's organic farm in Marin.*

*18% service charge for parties of six or more.*
*In consideration of our guests, please refrain from using your cell phone in the dining room.*

Courtesy of Greens, San Francisco, CA

# Dinner Menus

A DINNER menu is usually a combination of both à la carte and semi à la carte items. Bellini's Ristorante Italiano® (Fig. 4-7) offers appetizers, salads, soups, and sides as à la carte items. Its semi à la carte choices include pasta classics, vegetarian entrées and meatless pastas, or entrées, served with a salad.

A dinner menu usually has more appetizers and entrées than a luncheon menu. The type of service used in a restaurant offering a dinner menu may be American, French, or Russian.

In *American service*, there is one server who takes the order and brings it to the table. The table is then cleared and reset by a buser.

*French service* is sometimes used in high-end restaurants. This type of service may involve table-side cooking. A *guéridon*, or cart, which comes with a heating unit called a *réchaud*, is used. Most items are uncooked or semi-prepared and are brought from the kitchen, placed on the *guéridon*, cooked on the *réchaud*, and served to the patron. French service requires two servers: a *chef du rang*, or captain, and a *commis du rang*, or assistant. The captain takes the order, does the table-side cooking, and brings the beverages, appetizers, entrées, and desserts to the table. The assistant brings the bread and butter, clears each course, crumbs the table, and serves the coffee or tea. In many high-end restaurants there is also a *sommelier*, or wine steward, who makes wine recommendations, takes the order, presents, and serves the wine to the guest.

In *Russian service* the entrée, vegetables, and potatoes are prepared in the kitchen, placed on a silver or wooden platter, and then served on the guest's plate at the table. In modified Russian service, which is sometimes used in seafood or specialty restaurants, the server serves the entrée from a casserole using a serving spoon and fork.

# Tasting Menus

THE tasting menu is prix fixe in style and is usually an added feature to the dinner menu. Tasting menus are popular in white-tablecloth establishments and are expensive. Often this type of menu includes several courses ranging from five-course up to eight-course tastings. Within each course the patron usually has a choice of two offerings from which to choose, and each course is traditionally paired with a selected wine. Restaurants customarily charge extra for tasting menus that are paired with selected wines. The tasting menu in Figure 4-8 offers a prix-fixe menu with a choice of either a five-course tasting menu with or without wine, or a Grand Tasting, which consists of eight courses with a menu that changes every day depending on the daily market and the chef's signature offerings. Wine pairings are also offered and are specially selected by the sommelier.

## Special Occasion Menus

THE special-occasion menu is prix fixe in style and includes a choice of appetizer, soup, salad, and entrée, and may also offer an alcoholic beverage (Fig. 4-9). For the most part, the special-occasion menu should display a theme or season on the cover of the menu, and the food items and/or garnishes should be typical of that particular season.

The décor of the restaurant should carry the theme of the special occasion as well, whether it is an Easter, Mother's Day, Thanksgiving, or Christmas, theme. Cornucopias may be displayed for Thanksgiving; spring floral bouquets for Easter or Mother's Day; and poinsettias for Christmas. American-style service is usually used for special occasions.

## Ethnic Menus

AN ethnic menu may be semi à la carte or à la carte. In most cases, an ethnic menu offers selections that are representative of the cuisine from a particular region or country, such as Italy, Portugal, and France. A French menu from Restaurant Daniel® in New York City might offer these items: Marinated Raw Tuna and Crispy Sweetbreads with Tomato Sauce Celery Leaves, Purslane and Hazlenuts; Maine Peeky Toe Crab Salad in a Light Tomato Gelée with Fennel and Avocado; and Roasted Beef Medallion Wrapped with Pancetta and Black Truffle Braised Potato and Porcini Gratin with Haricots Verts. The descriptions of the appetizers, soups, salads, entrées, vegetables, potatoes, and desserts are often written in the language

**Figure 4-7. Dinner Menu**

# Bellini's
## RISTORANTE ITALIANO

## APPETIZERS

**Toasted Ravioli**    $8.00
Eight cheese filled ravioli, lightly breaded, fried and topped with marinara & melted mozzarella. Spicy.

**Bruschetta Bread**    $8.00
Topped with zucchini, summer squash, yellow and red tomatoes, olives, basil olive oil and garlic. Topped with grated pecorino.

**Mozzarella Marinara**    $9.00
Creamy mozzarella lightly breaded, sauteed and topped with our homemade marinara.

**Tuscan Farmers Appetizer**    $9.00
Cannellini beans simmered with carmelized onions, garlic, prosciutto over homemade Italian toast.

**Florentine Bread**    $9.00
Homemade Italian bread, toasted. Topped with spinach & artichoke heart dip.

**Portabello Mushroom**    $9.00
Stuffed with a homemade vegetable bread stuffing topped with mozzarella and baked.

**Fried Calamari**    $9.00
Lightly battered and fried, topped with banana peppers. Served with our homemade marinara sauce.

**Calamari Fritti**    $9.00
Calamari cutlets, lightly breaded, sauteed and topped with a lemon butter & white wine milanese sauce.

**Mussels Bianco or Marinara**    $10.00
Mussels with oil, garlic and lemon, or our homemade marinara or cream sauce.

**Little Necks on the Half Shell**    $10.00
On the half shell served with our own house spicy *cocktail sauce.

**Clams Casino**    $10.00
Fresh clams baked with seasoned bread crumbs and pancetta.

**Raw Oysters**    $10.00
On the half shell served with our own house spicy *cocktail sauce.

**Shrimp Cocktail**    $12.00
Four jumbo shrimp served with our own house spicy *cocktail sauce.

**Oysters Florentine**    $12.00
Fresh shucked oysters with spinach and marscapone cheese.

*Alcohol used in preperation of Cocktail Sauce*

## SALADS

**House**    $6.00
Fresh romaine, tomatoes, carrots, red cabbage, onions and peppers topped with our house Italian dressing and croutons.

**Caesar**    $7.00
Fresh romaine tossed with our homemade Caesar dressing, croutons and romano cheese. (Dressing contains anchovy paste)

**Caprice**    $9.00
Homemade fresh buffalo mozzarella with sliced tomato, basil and drizzled with olive oil.

**Antipasto for 2**    $12.00
Eggplant, prosciutto, olives, chicken pesto, roasted red peppers, artichoke hearts and buffalo mozzarella.

## SOUPS

**Baked Minestrone**    $6.00
A hearty vegetable soup topped with our homemade Italian toast glazed with mozzarella.

**Baked Onion**    $6.00
Carmelized onions, beef broth and a cheese crouton.

**Lobster Bisque**    $9.00
Made with fresh Maine lobster meat, sherry & cream.

**Figure 4-7. Dinner Menu (Continued)**

## PASTA CLASSICS

*Served with homemade breads & house salad*
*Wine Suggestions appear with each entree*
*for your convenience*

**Rigatoni, Broccoli & Chicken**    $14.00
Chicken tenders sauteed with broccoli in a cream sauce.
*Wine suggestion: EOS Chardonnay*

**Fettuccine Chicken & Mushrooms**    $14.00
Chicken tenders sauteed with prime white mushrooms in
a cream sauce.
*Wine suggestion: Falesco Vitiano Bianco*

**Fettuccine with Meatballs**    $14.00
Our homemade meatballs simmered in our marinara sauce.
*Wine suggestion: Pietrafitta Chianti*

**Fettuccine with Chicken Pesto**    $15.00
Chicken tenders sauteed with pesto sauce and tossed with
fettuccine.
*Wine suggestion: Botromagno Gravina*

**Fettuccine Bellini**    $15.00
Prosciutto ham & fresh tomato slices sauteed in a vodka
cream sauce & a touch of crushed red pepper.
*Wine suggestion: Falesco Vitiano Bianco*

**Fettuccine Carbonara**    $15.00
Carmelized onions, peas, prosciutto, fresh egg &
Romano cheese in a cream sauce.
*Wine suggestion: Botromagno Gravina*

**Fettuccine with Prosciutto,**
**Spinach & Mushrooms**    $15.00
In a delicate cream sauce.
*Wine suggestion: EOS Chardonnay*

**Fettuccine with Bolognese**    $15.00
Ground sweet Italian sausage simmered in
our marinara sauce.
*Wine suggestion: Allegrini Valpolicella Classica*

**Ravioli Bolognese**    $15.00
Cheese stuffed ravioli topped with bolognese sauce and
melted mozarella.
*Wine suggestion: Allegrini Valpolicella Classica*

**Tortellini Bolognese**    $15.00
Cheese tortellini topped with bolognese sauce, and melted
mozzarella.
*Wine suggestion: Allegrini Valpolicella Classica*

**Joseph's Special Lasagna**    $16.00
Lasagna noodles layered with ricotta, Italian sausage and
mozzarella.
*Wine suggestion: Pietrafitta Chianti*

### ADD VEGETABLES TO YOUR PASTA CLASSIC

| | |
|---|---|
| Broccoli | $2.00 |
| Mushrooms | $2.00 |
| Tomatoes | $2.00 |
| Spinach | $2.00 |

## VEGETARIAN ENTREES & MEATLESS PASTAS

*Served with homemade breads & house salad*

**Rigatoni or Fettuccine**    $13.00
Topped with our homemade marinara sauce.
*Wine suggestion: Pietrafitta Chianti*

**Manicotti**    $14.00
Pasta tubes stuffed with ricotta cheese baked
in marinara sauce & topped with mozzarella.
*Wine suggestion: Pietrafitta Chianti*

**Gnocchi**    $14.00
Potato & flour pasta dumplings baked in the
oven with marinara sauce & mozzarella.
*Wine suggestion: Allegrini Valpolicella Classica*

**Fettuccine with Pesto Sauce**    $14.00
A fresh basil sauce with pureed pine nuts,
Romano cheese, olive oil and garlic.
*Wine suggestion: Falesco Vitiano Bianco*

**Baked Rigatoni**    $14.00
Rigatoni baked in marinara sauce, glazed with
melted mozzarella.
*Wine suggestion: Pietrafitta Chianti*

**Fettuccine Alfredo**    $14.00
The Italian classic from Rome!
Fettuccine sauteed in a delicate cream sauce.
*Wine suggestion: Botromagno Gravina*

**Pasta Primavera**    $15.00
Fresh assorted garden vegetables served over
fettuccine with your choice of sauce: olive oil
and garlic, marinara or cream sauce.
*Wine suggestion: EOS Chardonnay*

**Eggplant Parmigiana**    $15.00
Hand cut for size & perfection. Lightly breaded,
oven baked in marinara sauce glazed with a
mozzarella cheese.
*Wine suggestion: Pietrafitta Chianti*

## SIDES

| | |
|---|---|
| Fries | $3.00 |
| Meatballs | $6.00 |
| Spinach | $6.00 |
| Alfredo | $6.00 |
| Bolognese | $6.00 |
| Broccoli | $6.00 |

*Substitutions are subject to price change. When sharing a dinner we apply a
$5 plate charge (without a salad) or $6 for each additional salad.*

Courtesy of Bellini's Ristorante Italiano®, North Conway, NH

**Figure 4-8. Tasting Menu**

DANIEL

## SEASONAL TASTING MENU

Five-course tasting menu - $132
Paired with wine - $65 supp.

**Foie Gras** Terrine with Sauternes
Medjool Date Carpaccio with Lucuma, Mâche and Almond Vinaigrette
or
Terrine of **Muscovy Duck** "à l'Orange"
Pickled Ramps, Frisée, Lillet Gelée and Sicilian Pistachio
Gewürztraminer "Altenbourg", Paul Blank 2004

🐦

A Tasting of **Peeky Toe Crab:**
"En Gelée" with Beets, In a Salad with Avocado and Wasabi
and a Crispy Cake with Orléans Mustard
or
Cured **Fluke** with Watercress Mousseline
Carrot Confit, Italian Sturgeon Caviar and Citrus Crème Fraîche
Tement Sauvignon Blanc, Styria 2004

🐦

Pan Roasted **Dover Sole** with Hon Shemeji Mushrooms
Braised Swiss Chard and a Marcona Almond Emulsion
or
Slow Baked **Grouper** "Grenobloise" with Cauliflower
Romanesco and Aged Balsamic-Bordelaise Sauce
Savigny-Les-Beaune "Aux Fourches" Maison Champy 2003

🐦

Seared **Beef** Rib Eye and Braised Short Ribs
Bone Marrow Crusted Tardivo Radicchio and Creamy Celery
or
Roasted Colorado Loin of **Lamb** with Stewed Fennel
Crispy "Socca", Sicilian Olive Cake and Lemon Musto Oil
Vasse Felix Cabernet Sauvignon, Magaret River 2002

🐦

Caramel **Pear "Suzette"** with Grand Marnier Baba
Orange Blossom Mille Crêpe and Earl Grey Ice Cream
Royal Tokaji, Tokaji Aszü "5 Puttonyos" 2000
or
Chocolate **Caramel** Millefeuille with Vanilla Confiture de Lait
"Fleur de Sel" Caramel Ice Cream
Maury, Domaine de la Coume du Roy "Cuvée Agnès" 1998

---

## GRAND TASTING

An eight-course menu inspired by the daily market
and the Chef's signature Winter offerings - $175

Wine pairings specially selected by our Sommelier - $85

---

Tasting menus are prepared until 10:30 pm, for the entire table only

**Courtesy of Restaurant Daniel, New York, NY**

**Figure 4-9. Special Occasion Menu**

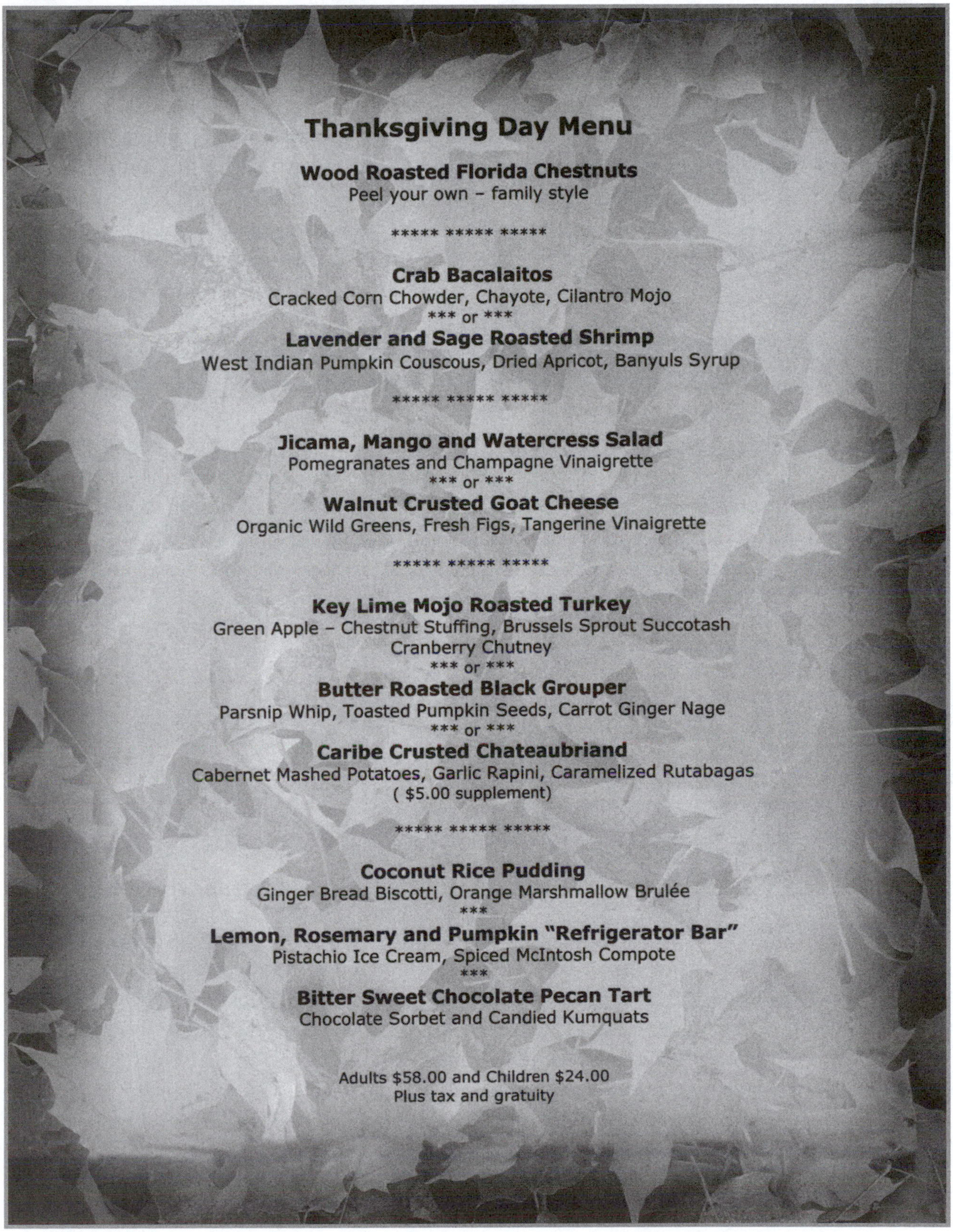

## Thanksgiving Day Menu

**Wood Roasted Florida Chestnuts**
Peel your own – family style

\*\*\*\*\* \*\*\*\*\* \*\*\*\*\*

**Crab Bacalaitos**
Cracked Corn Chowder, Chayote, Cilantro Mojo
\*\*\* or \*\*\*
**Lavender and Sage Roasted Shrimp**
West Indian Pumpkin Couscous, Dried Apricot, Banyuls Syrup

\*\*\*\*\* \*\*\*\*\* \*\*\*\*\*

**Jicama, Mango and Watercress Salad**
Pomegranates and Champagne Vinaigrette
\*\*\* or \*\*\*
**Walnut Crusted Goat Cheese**
Organic Wild Greens, Fresh Figs, Tangerine Vinaigrette

\*\*\*\*\* \*\*\*\*\* \*\*\*\*\*

**Key Lime Mojo Roasted Turkey**
Green Apple – Chestnut Stuffing, Brussels Sprout Succotash
Cranberry Chutney
\*\*\* or \*\*\*
**Butter Roasted Black Grouper**
Parsnip Whip, Toasted Pumpkin Seeds, Carrot Ginger Nage
\*\*\* or \*\*\*
**Caribe Crusted Chateaubriand**
Cabernet Mashed Potatoes, Garlic Rapini, Caramelized Rutabagas
( $5.00 supplement)

\*\*\*\*\* \*\*\*\*\* \*\*\*\*\*

**Coconut Rice Pudding**
Ginger Bread Biscotti, Orange Marshmallow Brulée
\*\*\*

**Lemon, Rosemary and Pumpkin "Refrigerator Bar"**
Pistachio Ice Cream, Spiced McIntosh Compote
\*\*\*

**Bitter Sweet Chocolate Pecan Tart**
Chocolate Sorbet and Candied Kumquats

Adults $58.00 and Children $24.00
Plus tax and gratuity

Courtesy of Chef Allen's, Aventura, FL

used in the country from which the cuisine is derived. An accompanying English translation should appear for those who wish to experience the cuisine but do not have a grasp of the language.

Acquiring certain ingredients for items on ethnic menus may be problematic. It is always prudent to carefully research the availability, costs, and delivery time of these products before producing or printing the menu. Ethnic menus can be moderate to high in price depending on the restaurant's concept and cuisine. A French classical menu in a white-tablecloth restaurant will generally be more expensive than a menu used in a Portuguese restaurant. The décor is also extremely important in ethnic restaurants. Brightly colored tiles, servers dressed in traditional costumes, and mariachi music playing in the background are anticipated and appreciated by diners at a Mexican restaurant.

The style of service in ethnic restaurants is usually American, although. French restaurants might offer French service, and high-end restaurants in this category might even offer Russian service. Frontera Grill® in Chicago, Illinois (Fig. 4-10), offers semi à la carte and à la carte items on its menu. The specialties and entrées come with a variety of accompaniments. À la carte items consist of items from the "Sustainable" Mexican Seafood Bar, which include items from both the small dish (platillos pequenos) and the "extras" categories.

# Specialty Menus

A SPECIALTY menu is usually a combination of both à la carte and semi à la carte items. Appetizers, soups, salads, and desserts are à la carte. The entrées come with vegetables, and potato or rice. For the most part, specialty houses offer steak, seafood, or chicken. It is imperative that these food items are cross-utilized throughout the menu, especially fish or seafood, because these items are highly perishable and very expensive. *Cross-utilization* means that food listings should be prepared in a variety of ways. For example, scallops served as an entrée might also be used in a chowder or a seafood casserole. A seafood specialty restaurant usually employs a number of cooking techniques, such as baking, broiling, frying, grilling, poaching, sautéing, smoking, and steaming. In planning a menu for a specialty restaurant, it is important to remember to offer items such as chicken or beef as well, to accommodate those customers who do not like seafood or who are allergic to it. The most important factor is serving seafood is freshness. Seafood should be purchased on a daily basis, preferably from local fisheries, if location permits. Steaks served in a specialty house should be USDA Prime or USDA Choice.

The type of service used in a specialty house is usually American. However, in many seafood houses, a number of dishes are served in casseroles, which usually requires modified Russian service. The menu in Figure 4-11 is à la carte and semi à la carte. The à la carte items consist of appetizers, soup, salad, steak enhancements, and desserts. Semi à la carte choices include a salad or a cup of soup, and one side dish with the entrée.

# Catering Menus

THE catering business is one of the fastest-growing segments in the restaurant industry. Restaurants, hotels, colleges, universities, and even quick-service operations have begun to cater to expand their overall profits. Catering operations generally provide food and beverages that are prepared from a central kitchen. The major advantage of having a function catered is that everything is provided for and guests can sit back and enjoy the event without any overall concerns. The catering menu is generally a set menu. The menu listings are selected by the chef and the catering banquet manager of the restaurant or the hotel. The arrangement of courses on the menu is set as well. In most cases the menu begins with light food items and then proceeds to heavier items. Catered meals can be simple to elaborate, from a simple breakfast buffet, a special theme menu, a complete luncheon or dinner buffet, to elaborate presentation stations that might include a raw bar, cheese display, Caribbean tapas bar, and individual carving stations (Fig. 4-12). The prices for a catering function can be expensive because the operation that is featuring the event provides everything, including the function space, tables, chairs, eating utensils and flatware, and possibly even entertainment.

**Figure 4-10. Ethnic Menu**

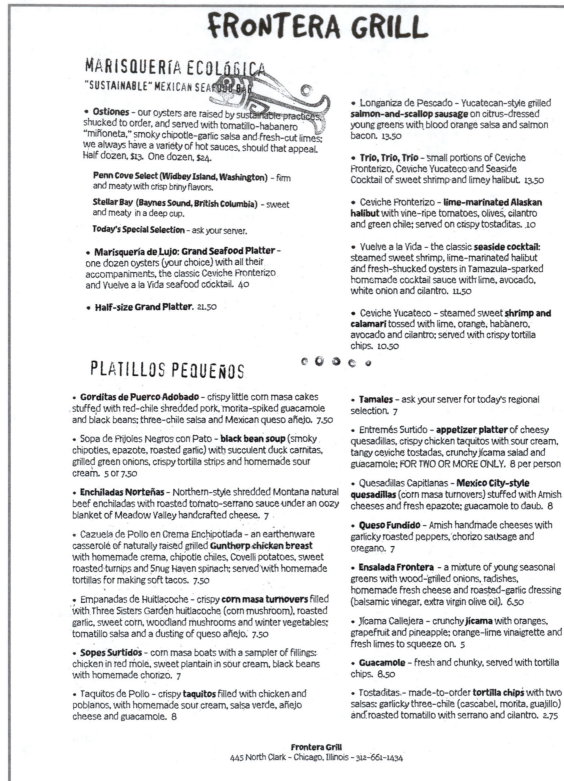

# FRONTERA GRILL

## MARISQUERÍA ECOLÓGICA
### "SUSTAINABLE" MEXICAN SEAFOOD BAR

• **Ostiones** - our oysters are raised by sustainable practices, shucked to order, and served with tomatillo-habanero "miñoneta," smoky chipotle-garlic salsa and fresh-cut limes; we always have a variety of hot sauces, should that appeal. Half dozen, $13. One dozen, $24.

**Penn Cove Select (Widbey Island, Washington)** - firm and meaty with crisp briny flavors.

**Stellar Bay (Baynes Sound, British Columbia)** - sweet and meaty in a deep cup.

**Today's Special Selection** - ask your server.

• **Marisquería de Lujo: Grand Seafood Platter** - one dozen oysters (your choice) with all their accompaniments, the classic Ceviche Fronterizo and Vuelve a la Vida seafood cocktail. 40

• **Half-size Grand Platter.** 21.50

• Longaniza de Pescado - Yucatecan-style grilled **salmon-and-scallop sausage** on citrus-dressed young greens with blood orange salsa and salmon bacon. 13.50

• **Trio, Trio, Trio** - small portions of Ceviche Fronterizo, Ceviche Yucateco and Seaside Cocktail of sweet shrimp and limey halibut. 13.50

• Ceviche Fronterizo - **lime-marinated Alaskan halibut** with vine-ripe tomatoes, olives, cilantro and green chile; served on crispy tostaditas. 10

• Vuelve a la Vida - the classic **seaside cocktail:** steamed sweet shrimp, lime-marinated halibut and fresh-shucked oysters in Tamazula-sparked homemade cocktail sauce with lime, avocado, white onion and cilantro. 11.50

• Ceviche Yucateco - steamed sweet **shrimp and calamari** tossed with lime, orange, habanero, avocado and cilantro; served with crispy tortilla chips. 10.50

## PLATILLOS PEQUEÑOS

• **Gorditas de Puerco Adobado** - crispy little corn masa cakes stuffed with red-chile shredded pork, morita-spiked guacamole and black beans; three-chile salsa and Mexican queso añejo. 7.50

• Sopa de Frijoles Negros con Pato - **black bean soup** (smoky chipotles, epazote, roasted garlic) with succulent duck carnitas, grilled green onions, crispy tortilla strips and homemade sour cream. 5 or 7.50

• **Enchiladas Norteñas** - Northern-style shredded Montana natural beef enchiladas with roasted tomato-serrano sauce under an oozy blanket of Meadow Valley handcrafted cheese. 7

• Cazuela de Pollo en Crema Enchipotlada - an earthenware casserole of naturally raised grilled **Gunthorp chicken breast** with homemade crema, chipotle chiles, Covelli potatoes, sweet roasted turnips and Snug Haven spinach; served with homemade tortillas for making soft tacos. 7.50

• Empanadas de Huitlacoche - crispy **corn masa turnovers** filled with Three Sisters Garden huitlacoche (corn mushroom), roasted garlic, sweet corn, woodland mushrooms and winter vegetables; tomatillo salsa and a dusting of queso añejo. 7.50

• **Sopes Surtidos** - corn masa boats with a sampler of fillings: chicken in red mole, sweet plantain in sour cream, black beans with homemade chorizo. 7

• Taquitos de Pollo - crispy **taquitos** filled with chicken and poblanos, with homemade sour cream, salsa verde, añejo cheese and guacamole. 8

• **Tamales** - ask your server for today's regional selection. 7

• Entremés Surtido - **appetizer platter** of cheesy quesadillas, crispy chicken taquitos with sour cream, tangy ceviche tostadas, crunchy jícama salad and guacamole; FOR TWO OR MORE ONLY. 8 per person

• Quesadillas Capitlanas - **Mexico City-style quesadillas** (corn masa turnovers) stuffed with Amish cheeses and fresh epazote; guacamole to daub. 8

• **Queso Fundido** - Amish handmade cheeses with garlicky roasted peppers, chorizo sausage and oregano. 7

• **Ensalada Frontera** - a mixture of young seasonal greens with wood-grilled onions, radishes, homemade fresh cheese and roasted-garlic dressing (balsamic vinegar, extra virgin olive oil). 6.50

• Jícama Callejera - crunchy **jícama** with oranges, grapefruit and pineapple; orange-lime vinaigrette and fresh limes to squeeze on. 5

• **Guacamole** - fresh and chunky, served with tortilla chips. 8.50

• Tostaditas - made-to-order **tortilla chips** with two salsas: garlicky three-chile (cascabel, morita, guajillo) and roasted tomatillo with serrano and cilantro. 2.75

**Frontera Grill**
445 North Clark - Chicago, Illinois - 312-661-1434

## Figure 4-10. Ethnic Menu (Continued)

DINNER MENU FOR DECEMBER 27 – JANUARY 28, 2006

# ESPECIALIDADES

- Pato en Mole Poblano – adobo-marinated, wood-grilled **Gunthorp duck breast** in Mexico's famous fiesta sauce; mole poblano; classic Mexican white rice, salsa of caramelized fennel, figs and jícama. 21.50

- Pollo Encalabazado – **Gunthorp chicken breast** (garlic and serrano-marinated and wood-grilled) in poblano-spiked, creamy-smooth butternut sauce with yucca-butternut mash and pea tendril-friseé salad. 20.50

- Puerco en Tinga Poblana – grill-roasted **Maple Creek pork loin** served with classic Pueblan pork tinga (roasted tomatoes, smoky chipotle chiles, chorizo sausage and red-skin potatoes); topped with avocado and homemade fresh cheese. 20

- **Tamal Azteca** – layered tortilla "lasagne" filled with corn, calabacitas, nopales and Samuel's handcrafted cheese; garlicky roasted tomato-guajillo sauce, grilled local oyster mushrooms and crispy beets complete the picture. 17

- Salmón en Mole Verde Queretano – **wild Alaskan coho salmon** with Querétaro-style green mole of sesame seeds, almonds, peanuts, poblanos, plantains and sweet spices; Bill's winter spinach and herby green rice. 21.50

- Platillo del Día - ask your server for details on today's special offering.

- Caldo de Siete Mares – a big hearty braise of **scallops, mussels, mahimahi and squid** with rich guajillo chile broth, roasted chayote and grilled green beans. 22.50

- Pescado al Chilaca – garlic-marinated, grilled fresh **day-boat catch** with rustic sauce of fresh corn, cilantro and chilaca chiles; garlicky potato-huitlacoche enchilada and watercress salad 22

- Carne Asada - **Montana Natural rib steak**, marinated in spicy red chile and wood-grilled, served with black beans, sweet plantains with sour cream, and guacamole. 27

- Pollito a las Brasas – border-style, organic **Gunthorp rock hen**, half-boned, marinated in red chile, garlic and sweet spices, and grilled. Frijoles charros, charcoaled green onions, young greens. 20.50

- **Chiles Rellenos** - classic, soufflé-battered stuffed poblanos (one cheese, one minced-pork picadillo) with roasted tomato-chile sauce; black beans and Mexican rice. (limited supply) 19.50

# OTROS PLATILLOS

- **Enchiladas de Mole Rojo** – homemade tortillas rolled around chicken, doused with Oaxacan red mole; black beans. 16.50

- **Tamales de Frijol con Queso de Cabra** – black bean tamales filled with homemade goat cheese in a "guisado" of woodland mushrooms, organic roasted tomatoes, green chile and mint; watercress salad. 15.50

**Tacos al Carbón** - wood-grilled meat, poultry, fish or mushrooms sliced and served with roasted pepper rajas, two salsas, frijoles charros, guacamole, and homemade tortillas. 15.50

- Naturally raised **skirt steak** marinated with garlic and spices.
- Red chile-marinated **Maple Creek pork** (pastor style), with charcoaled pineapple, slab bacon and red onion (no rajas).
- Organic **Gunthorp chicken breast** marinated with fruit vinegar, spices and garlic.
- Tender **portobello** mushroom marinated with achiote and spice.
- Gunthorp **duck** marinated with red-chile adobo.
- Farm-raised **catfish** marinated with achiote and garlic.

# EXTRAS

- Frijoles Refritos – **black beans** fried with garlic, onion and epazote, topped with Mexican fresh cheese. 3.50

- Frijoles Charros – **pinto beans** simmered with bacon, poblanos, tomato and cilantro. 3.50

- Arroz a la Mexicana - traditional **Mexican rice** with a variety of flavors. Ask your server. 3.25

- **Arroz y Frijoles** – black beans and Mexican rice. 5

- **Salsa Habanera** - all you can eat—very spicy roasted habanero salsa with garlic and lime. 2.50

- Puré de Papas – rustic **mashed potatoes**. 4.25

- Cebollitas Asadas – **grilled green onions**. 1.50

- Plátanos con Crema - sweet fried **plantains** with homemade sour cream and fresh cheese. 5.50

- **Verduras en Escabeche** - homemade pickled jalapeños with carrots and cauliflower. 3

- Crema - thick and rich **cultured cream**, a little sour, homemade. 2.50

**Classic Mexican dishes vary from mild to spicy.**
**We always have spicy condiments for you to add if you wish.**

**Our goal is to serve you seasonal sustainably raised vegetables, meat and poultry;**
**and fish from sustainable fisheries. We support local, artisanal farmers.**

Courtesy of Frontera Grill, Chicago, IL

**Figure 4-11. Specialty Menu**

# Hereford House
Absolutely the best steak in Kansas
City... and I guarantee it!
Rod Anderson - Owner/operator

Ⓗ Selections marked with this icon represent
***Hereford House Signature Menu Items***
These items have been dubbed "house favorites" by both our culinary staff and customers alike.
We sincerely hope you will enjoy these and all of our menu selections.

## APPETIZERS

### ESCARGOT
Imported snails baked in mushroom caps with garlic herb butter
8.95

### CALAMARI
Flash fried, served crisp with marinara sauce
7.95

### Ⓗ STUFFED MUSHROOMS
Stuffed with crab and shrimp in a cream cheese filling
7.95

### SPINACH & ARTICHOKE DIP
Creamy spinach and hearts of artichoke served with crisp garlic baguette
7.25

### SHRIMP COCKTAIL
Served chilled with our zesty horseradish cocktail sauce
9.95

### Ⓗ HEREFORD HOUSE DRUMMIES
Served with tangy mild buffalo and ranch dipping sauce
8.95

### TEQUILA-LIME SHRIMP
Six marinated and grilled shrimp, served with house made Tequila Lime BBQ sauce and tri-colored tortilla chips
10.95

### CEDAR PLANK CRAB CAKES
Two jumbo lump crab cakes baked on Washington cedar, finished with a poblano pepper and garlic aioli
12.95

### Ⓗ COMBINATION PLATTER
Stuffed mushrooms, onion rings and flash fried calamari
19.95

### CHEESE AND SEASONAL FRUIT
Santa Fe goat cheese, Vermont white cheddar and a variety of seasonal fruit
Plate 8.95          Platter 16.95

## SOUP & SALAD

### HOUSE SALAD
3.95

### CAESAR SALAD
3.95

### STEAK SOUP

A Hereford House tradition
Cup 2.95          Bowl 4.50

### SOUP du JOUR
Chef's special recipe
Cup 2.95          Bowl 4.50

### CRAB & ASPARAGUS SALAD
Spinach tossed in cilantro lime vinaigrette dressing, topped with grilled asparagus, grilled tomatoes and blue lump crab
11.95

### HEREFORD HOUSE CLUB
A bed of lettuce topped with smoked turkey, bacon and tomatoes, accompanied by black olives, cheddar cheese and hard boiled eggs
10.95

### CHICKEN SALAD
Iceberg romaine mix, carrots, tomatoes, red and green onion and cheddar cheese, tossed in honey mustard dressing. Your choice of crispy fried or grilled chicken
10.95

## MAIN COURSE

All entrees are served with house salad, Caesar salad or cup of soup and choice of: baked potato, french fries, twice baked potato, mashed potatoes, cheddar ranch potatoes, rice pilaf or cut green beans.

### STEAK

#### FILET MIGNON
6 oz. 24.95          8 oz. 28.95          10 oz. 32.95

#### TOP SIRLOIN
8 oz. 17.95          12 oz. 21.95

#### KANSAS CITY STRIP
10 oz. 23.95          14 oz. 27.95          18 oz. 31.95

#### RIBEYE
16 oz. 27.95

#### T-BONE
20 oz. 34.95

#### DELMONICO STEAK
(Bone-in KC strip)
16 oz. 28.95

## SIGNATURE DISHES

### Ⓗ PRIME RIB
Oven roasted with signature seasoning.
10 oz. 20.95          14 oz. 24.95          18 oz. 28.95

### Ⓗ STEAK OSCAR
Our 60 oz. filet, served with our famous cedar plank crab cake and topped with bearnaise sauce and asparagus spears
32.95

### Ⓗ STEAK DIJON
Our 6 oz. filet topped with dijon mustard and caramelized brown sugar, creating a unique and delicious combination
26.95

**Figure 4-11. Specialty Menu (Continued)**

(H) BLACK & BLEU STRIP

Our 10 oz. Kansas City strip topped with cracked black pepper and bleu cheese
crumbles
25.95

(H) BLACKENED RIBEYE

Our 16 oz. ribeye steak, seasoned with our Cajun seasoning
28.95

(H) HICKORY GRILLED CHICKEN

Twin boneless grilled chicken breasts, served with a side of bearnaise sauce
14.95

(H) CHOPPED STEAK

Fresh ground sirloin, hand-pattied and topped with mushrooms and flash fried onions
14.95

(H) BBQ RIBS

A full slab of St. Louis style pork ribs, glazed with barbecue sauce
18.95

## SEAFOOD

CEDAR PLANK SALMON

19.95

TWIN LOBSTER TAILS

37.95

BAKED STUFFED SHRIMP

23.95

FILET & LOBSTER TAIL

37.95

FILET & STUFFED SHRIMP

29.95

STEAK ENHANCEMENTS

Your Choice 3.95

Baked Sweet Potato, Sauteed Spinach, Sauteed Portobello Mushrooms, Sauteed Asparagus Your Choice 2.00
Cracked Black Pepper & Bleu Cheese Sauce, Bearnaise Sauce, Dijon Mustard & Brown Sugar Glaze,
Cabernet Mushroom Sauce

## TEMPERATURE GUIDE

RARE: Cool red center
MEDIUM RARE: Warm red center
MEDIUM: Hot pink center
MEDIUM WELL: Slight pink center
WELL DONE: Cooked throughout
*Consuming raw or undercooked meats, poultry, seafood, or eggs may increase your risk of a foodborne illness.

## NIGHTLY FEATURES

SUNDAY
PRIME RIB
10 oz. 17.95    14 oz. 21.95    18 oz. 25.95
MONDAY

T-BONE
24.95

TUESDAY
STEAK OSCAR
29.95

WEDNESDAY
FILET & LOBSTER TAIL
34.95

THURSDAY
BLACKENED RIBEYE
25.95

FRIDAY
BACON WRAPPED TENDERLOIN & TEQUILA BBQ SHRIMP
24.95

SATURDAY
DELMONICO STEAK
25.95

CHOCOLATE CARAMEL CAKE

This house favorite starts with Devils food chocolate cake dredged with caramel,
a layer of chocolate truffle mousse is added and glazed with a chocolate ganache,
accented with almonds. Served on a bed of berry coulis then topped with a peach coulis.
$4.95

HAAGEN-DAZS SUNDAE

Haagen-Dazs vanilla ice cream, served with your choice of Ghiradelli Chocolate
or Caramel sauce, topped with whipped cream and a cherry.
$3.95

CARROT CAKE

A traditional carrot cake with a twist. Candied English walnuts accent this moist recipe with pineapple
and coconut, layered with a white chocolate cream cheese filling.
Topped with a brown sugar glaze and toasted candied walnuts.
$4.95

WHITE CHOCOLATE BREAD PUDDING

A New Orleans style recipe, made with Italian bread cooked in a white chocolate custard,
accented with white chocolate ganache and drizzled in caramel sauce. Served warm.
$5.95

4 - BERRY COBBLER

Raspberries, strawberries, blueberries and blackberries, served warm and topped with a strawberry scone and vanilla ice cream.
$4.95

VANILLA CHEESECAKE

Served on a pool of peach coulis and topped with berry coulis.
$4.95

CREME BRULEE

Chef's selection offered occasionally on the menu.
Ask your server for details.
$4.95

Courtesy of Hereford House, Kansas City, MO

**Figure 4-12. Excerpt from a Catering Menu**

HYATT
REGENCY
NEWPORT ®
HOTEL AND SPA – RHODE ISLAND

# breakfast buffet

All Breakfast Buffets include Starbucks® Coffee, Tea Selection, Soy Milk and Flavored Syrups

**BREAKFAST BUFFET #1**     $25.00 per guest

Selection of Chilled Juices

Sliced Fresh Seasonal Fruit and Berries

An assortment of Danish, Croissants, Muffins and Breakfast Baguettes

Flavored Butters, Jams and Preserves

Freshly Scrambled Eggs

Crisp Bacon

Oven-Roasted Potatoes

**BREAKFAST BUFFET #2**     $17.00 per guest

Selection of Chilled Juices

Sliced Fresh Seasonal Fruit and Berries

An assortment of Danish, Croissants, Muffins and Breakfast Baguettes

Flavored Butters, Jams and Preserves

One Goat Island, Newport,
Rhode Island 02840 • 401 851 1234
• newport.hyatt.com
All Prices Subject to 16% Service Charge,
5% Administrative Fee and 8% State Sales Tax
• November 2005

# themed breaks

**HIGH ENERGY**     $15.00 per guest

Assorted Nutri-Grain® and Granola Bars

Individual Fat Free Yogurts

Whole Fresh Fruit

Trail Mix

Fruit Smoothies

Coffee Presentation with Flavored Syrups

Bottled Water & Airforce® Nutrisodas®

**POLAR FREEZE**     $16.00 per guest

An Assortment of Favorite Ben & Jerry's® Bars

Locally made Specialty Italian Ices

Stewart's® Root Beer & Assorted Sodas

Coffee Presentation with Flavored Syrups

# lunch buffets

**THE FEDERAL HILL**     $30.00 per guest

Minestrone Soup

The Classic Italian Antipasto Bar

Traditional Caesar Salad with Garlic Croutons

A Selection of Brick-Oven Pizzas presented hot on Butcher's Blocks:

BBQ Chicken with Caramelized Red Onions, Fresh Tomato

Basil & Mozzarella and Double Pepperoni with Flaked Red Pepper and Parmigiano-Reggiano Cheese

Baked Orecchiette Pasta with Grilled Breast of Chicken enveloped in a rich Vodka Tomato Cream Sauce

Tiramisu, Biscotti

**THE THAMES STREET**     $34.00 per guest

Corn Chowder

Westport Rivers Field Greens, Vine-Ripened Tomatoes & Fresh Mozzarella

Asian Lo Mein Salad tossed with Chinese Vegetables & Spicy Peanut Dressing

Stillwater Spa Slaw

Sliced Cajun-Blackened Chicken Breast with Hot Honey Mustard

Grilled Sliced Flank Steak marinated in Oyster Sauce, Rice Wine Vinegar, Garlic and Ginger

Whole-Roasted Filet of Atlantic Salmon with a Herb-Crumb Topping

Artisan Bread Display

French Apples Carmel Tart

Boston Cream Cake

# dinner buffets

**THE GOAT ISLAND CLAMBAKE**     $75.00 per guest

This authentically prepared New England Clambake includes our Chef's ceremonial unveiling of the Clambake along with a short presentation of the history of the Clambake tradition in New England

Goat Island Clam Chowder with traditional Oyster Soda Crackers

Farm Greens layered with Vegetables, Selection of Dressings

Platters of Pesto-Brushed, Lightly-Grilled Vegetables served

**Figure 4-12. Excerpt from a Catering Menu (Continued)**

with Tuscan Olive Oil and Barrel-Aged Modena Balsamic Vinegar

Steamed 1½ Pound Hard Shell Lobster Steamers and Mussels with Drawn Butter and Clam Broth

Wood-Grilled Sirloin Steak with a French Shallot Marmalade

Grilled Basil Chicken Served with a Roasted Red Pepper Coulis

Smoke House Chorizo Sausage, Caramelized Onions and Sweet Peppers

Red Bliss Potatoes and Native Butter n' Sugar Corn on the Cob

Hot Peach and Blueberry Cobbler with Vanilla Bean Ice Cream

**THE NEWPORT BRIDGE**     $62.00 per guest
**DINNER BUFFET**

The Dockside Salad, Farm-Raised Lettuces, Hearts of Palm Artichokes, English Cucumbers, Asparagus, Egg, Tomato and Avocado with a Creamy Dijon Dressing

Sliced Vine-Ripe Tomatoes, Fresh Mozzarella and Opal Basil with Bermuda Onions, Spice Sprouts, Spanish Olive Oil and White Balsamic Vinegar

Maple Mustard-Glazed Pork Tenderloin with a Spiced Apple Compôte

Grilled Atlantic Salmon Filet with a Three Melon and English Cucumber Relish

Herb-Crusted New York Strip Loin with a Madeira Sauce and Crispy Battered Vidalia Onions

Yukon Gold Mashed Potatoes/Oven-Roasted Root Vegetables

Better Than Your Mother's Chocolate Cake Fresh Fruit Tart Almond Macaroons

## presentation stations

Narragansett Bay Raw Bar    $400.00 per display
       (100 pieces per display)

Jumbo Shrimp, Oysters on the Half Shell, Jonah Crab Claws and Little Neck Clams served with Cocktail Sauce, Champagne Mignonette and Specialty Hot Sauces

Federal Hill Antipasto     $13.00 per guest

A Classic display of Capicola Ham, Hard Salami, Mortadella, Prosciutto, Artichoke Hearts, Kalamata Olives,

Roasted Peppers, Pepperoncini, Provolone Cheese, Barrel-aged Balsamic & Herb Foccacia Bread

Crudite       $5.00 per guest

An Array of Garden Vegetables with Garlic-Spinach, Onion and Hummus Dips

International Cheese Display    $7.00 per guest

Imported and Domestic Cheeses served with French Bread and Lavosh

Caribbean Tapas Bar     $12.00 per guest

Fresh Mini Corn Tales with Lime, Tostones & Mohito, Stuffed Savory Plantain Pinwheels, Black Beans & Tropical Fruits with Queso Blanco Salsa, Conch Salad with Pickled Onions, Sweet Peppers and Watermelon, Chilled Muscles with Salsa Verde, Chilled Rice & Pea Salad

*Presentation Stations Prepared for a Minimum 35 Guests

## carving stations

**ROASTED TURKEY BREAST***    $260.00 (serves 20)
Served with Cranberry-Orange Relish, Herbed Dijon Aioli and Silver Dollar Rolls

**ROASTED BEEF TENDERLOIN***    $350.00 (serves 25)

Served with Caramelized Cipolini Onion Marmalade, Dijon Mustard and Potato Rolls

**MAPLE GLAZED HAM***    $375.00 (serves 40)

Served with Rum Raisin Sauce &Hot Cross Buns

**PEPPER CRUSTED STRIP LOIN***    $450.00 (serves 40)

Served with Creamed Horseradish, Whole Grain and Dijon Mustard and Assorted Rolls

**ROASTED LEG OF LAMB***    $375.00 (serves 25)

Served with Minted Apple Chutney and Seeded Rolls

*requires an attendant at $100 each plus tax

Courtesy of Hyatt Regency Hotel and Spa, Newport, RI

# Room Service Menus

THE room service menu can be à la carte, semi à la carte, or prix fixe. The menu may consist of a complete wine list and liquor list, appetizers, soups, salads, hot and cold entrées, hot and cold sandwiches, accompaniments, and an assortment of desserts. Guests phone in orders that are prepared, placed on a service tray or table, and then delivered to the guests' rooms. Menu items on the room service menu may be more expensive than the same items on the actual dining room menu.

It is important that room service items have good hot and cold holding qualities. Items that might be listed on a room service menu could include stuffed filet of sole with a tossed salad or a filet mignon with a baked potato and garden salad. The room service menu should also include items that cater to both adults and children. "Pizza for one" and burgers are frequently included as choices that appeal to both groups. The menu in Figure 4-13, courtesy of the Equinox Resort & Spa®, is a combination à la carte and semi à la carte menu. The yogurt, cold cereals, breakfast breads, juice, milk, hot beverages, and a few breakfast items, such as buttermilk pancakes and Belgian waffles with berries, are à la carte. Semi à la carte items include the continental breakfast, the "Equinox," and the omelet.

# Institutional Menus

THE institutional menu is utilized in hospitals, health care centers, schools, colleges, universities, correctional facilities, and military facilities. The institutional menu must be nutritionally balanced and include items from each of the recommended food groups (grains, vegetables, fruit, oils, dairy, and meats, beans, fish, and nuts) at every meal.

Most institutions, especially hospitals, use a cyclical menu to alleviate boredom. **A cyclical menu** is one that has different items on the menu each day for a period of two to five weeks. Many hospitals have a one- to two-week cycle, while most schools and universities have a four- to five-week cycle for their menus. Today a large number of institutional food operations pay an annual fee to professional foodservice companies, such as ARAMARK® and SODEXHO®, to run their foodservice operations. Chefs who prepare institutional menus, especially in hospitals, must have a solid culinary background and knowledge of special diets, such as cardiac, diabetic, liquid,

**Figure 4-13. Room Service Menu**

# THE EQUINOX

---

Last Name

---

Number of Guests

**Breakfast:**

❑ **The Continental** $10

*Basket of fresh muffins, croissant, danish and cup of fresh fruit.*

❑ **The Equinox** $14

*Two eggs your style, apple smoked bacon or sausage, breakfast potatoes and toast.*

(Select: ❑ White    ❑ Wheat    ❑ Rye)

❑ Bacon    ❑ Sausage    ❑ Chicken Sausage

❑ Scrambled    ❑ Poached    ❑ Boiled    ❑ Up

❑ Over Easy    ❑ Over Medium    ❑ Whites Only

**With The Continental or The Equinox, please select one cold and one hot beverage:**

❑ Freshly Squeezed Orange Juice    ❑ Grapefruit

❑ Cranberry    ❑ Apple    ❑ Tomato    ❑ Vegetable

❑ Whole Milk    ❑ 2% Milk    ❑ Skim Milk

❑ Starbucks Coffee    ❑ Decaffeinated Coffee    ❑ Tazo Tea

(With: ❑ Whole Milk    ❑ Skim Milk    ❑ Half and Half)

❑ **Omelet** $12

*Served with breakfast potatoes and toast.*

(Select: ❑ White    ❑ Wheat    ❑ Rye)

❑ Three Eggs    ❑ Eggbeaters    ❑ Egg Whites

Please Select Omelet Ingredients:

❑ Bacon    ❑ Ham    ❑ Peppers    ❑ Tomato

❑ Mushrooms    ❑ Onion    ❑ Cheese

*Applicable Vermont State Meals Tax and 18% service charge will be added.*

**A la Carte Breakfast:**

❑ Buttermilk Pancakes    $8

❑ Belgium Waffles with Berries    $8

❑ Warm Vermont Natural Cereal    $4

With: ❑ Maple Syrup

❑ Raisins    ❑ Brown Sugar    ❑ Milk

**Low Fat Flavored Yogurt:**    $3

❑ Strawberry    ❑ Blueberry

**Selection of Cold Cereals:**    $4

❑ Corn Flakes    ❑ Shredded Wheat    ❑ Frosted Flakes

With: ❑ Seasonal Berries    ❑ Bananas    $3

Milk: ❑ Whole    ❑ 2%    ❑ Skim

**Breakfast Breads:**

❑ Toast (Select: ❑ White    ❑ Wheat    ❑ Rye)    $2

❑ Bagel with Cream Cheese    $3

❑ Croissant    $3

❑ Muffin ( Select: ❑ Blueberry    ❑ Bran)    $2

❑ English Muffin    $2

**Juice:**    $4

❑ Freshly Squeezed Orange Juice    ❑ Grapefruit

❑ Cranberry    ❑ Apple    ❑ Tomato    ❑ V8

**Milk:**    $3

❑ Whole    ❑ 2%    ❑ Skim

**Hot Beverages:**

Small Pot: ❑ Starbucks Coffee    ❑ Decaffeinated Coffee    $4

❑ Small Pot Tazo Tea    $3

Large Pot: ❑ Starbucks Coffee    ❑ Decaffeinated Coffee    $7

❑ Large Pot Tazo Tea    $6

With:    ❑ Whole Milk    ❑ Skim Milk    ❑ Half and Half

**Courtesy of Equinox Resort & Spa, Manchester, VT**

and mechanical soft diets. A registered dietitian is also needed for consultation regarding nutritional food value and the recommended method of preparation. The institutional menus used at Miriam Hospital in Providence, Rhode Island, offer a restaurant-style menu that allows patients to freely choose from a number of selections (Fig. 4-14). Patients select from menu A one day, menu B the following day, and then menu C if necessary.

# Wine Menus

THE wine menu may be incorporated on the dinner menu or may be listed as a separate menu dedicated solely to wines. An extensive selection of wines, usually 20 or more, requires a separate wine list. The **cellar master** usually prepares the wine list.

The wine menu should include a variety of types and selections of wines that range in price. The name of the wine, its country of origin, the year of the vintage, its price, and the bin number are commonly included on a more extensive wine menu. A description of the style, taste, flavor, and pairing compatibility with certain foods may also be offered (Fig. 4-15). The Capital Grille®, in New York City, offers an award-winning wine list that features wines from geographic areas around the world: California, Washington State, France, Chile, Argentina, Germany, Austria, Spain, Australia, and Italy. A number of champagnes and sparkling wines are also listed on the menu. Figure 4-16 provides an excerpt from The Capital Grille®'s wine menu.

# Dessert Menus

DESSERT menus may be utilized to list and describe a restaurant's offerings. They may be used in and of themselves or in conjunction with a dessert tray or a dessert cart presentation. Displaying desserts on a tray or cart allows customers to view the restaurant's signature desserts and serves as an effective merchandising tool. When a restaurant's dessert offerings are fairly extensive, a separate menu may be required. Listings on this type of menu should have adequate descriptive copy. Some dessert menus also include a list of special coffees, teas, and after-dinner drinks for customers who may not want dessert after a rich meal (Fig. 4-17).

## Figure 4-14. Institutional Menu

### Lunch Menu A
**House Diet**
**Please Circle Items You Wish to Select.**

**Starters**

Chicken Noodle
Cream of Tomato
Vegetarian Vegetable
Matzoh Ball Soup
Chicken Broth

Cranberry Juice
Apple Juice
Grape Juice

Garden Salad with:
*French*
*Lite French*
*Italian*
*Lite Italian*
*FF Ranch*
*Caesar*

**Main Fare**
Vegetable Stir Fry w/Rice
Rst. Turkey w/Cornbread Stuffing/Gravy
New England Meat Loaf w/Gravy
Pepper Turkey Roll-Up Sandwich
Rare Roast Beef on Rye
All White Chicken Salad on White
Chicken Caesar Dinner Salad w/ Dressing
**No Gravy**

**Starches**
Mashed Potato
Confetti Rice
Maple Glazed Sweet Potato
Noodle Kugel
Penne Pasta
Marinara Sauce

**Sandwich Additions**
Potato Salad
Pasta Salad
Cole Slaw
Carrot Sticks
Potato Chips

**Vegetables**
Sweet Green Peas
Broccoli Florets
Sliced Carrots
Cut Sweet Corn
Green Beans

**Desserts**
**TMH** Chocolate Chip Cookie
Apple Crisp
Fruit Cup

Vanilla Parfait
Ice Cream
Gelatin

**Breads & Spreads**
Dinner Roll

Oyster Crackers
Margarine
Butter

**Hot Beverages**
Coffee
Decaf Coffee
Tea
Decaf Tea
Decaf. Herbal Tea

**Milk**
8oz. Lactaid
4oz. Whole Milk
4oz. 1% Milk

**Cold Beverages**
Coke
Ginger Ale
Sprite
Orange
Root Beer
Bottled Water

Diet Coke
Diet Ginger Ale
Diet Sprite

**Condiments**
Half & Half
Non Dairy Creamer
Sugar
Splenda

Salt
Pepper
Mrs. Dash
Lemon Juice

Mayonnaise
Mustard
Ketchup
Cranberry Sauce
Parmesan Cheese

Name:______________________ Room:________

Diet:______________________

### Dinner Menu A
**House Diet**
**Please Circle Items You Wish to Select.**

**Starters**

Chicken Noodle
Cream of Tomato
Vegetarian Vegetable
Matzoh Ball Soup
Chicken Broth

Cranberry Juice
Apple Juice
Grape Juice

Garden Salad with:
*French*
*Lite French*
*Italian*
*Lite Italian*
*FF Ranch*
*Caesar*

**Main Fare**
Grilled Seasoned Chicken Breast
Herbed Codfish w/ Lemon
Roast Leg of Lamb w/Gravy
Pepper Turkey Roll-Up Sandwich
Rare Roast Beef on Rye
Cottage Cheese w/ Fresh Cut Melon
Chicken Caesar Dinner Salad w/ Dressing
**No Gravy**

**Starches**
Mashed Potato
Confetti Rice
Maple Glazed Sweet Potato
Noodle Kugel
Penne Pasta
Marinara Sauce

**Sandwich Additions**
Potato Salad
Pasta Salad
Cole Slaw
Carrot Sticks
Potato Chips

**Vegetables**
Sweet Green Peas
Broccoli Florets
Sliced Carrots
Cut Sweet Corn
Green Beans

**Desserts**
**TMH** Chocolate Chip Cookie
Apple Crisp
Fruit Cup

Vanilla Parfait
Ice Cream
Gelatin

**Breads & Spreads**
Dinner Roll

Oyster Crackers
Margarine
Butter

**Hot Beverages**
Coffee
Decaf Coffee
Tea
Decaf Tea
Decaf Herbal Tea

**Milk**
8oz. Lactaid
4oz. Whole Milk
4oz. 1% Milk

**Cold Beverages**
Coke
Ginger Ale
Sprite
Orange
Root Beer
Bottled Water

Diet Coke
Diet Ginger Ale
Diet Sprite

**Condiments**
Half & Half
Non-Dairy Creamer
Sugar
Splenda

Salt
Pepper
Mrs. Dash
Lemon Juice

Mayonnaise
Mustard
Ketchup
Cranberry Sauce
Parmesan Cheese

Name:______________________ Room:________

Diet:______________________

### Breakfast Menu
**House Diet**
**Please Circle Items You Wish to Select.**

**Fruits and Juices**

Orange Juice
Cranberry Juice
Apple Juice
Prune Juice

Banana
Chilled Peaches
Fruit Cup

**Cereals**

Oatmeal
Cream of Wheat
Corn Flakes
Rice Crunchins
Cheerios

Shredded Wheat
Bran Flakes
Frosted Flakes
Froot Loops
Yogurt Parfait with Granola

**Main Fare**
Scrambled Eggs
Egg Beaters
Cheese Omelet
Texas French Toast with Syrup
Pancakes with Syrup
Cheese Blintzes
Cottage Cheese & Fresh Fruit Plate

**Side Dishes**
Home Fries
Maple Chicken Sausage
Grilled Turkey Ham

**Breads**
Corn Muffin
Blueberry Muffin
Bagel
Coffee Cake

**Spreads**
Margarine
Butter
Cream Cheese
Lite Cream cheese

**Hot Beverages**
Coffee
Decaf Coffee
Tea
Decaf Tea
Decaf Herbal Tea

**Milk**
8oz. Lactaid
8oz. Whole Milk
8oz. 1% Milk

**Cold Beverages**
Bottled Water

**Condiments**
Half & Half
Non-Dairy Creamer
Sugar
Splenda

Salt
Pepper
Mrs. Dash
Lemon Juice

Ketchup
Grape Jelly
Strawberry Jelly
Sour Cream

Name:______________________ Room:________

Diet:______________________

Courtesy of Miriam Hospital, Providence, RI

**Figure 4-15. Food and Wine Pairing Chart**

| Menu Listing | Wine Recommendations |
|---|---|
| Appetizers | Dry white, sherry, or Champagne |
| Entrée of: | |
| Beef | Vigorous, robust, full-bodied, hearty or spicy red |
| Chicken | Crisp, full-bodied white, or silky, soft red |
| Duck | Crisp, full-bodied white, or silky, soft red |
| Fish | Dry white, medium dry white |
| Ham | Rosé, dry white, medium dry white |
| Lamb | Vigorous, robust, full-bodied, hearty or spicy red |
| Pheasant | Vigorous, robust, full-bodied, hearty or spicy red |
| Pork | Rosé, dry white, medium dry white |
| Seafood | Dry white, medium dry white |
| Turkey | Crisp, full-bodied white, or silky, soft red, or Champagne |
| Veal | Crisp, full-bodied white, or silky, soft red |
| Venison | Vigorous, robust, full-bodied, hearty or spicy red |
| Desserts | Sweet wine or semisweet sparkling wine |

# Tea Menus

TODAY many hotels and white-tablecloth restaurants serve Low and High Teas. A Low Tea, sometimes referred to as light tea, includes a loose tea selection, crumpets, scones, pastries, and desserts. More elaborate Low Tea menus offer scones, crumpets, crustless sandwiches, desserts, candies, and petits fours. High Tea or Afternoon Tea is traditionally served in the late afternoon and can serve as a light meal. A High Tea consists of a variety of loose tea selections, scones, crumpets, tartlets, cookies, cakes, and sandwiches. Some hotels and restaurants also serve champagne at High Tea. High Tea is often more substantial than Low Tea and allows the establishment to merchandise food and beverages during off-peak hours. The Willard Intercontinental® in Washington, DC (Fig. 4-18) serves traditional High

Figure 4-16. Excerpt from a Wine Menu

# New York City Wine List

## CHAMPAGNE & SPARKLING WINES

| 1001 | Louis Roederer, Cristal Rosé, Reims, 1996 | $446 |
| 1002 | Salon, Blanc de Blancs, Le Mesnil, 1995 | 282 |
| 1003 | Louis Roederer, Cristal, Reims, 1999 | 275 |
| 1004 | Perrier-Jouët, Fleur de Champagne, Rosé, Epernay, 1999 | 251 |
| 1005 | Deutz, Cuvée William Deutz, Brut, Ay, 1996 | 231 |
| 1006 | Dom Pérignon, Brut, Epernay, 1996 | 222 |
| 1007 | Veuve Clicquot, La Grande Dame, Reims, 1996 | 222 |
| 1008 | Moët & Chandon, Brut Impérial, Rosé, Epernay, N.V. | 106 |
| 1009 | Bollinger, Special Cuvée, Brut, Ay, N.V. | 97 |
| 1010 | Veuve Clicquot, Yellow Label, Brut, Reims, N.V. | 96 |
| 1011 | Taittinger, La Française, Brut, Reims, N.V. | 94 |
| 1012 | Laurent-Perrier, Brut, Reims, N.V. | 79 |
| 1013 | Moët & Chandon, Brut Impérial, Epernay, N.V. | 79 |
| 1014 | Argyle, Extended Tirage Brut, Willamette Valley, 1993 | 78 |
| 1015 | Schramsberg, Blanc de Noir, Napa, 2001 | 69 |
| 1016 | Cristalino, Cava, Spain, N.V. | 28 |

## BURGUNDY, RED

| 1025 | Beaujolais-Villages, Beaujolais, Louis Jadot, 2004 | $29 |
| 1026 | Pinot Noir, Bourgogne, Joseph Drouhin, 2003 | 34 |
| 1027 | Hautes Côte de Beaune, Domaine des Echards, 2004 | 46 |
| 1028 | Moulin-à-Vent, Beaujolais, Olivier Merlin, 2004 | 59 |
| 1029 | St. Anour, Beaujolais, Cuvee Angelique, Domaine Clos De Carriers, 2001 | 64 |
| 1030 | Gevrey-Chambertin, Labouré-Roi, 2002 | 66 |
| 1031 | Meursault, Rouge, Rene Manuel, 2000 | 69 |
| 1032 | Aloxe-Corton, Domaine Francois Gay, 2000 | 75 |
| 1033 | Gevrey-Chambertin, Louis Jadot, 2002 | 83 |
| 1034 | Nuits-St.-Georges, Domaine Michel Gros, 2003 | 85 |
| 1035 | Volnay, Taillepieds, Domaine Marquis D'Angerville, 2001 | 86 |
| 1036 | Morey-Saint-Denis, Clos de la Bussiere, Premier Cru, Roumier, 2002 | 91 |
| 1037 | Vosne-Romanée, Premier Cru, Beaumont, Dominique Laurent, 2001 | 108 |
| 1038 | Chambolle-Musigny, Louis Latour, 1996 | 110 |
| 1039 | Pommard, Côte de Beaune, Arvelets, Premier Cru, Francois Parent, 2000 | 117 |
| 1040 | Clos de Vougeot, Grand Cru, Louis Latour, 1999 | 193 |
| 1041 | Romanée St.Vivant, Grand Cru, Les Quatre Journaux, Louis Latour, 1996 | 265 |

## BURGUNDY, WHITE

| 1042 | Mâcon-Lugny, Régnard, 2002 | $35 |
| 1043 | Bourgogne, Les Setilles, Olivier Leflaive, 2004 | 41 |
| 1044 | Pouilly-Fuissé, Louis Jadot, 2004 | 58 |
| 1045 | Puligny-Montrachet, Olivier Leflaive, 2003 | 83 |
| 1046 | Meursault, Louis Jadot, 2002 | 86 |
| 1047 | Corton-Charlemagne, Grand Cru, Louis Latour, 2001 | 139 |
| 1048 | Bâtard-Montrachet, Grand Cru, Domaine Jean-Noel Gagnard, 2001 | 272 |
| 1049 | Chevalier Montrachet, Grand Cru, Les Demoiselles, Louis Latour, 2001 | 312 |

## BORDEAUX, RED

| 1101 | Château Greysac, Haut-Médoc, 2000 | $44 |
| 1102 | Château Larose-Trintaudon, Haut-Médoc, 2000 | 44 |
| 1103 | Château de Cruzeau, Pessac-Léognan, Graves, 2000 | 57 |
| 1104 | Château Meyney, St.-Estèphe, 1998 | 59 |
| 1105 | Château Carignan, Prima, Premiere Cotes De Bordeaux, 2000 | 64 |
| 1106 | Château de Pez, St.-Estèphe, 2001 | 66 |
| 1107 | Château Coufran, Haut-Médoc, 2000 | 68 |
| 1108 | Château La Bastide Dauzac, Margaux, 2000 | 68 |
| 1109 | Château de Sales, Pomerol, 1998 | 72 |
| 1110 | Château Sociando-Mallet, Haut-Médoc, 1999 | 75 |
| 1111 | Château Clos des Jacobins, St.-Émilion, 1998 | 77 |
| 1112 | Château Gloria, St.-Julien, 1996 | 87 |
| 1113 | Château Bahans-Haut-Brion, Pessac-Léognan, 1996 | 97 |
| 1114 | Château La Gaffelière, St.-Émilion, 1998 | 97 |
| 1115 | Château Haut Batailley, Pauillac, 1998 | 99 |
| 1116 | Carruades de Lafite, Pauillac, 1996 | 110 |
| 1117 | Château Gruaud-Larose, St.-Julien, 1995 | 119 |
| 1118 | Château Trotanoy, Pomerol, 1997 | 121 |
| 1119 | Château Ducru-Beaucaillou, St.-Julien, 1999 | 127 |
| 1120 | Château Figeac, St.-Émilion, 1996 | 162 |
| 1121 | Château Brane-Cantenac, Margaux, 1998 | 182 |
| 1122 | Château Margaux, 1er Grand Cru Classé, Margaux, 1998 | 274 |
| 1123 | Château Mouton-Rothschild, 1er Grand Cru Classé, Pauillac, 1999 | 302 |
| 1124 | Château Latour, 1er Grand Cru Classé, Pauillac, 1998 | 335 |
| 1125 | Château Haut-Brion, 1er Grand Cru Classé, Pessac-Léognan, Graves, 1998 | 339 |
| 1126 | Château Lafite-Rothschild, 1er Grand Cru Classé, Pauillac, 1998 | 445 |

new york city

**Courtesy of The Capital Grille, New York, NY**

**Figure 4-17.  Dessert Menu**

## Desserts
### 8.00

**Creole "Opera" Cake**
*Thin layers of pecan génoise layered with chicory coffee
buttercream and dark chocolate ganache ~ topped with
bourbon chantilly and pecan praline cream*

**Crème Brûlée**
*Light and creamy vanilla bean custard with a crisp,
caramelized sugar crust*

**French Quarter Beignets**
*Traditional New Orleans beignets dusted with powdered sugar
~ served with warm café au lait sauce
and chocolate drizzles*

**🔥 Bananas Foster**
*A family classic: originally created by the Brennans*

**Passion Fruit Crêpes**
*Housemade crêpes filled with passion fruit curd and
California strawberries ~ topped with mixed berry granita and
caramelized orange reduction sauce*

**Creole Bread Pudding Soufflé**
*The richness of bread pudding whipped into a light fluffy soufflé
~ served with velvety bourbon whiskey sauce
(Please order in advance ~ additional $2.00)*

**🔥 Come visit us at our dessert kitchen**

**Chef's Selections of Cheeses**
*Consisting of American farmhouse cheeses and European
classics served with French bread and a toasted
pecan, sundried fruit and honey compote*
**12.50**

**COFFEE**

| | |
|---|---|
| FRESH ROASTED CHICORY COFFEE | 2.50 |
| DECAFFEINATED | 2.50 |
| ESPRESSO | 3.25 |
| CAPPUCCINO | 4.25 |
| ML WHOLE LEAF HOT TEA POUCH | 2.50 |

*Ask your captain about specialty coffee drinks*

**SINGLE MALT SCOTCH**

| | |
|---|---|
| CRAGGANMORE | 10.00 |
| DALMORE 12YR | 10.00 |
| DALWINNIE | 10.00 |
| GLENFIDDICH | 8.00 |
| GLENFIDDICH 18YR | 14.00 |
| GLENLIVET | 8.00 |
| GLENMORANGIE 10 YR | 8.00 |
| GLENMORANGIE PORT WOOD | 10.00 |
| GLENMORANGIE MADEIRA WOOD | 10.00 |
| GLENMORANGIE SHERRY WOOD | 10.00 |
| MACALLAN 12YR | 10.00 |
| MACALLAN 18YR | 25.00 |
| TALISKER | 12.00 |

**EAU DE VIE**

| | |
|---|---|
| MAROLO GRAPPA BAROLO | 20.00 |
| MAROLO GRAPPA BRUNELLO | 20.00 |
| MAROLO GRAPPA MOSCATO | 20.00 |
| PRIME UVE | 15.00 |

**CALVADOS**

| | |
|---|---|
| COEUR DE LION 1969 | 30.00 |
| CHATEAU BREUIL | 7.00 |

**SHERRY**

| | |
|---|---|
| DRY SACK | 7.00 |
| HARVEY'S BRISTOL CREAM | 6.00 |
| DOMECQ AMONTILLADO | 8.00 |

**COGNAC / ARMAGNAC**

| | |
|---|---|
| COURVOISIER NAPOLEON | 20.00 |
| HARDY NAPOLEON | 12.00 |
| HENNESSY XO | 20.00 |
| MARTELL CORDON BLUE | 30.00 |
| MARTELL VS | 8.00 |
| PIERRE FERRAND SELECTION | 20.00 |
| REMY MARTIN VSOP | 12.00 |
| REMY MARTIN XO | 25.00 |
| REMY MARTIN LOUIS XIII | 140.00 |
| LARRESSINGLE VSOP | 10.00 |

**CORDIALS**

| | |
|---|---|
| GODIVA, WHITE OR DARK | 7.00 |
| BAILEY'S IRISH CREAM | 7.00 |
| FRANGELICO | 7.00 |
| AMARULA CREAM | 8.00 |
| EXTASE | 17.00 |
| AMARETTO DI SARRONNO | 7.00 |
| GRAND MARNIER | 7.00 |
| GRAND MARNIER "150" | 40.00 |
| SAMBUCA ROMANA, WHITE OR BLACK | 7.00 |
| NAVAN VANILLA | 8.00 |

**PORTS**

| | |
|---|---|
| GRAHAM'S "6" GRAPE | 7.00 |
| DOW'S 20 YEAR OLD TAWNY | 10.00 |
| NOVAL 10 YEAR OLD TAWNY | 8.00 |
| SANDEMAN'S FOUNDER'S RESERVE | 6.00 |
| TAYLOR FLADGATE "LBV" 1999 | 8.00 |

*Ask your captain about vintage ports*

**DESSERT WINES**

| | |
|---|---|
| CHATEAU LA FORET SAUTERNE 2000 | 14.00 |
| COSENTINO "LATE HARVEST" VIOGNIER, NAPA 2002 | 12.00 |
| "DOLCE" DOLCE WINERY 2000 | 20.00 |
| VALCKENBERG "MADONNA" BEERENAUSLESE 1999/2000 | 20.00 |

**Courtesy of Commander's Palace, Las Vegas, NV**

**Figure 4-18. Tea Menu**

The history of Afternoon Tea began in France in the 1700s with what was known as "five o'clock tea." Just over a century later the practice became popular in England in the mid 1800s, when the Duchess of Bedford had trays of tea with bread, butter, and cake served in the mid-afternoon in order to stave-off her appetite until dinner, which was generally served as late as 9:00 p.m. As she began to invite other society ladies to join her, the Afternoon Tea became the 'in-thing' for the upper-class women. Along with tea, there would be small pastries with clotted cream or preserves, delicate sandwiches, and scones served. Though many people use the term "High Tea" to discribe this event, "High Tea" was actually served later and consisted of a full dinner meal. Tea was still served, but there would also be meats, fish or eggs, cheese, bread and butter, cake, and, on occasion, alcohol. It was more of a man's meal than a lady's social diversion.

---

*Afternoon Tea*
## Selection of Loose Teas by Mighty Leaf Tea Company

Himalayan Peak Darjeeling Organic
Vanilla Bean
Ti Kuan Yin
Jasmine Mist
Chamomile Citron
African Amber

Earl Gray Organic
Wild Blackberries
Marrakesh Mint
Green Tea Passion
Ginger Twist
Verbena

### Sandwiches
Smoked Salmon on Pumpernickel Bread
Egg Mayonnaise with Cress on White Bread
Cucumber and Cream Cheese on
Seven Grains Bread
Smoked Turkey with Havarti Dill Cheese on
Sour Dough Bread
Maryland Crab and Herb Mayonnaise in
Phyllo Cup

### Scones and Pastries
Orange and Raisin Scones served with Apricot and
Strawberry Jam, Lemon Curd and Devonshire Cream
Gianduja Chocolate Cake, Strawberry Tart,
Citrus Crème Brulèe, with Fresh Raspberries,
Almond Apricot Teacake, with Lemon Mousse

$32.00 per person
*****

### Sparkling Wine & Champagne by the Glass

Domaine Carneros, Brut, Carneros, California
$12

Lanson, Black Label, France
$15

Tattinger, La Francaise, Brut, France
$17

"My experience convinced me that tea is better than brandy"

Courtesy of Willard Intercontinental, Washington, DC

**Figure 4-19. Lounge Menu**

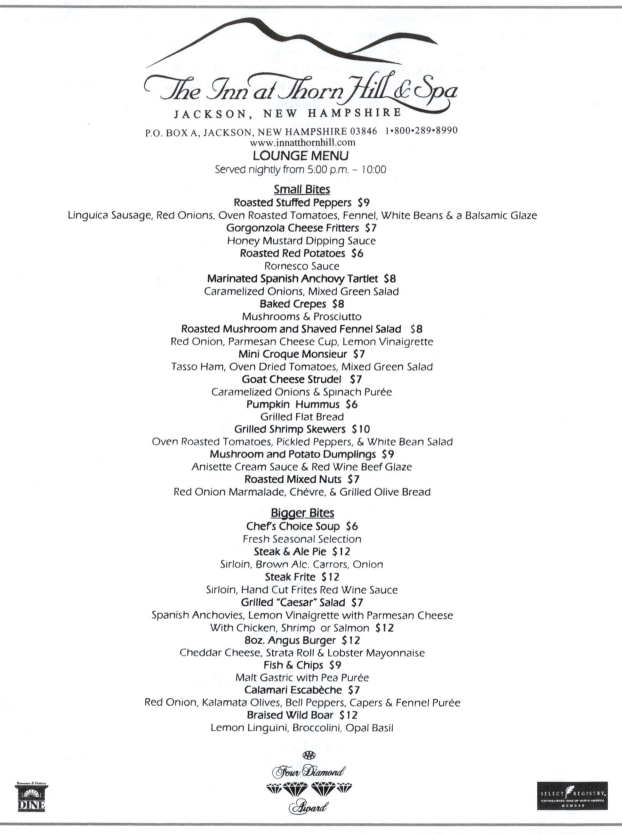

*The Inn at Thorn Hill & Spa*

JACKSON, NEW HAMPSHIRE

P.O. BOX A, JACKSON, NEW HAMPSHIRE 03846   1•800•289•8990
www.innatthornhill.com

### LOUNGE MENU
Served nightly from 5:00 p.m. – 10:00

#### Small Bites

**Roasted Stuffed Peppers  $9**
Linguica Sausage, Red Onions, Oven Roasted Tomatoes, Fennel, White Beans & a Balsamic Glaze

**Gorgonzola Cheese Fritters  $7**
Honey Mustard Dipping Sauce

**Roasted Red Potatoes  $6**
Romesco Sauce

**Marinated Spanish Anchovy Tartlet  $8**
Caramelized Onions, Mixed Green Salad

**Baked Crepes  $8**
Mushrooms & Prosciutto

**Roasted Mushroom and Shaved Fennel Salad  $8**
Red Onion, Parmesan Cheese Cup, Lemon Vinaigrette

**Mini Croque Monsieur  $7**
Tasso Ham, Oven Dried Tomatoes, Mixed Green Salad

**Goat Cheese Strudel  $7**
Caramelized Onions & Spinach Purée

**Pumpkin Hummus  $6**
Grilled Flat Bread

**Grilled Shrimp Skewers  $10**
Oven Roasted Tomatoes, Pickled Peppers, & White Bean Salad

**Mushroom and Potato Dumplings  $9**
Anisette Cream Sauce & Red Wine Beef Glaze

**Roasted Mixed Nuts  $7**
Red Onion Marmalade, Chévre, & Grilled Olive Bread

#### Bigger Bites

**Chef's Choice Soup  $6**
Fresh Seasonal Selection

**Steak & Ale Pie  $12**
Sirloin, Brown Ale. Carrors, Onion

**Steak Frite  $12**
Sirloin, Hand Cut Frites Red Wine Sauce

**Grilled "Caesar" Salad  $7**
Spanish Anchovies, Lemon Vinaigrette with Parmesan Cheese
With Chicken, Shrimp or Salmon  $12

**8oz. Angus Burger  $12**
Cheddar Cheese, Strata Roll & Lobster Mayonnaise

**Fish & Chips  $9**
Malt Gastric with Pea Purée

**Calamari Escabèche  $7**
Red Onion, Kalamata Olives, Bell Peppers, Capers & Fennel Purée

**Braised Wild Boar  $12**
Lemon Linguini, Broccolini, Opal Basil

*Four Diamond Award*

**Courtesy of The Inn at Thorn Hill, Jackson, NH**

Tea that includes a variety of teas, sandwiches, and an assortment of scones and pastries. Sparkling wine and champagne by the glass are also offered at an additional cost.

## Lounge Menus

A LOUNGE menu may be à la carte or semi à la carte. The à la carte items consist of appetizers, soups, salads, and sandwich items. The entrée selections are semi à la carte and are served with vegetable, potato, or rice. Lounge menus are usually found in hotels, inns, and spas where patrons can select food items that are easily prepared and less expensive than in the dining room. Most times patrons utilize lounge service in the late afternoon or late evening, which allows the establishment to market light foods and beverages at times when the demand for full-service meals is down. The lounge menu used at The Inn at Thorn Hill® in Jackson, New Hampshire (Fig. 4-19) serves "Small Bites," or appetizers, and "Bigger Bites," such as soup, Steak & Ale Pie, and Calamari Escabeche à la carte.

Semi à la carte items include the Steak Frite and the Braised Wild Boar served with Lemon Linguini, Broccolini, and Opal Basil.

# For Review and Discussion

1. What is a **semi à la carte** menu?

2. What is a **prix-fixe** menu?

3. Describe the characteristics of the luncheon menu.

4. Discuss American, French, and modified Russian service.

5. Explain the principal characteristics of the special occasion menu.

6. What are the considerations that should be taken into account when planning an ethnic menu?

7. Explain the principal elements of the specialty menu.

8. What are the major characteristics of an institutional menu?

9. What are the elements that should be considered when designing a wine menu?

10. Explain the difference between Low and High Tea.

*Part 2*

# FINANCIAL ASPECTS OF MENU PLANNING

# Chapter 5

# THE YIELD TEST

YIELD tests are an essential part of determining the profitability of a menu item. This chapter discusses the types of yield tests, how to do a yield test, and their importance.

## Objectives

❏ To define yield tests

❏ To explain how to use yield tests within the foodservice industry

❏ To discuss how a yield test is used when planning menus

❏ To calculate the cost of a yield test

# Defining the Yield Test

A **yield test** is used to determine the amount of **edible product (EP)** (also referred to as yield) and the amount of **waste product (WP)** of a particular food item.

It is essential for a menu planner to know the amount of EP in food items to avoid purchasing an item that yields very little EP and produces WP that cannot be used. The higher the yield of a food item, the greater the number of portions that will be available and the higher the profit.

Yield tests should be done at least three times for every food item used in a foodservice operation. Management and chefs should know how much each food item yields. Since foods vary in terms of their perishability, the amount of yield varies from one delivery to the next. Food items that have a high perishability factor such as meats, poultry, produce, fruits, and seafood should have yield tests on a regular basis.

Management must be demanding when setting specifications for food items. Specifications determine a standard of quality in a food product. Examples of such factors include:

- **Weight**
- **Color**
- **Shape**
- **Grade**
- **Texture**
- **Size**
- **Odor**
- **Packaging**
- **Product temperature**
- **Yield grade**

It is these specifications that help to determine the quality of food.

A yield test should be conducted under two conditions: (1) in a controlled environment and (2) during actual production time. A **controlled environment** exists when the individual conducting the yield test is not distracted by anything or anyone, is not rushed, and has all the necessary equipment to perform the test. A yield test that is performed during actual production provides a **noncontrolled environment** because distractions exist.

The reason for conducting a yield test under each of these conditions is to provide management with both the maximum and minimum yield that a product can produce. The actual yield is always lower until management trains employees to cut and serve food items properly in order to gain a better yield.

## Types of Yield Tests

THERE are two basic types of yield tests:

1. **A convenience food yield test**
2. **A fresh food yield test**

## Convenience Food Yield Test

The **convenience food yield test** is done on food items that have been prepackaged into cans, bags, and boxes. This test consists of opening packages and weighing the amount of edible product. **Packing** is the extra filling placed inside a convenience food product to keep its quality.

This test determines if the amount of packaging is within the specifications stated. If the amount of packing is different than the specifications stated management is losing money by paying for excess packing. The Food and Drug Administration has set standards for the amount of packing used in all canned products.

## Fresh Food Yield Test

The **fresh food yield test** (see Fig. 5-1) is done on food items that are purchased in an unaltered, fresh state. This test consists of weighing food items both before starting any type of preparation, and after completing the final preparation. This test is completed in eight steps:

1. **The fresh food product is weighed as it is received.**
2. **The fresh food product is weighed after it comes out of storage. Most foods lose weight during storage through evaporation.**
3. **Any undesirable parts, such as fat, bones, outer leaves, etc., are trimmed.**
4. **The fresh food product is washed and weighed. (At this point, the convenience food yield test also can be calculated).**
5. **The food is prepared and cooked. The food is weighed to determine the amount of weight loss caused through shrinkage during the cooking stage.**

## Figure 5-1. Yield Test Card

Item_____ Grade_____ Date_____

Pieces_____ Weight_____ lb_____ oz Average Wt._____ lb_____oz

Total Cost $_____ at $_____ per_____ Purveyor_____

| Breakdown | No. | Weight | | Ratio to Total Weight | Value per Pound | Total Value | Cost of ea. | | Portion | | Cost Factor per | |
|---|---|---|---|---|---|---|---|---|---|---|---|---|
| | | lb | oz | | | | lb | oz | Size | Value | lb | Por. |
| | | | | | | | | | | | | |
| | | | | | | | | | | | | |
| | | | | | | | | | | | | |
| | | | | | | | | | | | | |
| | | | | | | | | | | | | |
| | | | | | | | | | | | | |
| | | | | | | | | | | | | |
| Total | | | | | | | | | | | | |

$$\text{Cost Factor per lb or Portion} = \frac{\text{Ready-to-Eat Value per lb or Portion}}{\text{Purchase Price per lb}}$$

### Cooking Loss

To find ready-to-eat value of cuts at a new market price, multiply new price per lb by the cost factor.

Item_____

Portion Size_____ Cooked_____ hr_____ min at_____degrees

Portion Cost Factor_____ Cooked_____ hr_____ min at_____degrees

| Breakdown | No. | Weight | | Ratio to Total Weight | Value per Pound | Total Value | Ready-to-Eat Value per | | Ready-to-Eat Portion | | Cost Factor per | |
|---|---|---|---|---|---|---|---|---|---|---|---|---|
| | | lb | oz | | | | lb | oz | Size | Value | lb | Por. |
| Original Weight | | | | | | | | | | | | |
| Loss in Trimming | | | | | | | | | | | | |
| Trimmed Weight | | | | | | | | | | | | |
| Loss in Cooking | | | | | | | | | | | | |
| Cooked Weight | | | | | | | | | | | | |
| Bones and Trim | | | | | | | | | | | | |
| Loss in Slicing | | | | | | | | | | | | |
| Salable Meat | | | | | | | | | | | | |

$$\text{Cost Factor per lb or Portion} = \frac{\text{Ready-to-Eat Value per lb or Portion}}{\text{Purchase Price per lb}}$$

6. The food product is cut into portion sizes.

7. The food product is cut to determine the amount of edible product lost during the portioning or carving stage.

8. Once the food item has been cut into the total number of portions, the amount of waste product is totaled.

# Calculating a Yield Test

## Step 1

Establish the AP weight. The **AP weight** is the as purchased weight of the raw product. Weigh the product.

## Step 2

Calculate the amount of waste. Weigh all waste product, such as bones, fat, outer leaves, and so forth.

## Step 3

Calculate the edible product.

$$\textbf{AP weight} - \textbf{Waste product} = \textbf{Edible product}$$

For example:

$$10 \text{ lb} - 3 \text{ lb} = 7 \text{ lb}$$

## Step 4

Convert the edible product unit of measurement (possibly pounds to ounces), if the single portion size to be served is different from the edible product amount.

$$\textbf{Edible product} \times \textbf{16 oz (1 lb)} = \textbf{Total number of portions}$$

For example:

$$7 \text{ lb} \times 16 \text{ oz} = 112 \text{ oz}$$

# Step 5

Calculate the number of individual portions available. Then divide the total number of portions available by the individual portion size to get the number of portions available. For example:

$$112 \text{ oz} \div 4 \text{ oz} = 28$$

# Step 6

Establish the individual portion cost. Take the total cost and divide it by the total number of portions. This equals the individual portion cost. For example:

$$\$20 \div 28 = \$0.72$$

## Practice Problem

**1.** AP Weight 30 lb
AP Price $5.95 lb      Total Extension_____
Waste 3 lb      Total # of Portions_____
Portion Size 3 oz      Portion Cost_____

**2.** AP Weight 19 lb
AP Price $8.77 lb      Total Extension_____
Waste 2 lb      Total # of Portions_____
Portion Size 6 oz      Portion Cost_____

**3.** AP Weight 315 lb
AP Price $1.75 lb      Total Extension_____
Waste 20.5 lb      Total # of Portions_____
Portion Size 10 oz      Portion Cost_____

**4.** AP Weight 35 lb
AP Price   $1.50 lb      Total Extension_____
Waste 15 lb      Total # of Portions_____
Portion Size 4 oz      Portion Cost_____

**5.** AP Weight 25 lb
AP Price $6.95 lb       Total Extension _____
Waste 2.5 lb          Total # of Portions_____
Portion Size 5 oz    Portion Cost_____

**6.** AP Weight 50 lb
AP Price $5.00 lb       Total Extension_____
Waste 5 lb            Total # of Portions_____
 Portion Size 5 oz   Portion Cost_____

**7.** AP Weight 10 lb
AP Price $2.00 lb       Total Extension_____
Waste 2 lb            Total # of Portions_____
Portion Size 4 oz    Portion Cost_____

**8.** AP Weight 65 lb
AP Price $0.95 lb       Total Extension_____
Waste 5 oz           Total # of Portions_____
Portion Size 10 oz   Portion Cost_____

## Answers

**1.** Total Extension $178.50
Total  # of Portions 144
Portion Cost $1.24

**2.** Total Extension $166.63
Total # of Portions 45
Portion Cost $3.70

**3.** Total Extension $551.25
Total # of Portions 471
Portion Cost $1.17

**4.** Total Extension $52.50
Total # of Portions 80
Portion Cost $0.66

**5.** Total Extension $173.75
Total # of Portions 72
Portion Cost $2.41

**6.** Total Extension $250.00
Total # of Portions 144
Portion Cost $1.74

**7.** Total Extension $20.00
Total # of Portions 32
Portion Cost $0.63

**8.** Total Extension $61.75
Total # of Portions 103
Portion Cost $0.60

# Edible Yields Percentage

Table 5.1 provides edible yields information that follows has been prepared by the Nutritional and Technical Services Division and the Human Nutrition Information Service of the U.S. Department of Agriculture and the National Marine Fisheries Service of the U.S. Department of Commerce.

**Table 5-1. Edible Yields**

| EDIBLE YIELDS PERCENTAGE AFTER COOKING | |
|---|---|
| **BEEF** | **ONE POUND AS PURCHASED = EDIBLE (COOKED) YIELD (%)** |
| Brisket, corned (boned) | = 70% |
| Brisket, fresh (boned) | = 69% |
| Ground meats (26% fat) | = 72% |
| Ground meats (20% fat) | = 74% |
| Ground meats (15% fat) | = 75% |
| Ground meats (10% fat) | = 76% |
| Roast, chuck (without bone) | = 63% |
| Roast, chuck (with bone) | = 54% |
| Rump (without bone) | = 68% |
| Rump (with bone) | = 62% |
| Steak, flank | = 73% |
| Steak, round (without bone) | = 63% |
| Stew meat | = 61% |
| **POULTRY** | **ONE POUND AS PURCHASED = EDIBLE (COOKED) YIELD (%)** |
| Chicken breast halves | = 66% w/skin |
| (approx. 6.1 oz with ribs) | = 56% w/o skin |
| Chicken breast halves | = 55% w/skin |
| (approx. 7.5 oz with backs) | = 47% w/o skin |
| Turkey | = 53% w/skin |
| Turkey | = 47% w/o skin |
| **OTHER MEATS** | |
| Lamb chops (shoulder, with bone) | = 46% |

| | |
|---|---|
| Lamb roast (leg, without bone) | = 61% |
| Lamb roast (shoulder, without bone) | = 54% |
| Lamb stew meat | = 65% |
| Veal cutlets | = 54% |
| Pork chops, loin | = 54% |
| Pork roast (leg, without bone) | = 57% |
| Pork roast (leg, with bone) | = 46% |
| Pork loin (without bone) | = 58% |
| Pork loin (with bone) | = 45% |
| Shoulder/boston butt (without bone) | = 60% |
| Shoulder/boston butt (with bone) | = 52% |
| Shoulder/picnic (without bone) | = 57% |
| Shoulder/picnic (with bone) | = 42% |
| Canadian bacon | = 69% |
| Ham (without bone) | = 63% |
| Ham (with bone) | = 53% |

| **FRESH VEGETABLES AND FRUITS** | **ONE POUND AS PURCHASED = EDIBLE YIELD (%)** |
|---|---|
| Apples | = 91% |
| Apricots | = 93% |
| Asparagus | = 53% |
| Avocados | = 67% |
| Bananas | = 65% |
| Beans, green | = 88% |
| Beans, lima | = 44% |
| Beans, wax (yellow) | = 88% |
| Beet greens | = 48% |
| Beets | = 77% |
| Broccoli | = 81% |
| Brussels sprouts | = 76% |
| Cabbage | = 87% |
| Cabbage, red | = 64% |
| Cantaloupe | = 52% |

*(Continues)*

| FRESH VEGETABLES AND FRUITS | ONE POUND AS PURCHASED = EDIBLE YIELD (%) |
|---|---|
| Carrots | = 70% |
| Cauliflower | = 62% |
| Celery | = 83% |
| Chard, Swiss | = 92% |
| Cherries | = 98% |
| Chicory | = 89% |
| Collards | = 57% |
| Corn, on the cob | = 33% |
| Cranberries | = 95% |
| Cucumbers | = 84% |
| Eggplant | = 81% |
| Endive, escarole | = 78% |
| Grapefruit | = 52% |
| Grapes | = 97% |
| Honeydew melon | = 46% |
| Kale | = 67% |
| Lemons | = 43% (3/4 c juice) |
| Lettuce, head | = 76% |
| Lettuce, leaf | = 66% |
| Lettuce, romaine | = 64% |
| Limes | = 47% (7/8 c juice) |

| FRESH VEGETABLES AND FRUITS | ONE POUND AS PURCHASED = EDIBLE YIELD (%) |
|---|---|
| Mangoes | = 69% |
| Mushrooms | = 98% |
| Mustard greens | = 93% |
| Nectarines | = 91% |
| Okra | = 87% |
| Onions, green | = 83% |
| Onions | = 88% |
| Oranges | = 71% |

*(Continues)*

*(Continued)*

| | |
|---|---|
| Papaya | = 67% |
| Parsley | = 92% |
| Parsnips | = 83% |
| Peaches | = 76% |
| Pears | = 92% |
| Peas, green | = 38% |
| Peppers, green | = 80% |
| Pineapple | = 54% |
| Plantains, ripe | = 65% |
| Plums | = 94% |
| Potatoes, white | = 81% |
| Pumpkin | = 70% |
| Radishes | = 94% |

| FRESH VEGETABLES AND FRUITS | ONE POUND AS PURCHASED = EDIBLE YIELD (%) |
|---|---|
| Raspberries | = 96% |
| Rhubarb | = 86% |
| Rutabagas | = 85% |
| Spinach | = 88% |
| Squash, summer | = 95% |
| Squash, zucchini | = 94% |
| Squash, acorn | = 70% |
| Squash, butternut | = 84% |
| Squash, Hubbard | = 64% |
| Strawberries | = 88% |
| Sweet potatoes | = 80% |
| Tangerines | = 74% |
| Tomatoes | = 99% |
| Tomatoes, cherry | = 97% |
| Turnips | = 70% |
| Watercress | = 92% |
| Watermelon | = 57% |

## Software Packages

*THE Book of Yields* Accuracy in Food Costing and Purchasing CD-ROM, 7th edition, by Francis T. Lynch: © 2008 John Wiley & Sons, Inc. ISBN: 978-0-470-16764-9 www.chefdesk.com

"ExecuChef,™" by Susan Schaeffer: www.ExecuChef.com

# For Review and Discussion

1. Define **yield test**.

2. List five types of waste that can be produced during a yield test.

3. What do the abbreviations AP, WP, and EP mean?

4. What is the formula used to find a portion cost?

# Chapter 6

# STANDARD RECIPES

STANDARD recipes are needed to produce a standard-quality food product. This chapter discusses a variety of methods for writing recipes, the techniques for standardizing recipes, and the importance of standardization.

*Objectives*

❑ To stress the importance of using standardized recipes

❑ To show standard recipe card format

❑ To identify the elements of a recipe card

❑ To illustrate a variety of methods for recipe creativity

# Defining Standard Recipes in the Industry

A **standard recipe** is the only recipe used to prepare a particular menu item. The object of writing, maintaining, and using standardized recipes is to guarantee a consistent quality product.

When customers enjoy the food they eat at a restaurant, they want to repeat the experience upon returning. Customers expect the food quality to be as good (or even better than) the quality they experienced most recently. A foodservice operation that does not duplicate the same food quality every time the product is made and served disappoints its customers. In today's competitive world, customers will not tolerate inconsistent food quality from a foodservice operation. Customers expect the best quality of food that their money can buy, and competition demands that the foodservice operation meet those expectations. By standardizing recipes, a foodservice operation is able to meet customers' demands and remain competitive in the industry. In terms of profit, a foodservice operation cannot afford to disappoint its customers by serving an inconsistent product.

The fast food industry, with its standards of quick service, low prices, and organized systems of producing a consistent quality of food, has taught the foodservice industry and the consumer the value of producing a standardized food product. To set a standard means to adapt food quality to a level or degree of excellence. The standardizing of recipes is one of the first steps in obtaining the level of excellence that customers come to expect. Some smaller foodservice operations do not use standardized recipe cards per se, because of the expense of writing, testing, and recording the recipes on index cards or in computer files. Hotels, institutions, foodservice chains, and larger restaurants use standardized recipes and systems because they can afford the expense and realize the value of having standardized recipes.

Chefs should know how to produce the items on a menu, and management should have a knowledge of how food items on a menu are prepared. If a chef cannot be at work, management often must take over. If management is not familiar with the preparation and cannot fill in for a chef, the food quality will lack consistency, causing customer dissatisfaction, loss of sales, and perhaps a damaged reputation.

There are different formats for recording recipes. Recipes can be written on plain sheets of paper, on index cards, or recorded in computer files. The format selected should be based on the system that provides the best support for the operation. When using standardized recipes, management must:

- **Ensure that there are no errors within the recipe.**
- **Test and retest the recipe to achieve excellent food quality.**
- **Keep recipes simple to read and to follow.**
- **Check that the recipes are grammatically correct.**
- **Use them.**

Management should select a standardized recipe card system that best fits the operation. A simple system is more useful and more successful than one that is complex. Standard recipes can be used most effectively when you are training cooks and management personnel.

## Recording Recipes

A recipe card (Fig. 6-1) should include this information:

- **Name of the recipe (item to be made)**
- **Portion size**
- **Yield (total portions and/or number of servings)**

### Figure 6-1.  Recipe Card Format

| Item _____ | | Menu Number _____ |
| Portions Size _____ | | Issue Number _____ |
| Yield _____ | | |

| Ingredients | Weight | Measure | Method of Preparation |
|---|---|---|---|
|  |  |  |  |

- **Index number for identification purposes**
- **Ingredients column**
- **Weight column**
- **Measurement column**
- **Directions or method of preparation column**
- **Picture of the finished product**

A picture of the finished product should appear with each recipe because it is true that "a picture is worth a thousand words." It is much easier to train a chef or a manager to prepare a recipe if the person has a picture in mind of how the finished product should look. Any presentation mistakes can be identified by referring to the recipe picture and corrected before the customer receives the menu item.

On recipe cards, the weight column refers only to ingredients that are expressed in ounces and pounds. The measure column refers to all other terms of measurement, such as taste, pinch, dash, teaspoons, tablespoons, cups, pints, quarts, gallons, and number 2 or number 10 cans. The method of preparation column must be written in a clear, grammatically correct fashion, with simple steps to follow. To save time for the chef, prerequisite tasks should be listed first (e.g., preheating the oven). Proceed with a step-by-step method for preparing the recipe (Figs. 6-2 and 6-3).

## Recipe Creativity

TO BE competitive in the foodservice industry, it is vital to provide the types of food that customers demand. Since customer food preferences are always changing, foodservice operations should often change their menus. The more profitable restaurants tend to pique customer curiosity by regularly preparing new and exciting dishes (perhaps as often as weekly). Successful foodservice operations experiment with recipes on a regular basis.

It is important to experiment to create sales and to add excitement to menus. First take a recipe and prepare according to the directions. Then make it a second time and change a few ingredients or the amounts of ingredients so that it becomes your way of making the recipe. Give the recipe to other chefs and tell them to prepare it first as is, then your way,

**Figure 6-2. New England Clam Chowder Recipe**

| Item New England Clam Chowder | | | Recipe Number S-1 |
| Portion Size 8-oz bowl | | | Portions 8 |
| Yield ½ gallon | | | |

| Ingredients | Weight | Measure | Method of Preparation |
| --- | --- | --- | --- |
| Shucked clams | 1 | quart | A. Drain clams, saving juice. |
| Chopped bacon | 8 | tablespoons | Chop clams, and reserve. |
| Sliced onions | 1 | cup | B. Cook bacon in a saucepan |
| Diced potatoes | 3½ | cups | until crisp. Do not drain grease. |
| Salt | ½ | teaspoon | Add onions and brown slightly. |
| Pepper | | pinch | C. Add potatoes, salt, pepper, |
| Hot water | 2 | cups | and water. Cook for 10 minutes. |
| Milk | 1 | quart | D. Add clams, milk, half and half, |
| Half and half | 1 | cup | and clam juice; cook until |
| Soda crackers | 8 | each | potatoes are tender, about 10 |
| | | | minutes. Do not overcook |
| | | | potatoes. |
| | | | E. Pour chowder over crackers |
| | | | in serving bowls. |

and finally, their own way. When the process is complete, you will have a recipe with three different variations. Finally, have employees taste the product and evaluate it. Listen to their suggestions and make changes as necessary.

Once employees are excited about the product, provide a few customers with samples each night. Ask them what they think of the product and how it might be improved. Allowing employees and customers to get directly involved in the planning and creation of menu items gives them a vested interest in the foodservice operation. Do this for about a month to get the customers and employees talking about the new food product. After everyone is talking about the product, have employees verbally suggest it to customers when describing the nightly special. *Do not place this product on the menu (verbal sales only)*! Wait until the product has become a good seller (by achieving 5 to 20 percent of sales for a night) before it is permanently placed on the menu. Not placing this product on the menu immediately, keeps the anticipation level high and adds to the excitement when the item actually appears on the menu.

**Figure 6-3. Roast Leg of Lamb Recipe**

| | |
|---|---|
| Menu Item <u>Roast leg of lamb</u> | Recipe Number <u>E-2</u> |
| Portion Size <u>6 oz</u> | Portions <u>8</u> |

| Ingredients | Quantity | Method of Preparation |
|---|---|---|
| Leg of lamb, bone in<br>  Olive oil<br>Dried rosemary<br>Garlic seasoning<br>Salt and pepper<br><br>Chicken stock<br><br><br><br>Fresh mint sprig<br>  and or mint jelly | 6 pounds<br>2 tablespoons (1 ounce)<br>1 tablespoon (½ ounce)<br>1 tablespoon (½ ounce)<br>2 tablespoons (1 ounce)<br><br>1/3 cup<br><br><br><br><br>As needed | Preheat oven to 325°F.<br>A. Place lamb on a rack in a shallow roasting plan.<br>B. Brush olive oil over lamb.<br>C. Rub rosemary, garlic, salt, and pepper onto lamb.<br>D. Roast for 3 hours or to an internal temperature of 155–165 degrees for medium. Do not cover lamb while it is cooking. Allow roast to stand 10–15 minutes, and then carve and serve.<br>  Deglaze roasting pan by adding chicken stock to drippings in pan.<br>Bring to a simmer, stirring to loosen caramelized drippings on bottom of pan. Ladle glaze over sliced lamb.<br>  Garnish by placing a mint sprig or a dollop of mint onto each plate. |

# For Review and Discussion

**1.** Why is it important to standardize recipes?

**2.** How does standardizing recipes increase the quality of menu items?

**3.** Which sector of the foodservice industry does a particularly good job in producing a standardized food product?

**4.** List three rules in making standardized recipes successful.

**5.** Name the items that are necessary on a standardized recipe card.

# Chapter 7

# RECIPE COSTING

RECIPE costing is the method used to determine the profit on food products. This chapter discusses the importance of costing out recipes, provides the methodology used to do so, and supplies examples of how to cost our recipes.

 *Objectives*

- ❏ To explain why recipe costing is necessary
- ❏ To identify different methods of reducing the food cost percentage
- ❏ To identify the elements in costing out a recipe
- ❏ To illustrate how to cost out a recipe

# Assigning the Task of Recipe Costing

THE majority of people who enter the foodservice industry do so to make a profit. To achieve this goal, it is necessary to "cost out" or assign a price to each ingredient. Although this task is not a difficult process, it is time consuming.

To begin the process, management should identify an individual who is responsible for overseeing the project from start to finish. The person must have a clear understanding of recipe costing and its relationship to food costing and profit. Although this coordinator may not be the only person working on the entire project, he or she is responsible for the completion of the task, which includes a complete analysis of the recipe costing system.

# The Importance of Recipe Costing

WHY is recipe costing necessary? To understand the full effect that recipe costing has on the amount of profit that a foodservice operation earns it is important to first understand the relationship between food cost and profit.

To obtain and maintain maximum profit, a foodservice operation must be aware of expenses. The four major expenses are:

1. **Food**
2. **Labor**
3. **Overhead**
4. **Profit**

**Food expense** is the cost of the food purchased. Some foodservice operations also include beverages in this category. **Labor expense** is the total cost of the labor force that a food service operation employs. **Overhead expense** consists of all other expenses except food, labor, and profit. Examples of overhead expenses are the cost of equipment, uniforms, laundry service, water, electricity, rent or mortgage, and taxes. **Profit** is considered as an accrual expense before any cash flow or sales. Once a sales transaction has taken place, all expenses have been paid, and there is money left in the cash register, there is a profit. It is then that profit is no longer considered to be an expense but rather an asset to the foodservice operation.

Once a cash flow has been established, the relationship of the three other expenses (food, labor, and overhead) to profit becomes inverse. An **inverse relationship** occurs, when one of the expenses increases or decreases, to affect the profit. For example, when the cost of food, labor, and overhead decrease, profit increases. The three major expense categories, plus profit, must equal 100 percent. Sales at 100 percent represent all the money that a foodservice operation can possibly make.

It is important that management establish an annual forecast of sales, profit, and expenses. The management personnel should track these costs on a daily, weekly, and monthly basis to obtain the projected annual profit. The management team cannot wait three or six months from the opening date to see if the business is making a profit. Even if a profit is being made, management still must evaluate the profit to see if it is up to the projected amount.

Most small family and independent foodservice operations are primarily concerned that there is enough money in the cash register at the end of the day to pay bills and to make a profit. There is nothing wrong with this philosophy, as long as the family still is interested in increasing daily profits. By understanding and implementing greater control of the three expense areas, this goal is possible.

Here are six guidelines for achieving a greater profit:

1. **Buy comparatively.** Purchase food from more than two purveyors or vendors. Occasionally purchase food from your regular purveyor's competition. Doing so will keep your relationship with your regular purveyor honest, and he or she will try harder to keep you as a satisfied customer.

2. **Do not always purchase a product with the lowest price.** Never sacrifice quality standards. Customers appreciate quality and will pay a higher price for a better food product.

3. **Keep track of pilferage.** Pilferage is the biggest contributor to a high food cost percentage. Employees often do not fully understand the implications of eating a food product without paying for it. The management team must decide what type of meal policy to implement and how to enforce it. Employees in the foodservice industry sometimes eat in the walk-in refrigerator if allowed to do so. Placing a lock on the walk-in when it is not being used and restricting access to the chefs can help control this problem. It is impossible to keep all employees from snacking or eating at a foodservice operation, but management must be aware of the effect of this problem on profit when it is not controlled.

4. **Train employees properly will help reduce *food* cost.** Food can be wasted because of employee accidents. The chef who burns the Lobster Newburgh, the service personnel who spill the sauce, and the bartender who incorrectly mixes a drink all contribute to an increase in the food cost percentage. Most accidents occur when people become careless about what they are doing. A proper training program teaches employees to take pride and care in their work. The greater the pride employees have in their work, the more care they are going to take in doing their jobs.

5. **Portion food in its proper portion size to control the food cost percentage.** When a chef serves an extra 2 or 3 ounces of a food product, the food cost percentage increases. When the customer is receiving more and paying less, the food cost that management has costed out will not be accurate.

6. **Forecast accurately.** Waste of food caused by overproduction is another factor that contributes to less profit. For controls on accurate forecasting, see Chapter 9.

# Guidelines for Costing Out a Recipe

To calculate the true cost of a recipe, it is necessary to understand how to round numbers. The general rule is to carry the number three places past the decimal point to the thousands place. If the number in the thousands place is five or greater, round up the number. For example, when the cost calculation of an ingredient is $1.248, the ingredient cost would be rounded up to $1.25. If the cost calculation of an ingredient equals $1.242, the cost would *not* be rounded up, and the cost of the ingredient would be $1.24. This guideline is applied to the recipes that are presented. The recipes also use these standard measurements:

| | |
|---|---|
| **3 teaspoons** | **= 1 tablespoon** |
| **2 tablespoons** | **= 1 ounce** |
| **6 teaspoons** | **= 1 ounce** |
| **1 ounce** | **= 28 grams** |
| **8 pints** | **= 1 gallon** |

# How to Cost Out a Recipe

ONCE a recipe has been selected, it needs to be recorded in a format that is easy to use for costing out recipes. (See Fig. 7-1 for an example.)

The form should contain this information:

A.  **Recipe name**

B.  **Recipe identification number**

C.  **Portion size**

D.  **Yield or number of portions**

E.  **Ingredients**

F.  **Waste percentage**

G.  **Edible portion (EP)**

H.  **As purchased (AP)**

I.  **Unit purchase price**

J.  **Conversion measure**

K.  **Ingredient cost**

L.  **Preliminary subtotal recipe cost**

M.  **Q factor of 1 percent (Place percentage in this box and then multiply the Q factor % by the preliminary subtotal recipe cost.)**

N.  **Q factor cost**

O.  **Subtotal recipe cost (Add Q factor cost to the preliminary subtotal recipe cost.)**

P.  **Portion cost (Divide the subtotal recipe cost by the total portions/yield.)**

Q.  **Additional cost (If this is an à la carte menu item, leave this box blank; if not, place the portion cost of the other menu items in this box.)**

R.  **Total recipe cost (Add any additional cost to portion cost; if there are no additional costs, the portion cost becomes the total recipe cost.)**

S.  **Desired overall food cost percentage (Retrieve this number from the annual profit and loss statement.)**

T.  **Preliminary selling price (Divide the total recipe cost by the desired food cost percentage.)**

U.  **Adjusted/actual selling price (based on what the customer is willing to pay)**

V.  **Adjusted/actual food cost percentage (Divide the total recipe cost by the adjusted/actual selling price.)**

**Figure 7-1. Recipe Costing From**

| A Recipe Name _____ | | | | | B Recipe ID No. _____ | |
|---|---|---|---|---|---|---|
| C Portion Size _____ | | | | | | |
| D Yield _____ | | | | | | |

| **E**<br>Ingredients | **F**<br>Waste<br>% | **G**<br>EP | **H**<br>AP | **I**<br>Unit Purchase<br>Price | **J**<br>Conversion<br>Measure | **K**<br>Ingredient<br>Cost |
|---|---|---|---|---|---|---|
| | | | | | | |
| | | | | | | |
| | | | | | | |
| | | | | | | |
| | | | | | | |

| | |
|---|---|
| **L** Subtotal | |
| **M** Q Factor % | |
| **N** Q Factor $ | |
| **O** Subtotal Recipe Cost | |
| **P** Portion Cost | |
| **Q** Additional Cost | |
| **R** Total Recipe Cost | |
| **S** Desired Food Cost % | |
| **T** Preliminary Selling Price | |
| **U** Adjusted/ Actual Selling Price | |
| **V** Adjusted/ Actual Food Cost % | |

# Recipe Heading

The recipe heading includes **A. Recipe Name, B. Recipe Identification Number, C. Portion Size,** and **D. Yield.**

## ❧ A. Recipe Name

Indicate the recipe name here. If the name is in a foreign language, include its English translation.

## ❧ B. Recipe Identification Number

Give each recipe an identification number so that the recipes can be organized in a systematic and easy to use method.

## ❧ C. Portion Size

Indicate the portion size here. The portion size is the amount of food or beverage that the customer will be served.

## ❧ D. Yield

The yield is the quantity of edible food or beverage that the recipe will make.

# Column E: Ingredients

List the ingredients in this column.

# Column F: Waste Percentage

Most recipes call for ingredients that are 100 percent edible (having no waste). The fact is, however, that most fresh food products, such as fruits, vegetables, poultry, fish, and seafood, have a certain percentage of waste.

To order the appropriate amount of food needed, the chef must calculate the amount of waste that the product has. For example, the recipe in Figure 7-2 calls for 32 ounces of 100 percent edible Romaine lettuce. A head of Romaine lettuce will have excess leaves and a core that will have to be trimmed. If the chef does not take into account the excess Romaine lettuce that has to be discarded, the yield will be less than the 32 ounces needed.

To calculate the amount of lettuce needed to yield 10 portions, the chef must establish the amount of waste that the head of Romaine lettuce will produce by performing a yield test. A yield test establishes the amount of edible product (EP) and the amount of waste product (WP).

# Column G: Edible Product Amount (EP)

The Edible Product (EP) column shows the amount of the ingredient in the recipe excluding waste.

# Column H: As Purchased Amount

The As Purchased (AP) amount is the amount of product purchased from the purveyor. This quantity usually includes a degree of waste. Products like salt, which do not have a waste amount, do not need to be evaluated.

Romaine lettuce has a waste of 20 percent and an EP amount of 32 ounces. To calculate the amount of Romaine lettuce that must be purchased (AP amount), the chef must use this formula:

$$AP = \frac{EP \times 100}{100\% - W\% \text{ (Waste percentage)}}$$

The waste amount is inserted into the formula as a whole number.

$$AP = \frac{32 \text{ oz}}{100 - 20} \times 100 = \frac{3{,}200 \text{ oz}}{80} = 40 \text{ oz}$$

The actual amount of Romaine lettuce that should be purchased for this recipe is 1.67 heads of lettuce; therefore, two heads of lettuce should be purchased.

# Column I: Unit Purchase Price Column

The Unit Purchase Price column lists the amount paid to the purveyor for an ingredient.

# Column J: Conversion Measure

The Conversion Measure column is where the conversion formula and the converting factor are recorded. The recipe AP amount is often expressed in ounces, whereas the AP price is expressed in pounds. When two different units of measurement are used, one must be converted so that they are the same. For example, in Figure 7-2, the AP amount of garlic required is 2 oz, and the cost of the garlic is $31.00 for 30 lb. The pounds must therefore be converted to ounces. Two methods can be used to convert the price per pound to ounces, but both methods must begin by answering the same question: "How much does 2 oz of garlic cost if 30 lb cost $31.00?" The price per pound is calculated in this way:

$$\$31.00 \div 30 \text{ lb} = \$1.03 \text{ lb}$$

In the first method, the menu planner calculates what percentage 2 oz is of 16 oz (1 lb); it equals .125. In other words, 2 oz is equivalent to 12.5 percent of 16 oz. Now that the same unit of measurement is derived in decimals, the garlic conversion factor (.125) is multiplied by the unit price ($1.03 lb.) per lb, for an ingredient cost of $0.12.

To use the second method, convert the Edible Portion (EP) unit of measurement to the As Purchased (AP) unit of measurement. The garlic is purchased by the pound and must be converted to the AP unit of measurement, which is in ounces. To accomplish this, divide $31.00 by 30 lb; the answer, $1.03, is the price per pound. Next divide $1.03 (the price per lb) by 16 oz (the number of ounces in a pound), to determine the cost of the item per ounce: $1.03 ÷ 16 = $0.06 per ounce. The unit of measurement derived, the ounce, is the same as the AP unit of measurement. To establish the ingredient cost for garlic, now multiply the cost per ounce by the AP quantity used in the recipe. Thus $0.06 oz × 2 oz = $0.12, is the ingredient cost.

## Column K: Ingredient Cost

The ingredient cost column is used to note the total cost of the ingredient used in the recipe. The converting factor and the unit price are multiplied to arrive at this figure. All of the ingredient costs in column K are added together to calculate a subtotal recipe cost, which is then written in column L, the subtotal recipe cost column.

## Column L: Subtotal of the Recipe Cost

Write the sum of all of the ingredient costs from column K in column L. This is the subtotal of the recipe cost column.

## Column M: Q Factor %

The **Q factor** is the price that the chef must charge to recover the cost of all of the ingredients that are too minor to calculate. For example, when a recipe calls for a dash or a pinch of an ingredient, this amount becomes too difficult to cost out, because the amount that a chef uses in a pinch or a dash is questionable and will differ from time to time.

One method that is used to recover the cost of a minor ingredient is to use a percentage factor. Since the amount of the ingredient to be used in this situation is questionable, we call this recovering cost factor a Q factor (**Q** stands for **questionable**).

The percentage amount of 1 percent is based on two facts:

1. **Most recipes do not have more than three Q factors.**
2. **The cost of these Q factor ingredients does not add up to 1 percent of the subtotal of the recipe.**

Thus it is important that the menu planner be selective when deciding on the Q factor. The exception to using more than 1 percent of the recipe subtotal would be if the ingredient were expensive, such as saffron.

## Column N: Q Factor in Dollars

The monetary value of the Q factor is calculated by multiplying the recipe subtotal by 1 percent. The answer is written in this column.

## Column O: Subtotal Recipe Cost

The subtotal recipe cost is calculated by adding the monetary value of the Q factor to the subtotal recipe cost. The answer is written in this column.

## Column P: Portion Cost

To calculate the portion cost (PC), divide the subtotal recipe cost by the total number of portions that the recipe yields.

## Column Q: Additional Costs

When a food item is to be sold as a semi à la carte item, the portion cost of any additional food items are cost out separately and are written in this column. For example, in Figure 7-2, the Caesar salad comes with a side of Italian bread. The menu planner calculates the portion cost of the slice of bread separately. The cost of additional items are added to the recipe subtotal cost column (column O), which determines the total recipe cost (column R). Another way of expressing the total recipe cost is by adding all of the costs of food items on the plate.

If customers are given a choice of a vegetable or starch, the menu planner must add the highest-priced vegetable or starch to the cost of the entrée. For example, most menus offer a choice of baked, mashed, or French fried potatoes with an entrée. The menu planner must cost out all three potato dishes in order to decide which one will be added to the portion cost of the entrée. The menu planner should not offer the customer a choice of vegetables that vary greatly in cost. Select vegetables that are similar in price in order to avoid having to charge too much for the entrée.

## Column R: Total Recipe Cost (Plate Cost)

The total recipe cost is calculated by adding the portion cost (column P) and the additional costs (column Q). This will give the cost of the food being placed on the plate.

## Column S: Desired Overall Food Cost Percentage

The desired overall food cost percentage is determined by management. The percentage is based on the annual food cost percentage that management desires to achieve in order to make the projected annual profit. The percentage will vary according to the foodservice concept and the annual profit and loss statement.

## Column T: Preliminary Selling Price

The preliminary selling price is established by dividing the total recipe cost (column R) by the desired overall food cost percentage (column S). It is called a preliminary selling price because most likely it is not the actual selling price that will be placed on the sales menu. It is the first price arrived at by maintaining a determined food cost percentage.

## Column U: Adjusted Actual Selling Price

The actual selling price is the selling price at which the product is sold on the menu. This price will differ from the preliminary selling price, because it is based on the dollar amount that the customer is willing to pay for the product. Other factors that influence the actual selling price are

- **Direct competition's price for the food product**
- **Demand (popularity) of the food product**
- **Availability of the food product**

The menu planner must examine all three factors before adjusting the preliminary selling price.

## Column V: Adjusted Actual Food Cost Percentage

Once the actual selling price has been readjusted either up or down, the menu planner can calculate the actual food cost percentage. This process is accomplished by dividing the total recipe cost (column R) by the actual selling price (column U).

The main objective for the menu planner in costing out recipes is to accurately calculate the cost of the food and to mark up the total recipe cost price to pay for labor cost and overhead cost, and to make a profit. The menu planner has to adjust the preliminary selling price to an actual selling price, which sometimes means lowering the profit margin made on the food product. If the preliminary selling price of barbecue chicken wings is $5.95, for example, and the chicken wings will not sell at that price because the customers will think that the price is too high or because the competition is selling chicken wings at $3.00, the price must be lowered in order to make the sale and to ensure customer satisfaction. The problem, however, is that this product is not making the profit needed to reach the annual projected profit margin. The menu planner must therefore compensate for the lower profit margin on the chicken wings. A way of recovering the $2.95 difference is to spread out the cost throughout the menu. This is known as **balancing the menu**.

Menus have a certain number of high food cost items and a certain number of low food cost items. Every foodservice operation would like to have only low food cost items on the menu in order to generate a better profit. Unfortunately, low food cost items are not always the choice of the majority of customers. Prime rib of beef is not the highest profit item on most menus, but it is one of the most popular choices. Keeping some high food cost items on the menu is necessary in order to keep patrons. However, in order to maintain a healthy profit margin, it is also necessary for a foodservice operation to maintain a good balance on the menu between high and low food cost items.

# Recipe Costing Software

RECIPE costing programs are available in a variety of software packages. These programs offer three advantages:

1. **The amount of time they save**
2. **Increased accuracy**
3. **The detailed reports that they are able to generate**

Some recipe costing software programs are very complex and expensive. These systems include more features, such as the ability to accommodate a number of recipes and menus for a variety of foodservice venues within a property. Less complex recipe software packages provide recipe costing on a smaller scale, possibly for one or two foodservice departments. A basic recipe costing software package usually allows for these tasks:

- **The generation of a list of inventory ingredients and their cost**
- **A summary of ingredient quantities**
- **A file storage system for the method of preparation of recipes**
- **A calculation of recipe costs and food costs percentages**
- **The ability to convert recipes to increase or decrease the yield**

## Figure 7-2.  Recipe Costing for Caesar Salad

**A.** Recipe Name: Caesar Salad
**C.** Portion Size: 3 oz

**B.** Recipe ID No.: S1
**D.** Yield: 10

| E. Ingredients | F. Waste % | G. EP | H. AP | I. Unit Purchase Price | J. Conversion Column | K. Ingredient Cost |
|---|---|---|---|---|---|---|
| Garlic | | | 2 oz | $31.00 for 30 lb | $31.00 ÷ 30 lb = $1.03 lb<br>$1.03 lb ÷ 16 oz = $0.06 oz<br>2 oz × $0.06 = $0.12 | $0.12 |
| Salt | | | 1 tsp | $8.79 for 24 24 oz rnds | $8.79 ÷ 24 rnds = $0.37 per 24 oz<br>$0.37 ÷ 24 oz = $0.02 oz<br>$0.02 oz ÷ 6 tsps = $0.003 tsp | When the value is less than $0.1 use Q factor |
| Anchovy fillets | | | 2 oz | $13.35 for 7 oz | $13.35 ÷ 7 oz = $1.91 oz<br>2 oz × $1.91 oz = $3.82 | $3.82 |
| Dijon mustard | | | 2 Tbsp | $31.58 for 6 24 oz jars | $31.58 ÷ 6 jars = $5.26 jar<br>$5.26 ÷ 24 oz = $0.22 oz<br>2 Tbsp = 1 oz | $0.22 |
| Olive oil | | | 2 oz | $79.00 for 3 gal | $79.00 ÷ 3 gal = $26.33 gal<br>$26.33 gal ÷ 128 oz = $0.21 oz<br>2 oz × $0.21 = $0.42 | $0.42 |
| Vinegar | | | 1 Tbsp | $11.22 for 4 gal | $11.22 ÷ 4 gal = $2.80 gal<br>$2.80 gal ÷ 128 oz = $0.02 oz<br>$0.02 oz ÷ 2 = $0.01 | $0.01 |
| Lemon juice | | | 2 oz | $43.74 for 4 gal | $43.74 ÷ 4 gal = $10.94 gal<br>$10.94 gal ÷ 128 oz = $0.09 oz<br>2 oz × $0.09 = $0.18 | $0.18 |
| Eggs | | | 5 each | $22.68 for 30 dozen | $22.68 ÷ 360 eggs = $0.06 egg<br>5 eggs × $0.06 = $0.30 | $0.30 |

## Figure 7-2. Recipe Costing for Caesar Salad (Continued)

**A.** Recipe Name: Caesar Salad
**C.** Portion Size: 3 oz

**B.** Recipe ID No.: S1
**D.** Yield: 10

| E. Ingredients | F. Waste % | G. EP | H. AP | I. Unit Purchase Price | J. Conversion Column | K. Ingredient Cost |
|---|---|---|---|---|---|---|
| Pepper | | | To taste | | | Q factor |
| Romaine lettuce | 20% | 2 lb = 32 oz | 32 oz ÷ .8 (80% yield) = 40 oz of Romaine lettuce. 1 head = 24 oz 40 oz ÷ 24 oz = 1.67 heads 2 heads of lettuce would be purchased | $18.00 for 24 heads | $18.00 ÷ 24 heads = $0.75 head 2 heads × $0.75 head = $1.50 | $1.50 |
| Croutons | | | 5 oz | $7.95 for 5 lb box | $7.95 ÷ 5 lb = $1.59 lb $1.59 lb ÷ 16 oz = $0.10 oz $0.10 oz × 5 oz = $0.50 | $0.50 |
| Parmesan cheese | | | 3 oz | $24.40 for 10 lb | $24.40 ÷ 10 lb = $2.44 lb $2.44 lb ÷ 16 oz = $0.15 oz 3 oz × $0.15 oz = $0.45 | $0.45 |
| | | | | | **L.** Subtotal | $7.52 |
| | | | | | **M.** Q factor 1% | $7.52 × .01 = $0.08 |
| | | | | | **N.** Q factor $ | $0.08 |
| | | | | | **O.** Subtotal Recipe Cost | $7.52 + $0.08 = $7.60 |
| | | | | | **P.** Portion Cost | $7.60 ÷ 10 = $0.76 |
| Italian Bread | | | | | **Q.** Additional Cost | $0.05 |

*(Continues)*

**Figure 7-2. Recipe Costing for Caesar Salad (Continued)**

| | | | | | R. Total Recipe Cost | $0.81 |
|---|---|---|---|---|---|---|
| | | | | | S. Desired food Cost % | .35 |
| | | | | | T. Preliminary Selling Price | $0.81 ÷ .35 = $2.31 |
| | | | | | U. Adjusted/Actual Selling Price | $3.95 |
| | | | | | V. Adjusted/ Actual Food Cost % | $0.81 portion cost ÷ $3.95 adjusted selling price = 20% |

# For Review and Discussion

**1.** Why is recipe costing necessary?

**2.** List three methods that may be used to lower a food cost percentage.

**3.** What do EP and AP have to do with recipe costing?

**4.** Define **Q factor**, and explain how it is used in the costing out of a recipe.

**5.** List three factors that influence the adjusted actual selling price.

# Part 3

# WRITING, DESIGNING, AND MERCHANDISING THE MENU

# Chapter 8

# CHARACTERISTICS OF A MENU

ONCE the menu has been costed out and final decisions have been made concerning food selection, the menu planner can begin to plan the organization and presentation of the menu. Decisions concerning paper, print, color, listing of items, size, and the cover design must be made. It is important that the menu planner have a basic knowledge about these menu mechanics to facilitate communication with the printer and to achieve the best results.

Balance, variety, composition, and descriptive copy of food and beverage items, truth-in-menu, and menu labeling also should be considered before materials are submitted for printing. This chapter discusses the characteristics of a menu at length.

## Objectives

❏ To introduce and explain the characteristics of a menu, which include paper, print, color, balance, variety, composition, descriptive copy, truth-in-menu, menu labeling, listing of items, size, and cover design

❏ To show how careful attention to menu presentation can help to merchandise menu items more effectively

# Issues for Consideration

THE menu planner must pay careful attention to these following items when preparing a menu:

- **Paper**
- **Print**
- **Color**
- **Balance**
- **Variety**
- **Composition**

- **Descriptive copy**
- **Truth-in-menu**
- **Menu labeling**
- **Listing of items**
- **Size**
- **Cover design**

# Paper

To begin the process of designing a menu, the menu planner selects the quality of paper desired. When choosing the paper, the menu planner must keep in mind how frequently the menu will be used. If the menu is going to be changed daily, then a paper that is less expensive and less durable, uncoated, and lightweight paper can be chosen. A menu that does not change often, however, would require a durable, coated, heavy stock, water-resistant, and stain-resistant paper. Durability is also an important consideration when selecting the paper for a cover.

When choosing paper, the menu planner must weigh four factors:

1. **Strength**
2. **Texture**
3. **Color**
4. **Opacity (Opacity refers to the property of paper that minimizes the "show-through" of printing to the back side of a sheet.)**

## Print

THE print on a menu should be sufficiently large and in a print that is easy to read.

There are many styles of type. The three that will be discussed are: roman, modern, and script. **Roman type** is characterized by a combination of thin and thick lines. It is easy to read and is used in newspapers, magazine articles, and books. Roman type should be used in the descriptive copy on the menu (Fig. 8-1).

**Modern type** does not have the thick and thin lines that are found in Roman type. Its letters are thick block letters (Fig. 8-1). Many government buildings use modern print on exterior signs. Modern type can be used for headings and subheadings on menus.

**Script type** looks like handwriting. Script is difficult to read and is used only for headings or subheadings on the menu (Fig. 8-1). Headings on the menu might be Appetizers, Soups, Salads, Entrées, and Desserts. Subheadings might consist of the names of the items offered, such as Stuffed Mushrooms as an appetizer or Sirloin Steak with Hollandaise Sauce for an entrée.

The menu planner must also decide on the type size. **Type size** is measured in points, starting with 6 points and going up to 192 points (Fig. 8-2). Most menus should be done in at least 12-point type. Smaller type is too

**Figure 8-1. Three Styles of Type: Roman, Modern, and Script**

# A B
Modern  Roman

*London Script*
**Commercial Script**

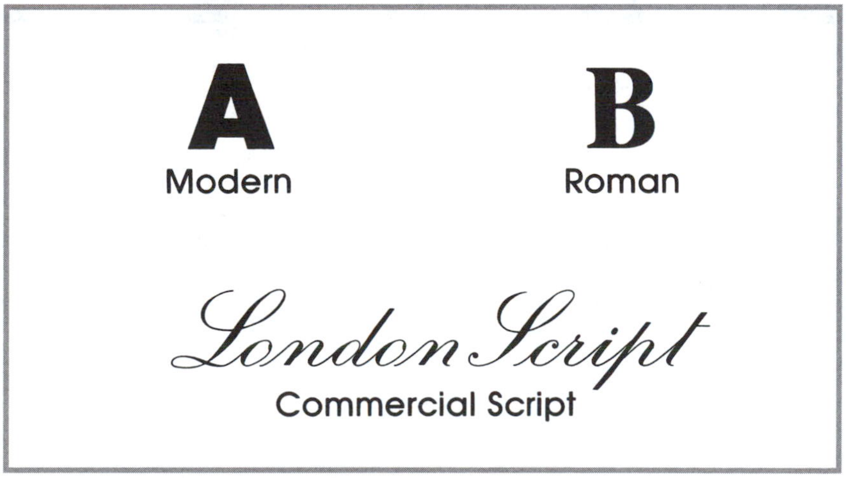

**Figure 8-2. Examples of Point Sizes**

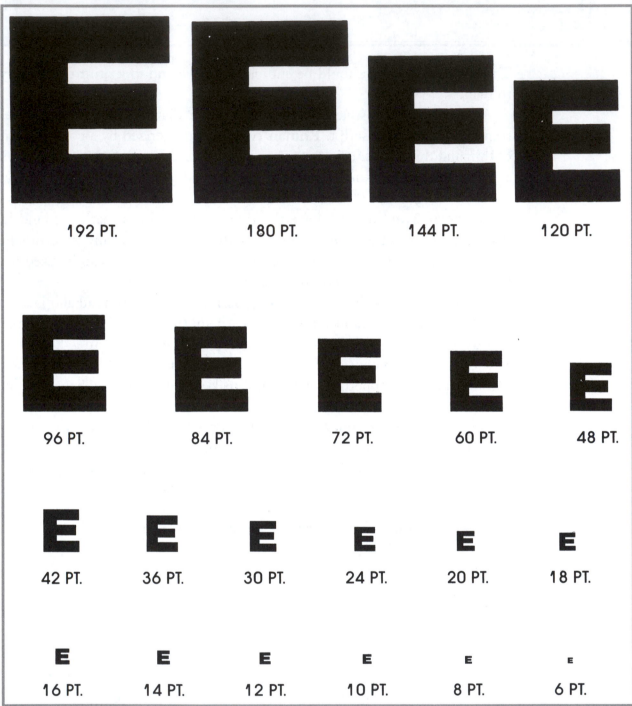

difficult to read. For the descriptive copy, space between lines must be allowed, called **leading.** Leading is also measured in points (Fig. 8-3). When there is no space between lines, this is referred to as **set solid.** It is important that the style of type be appropriate for the style of the restaurant. If the restaurant is modern, the menu should be modern as well.

**Figure 8-3. Samples of Leading**

■ Solid

Bananas Foster… A Brennan creation and now World Famous! Bananas sautéed in butter, brown sugar, cinnamon and banana liqueur, then flamed in rum. Served over vanilla ice cream. Scandalously Delicious!

■ 1-Point Leading

Bananas Foster… A Brennan creation and now World Famous! Bananas sautéed in butter, brown sugar, cinnamon and banana liqueur, then flamed in rum. Served over vanilla ice cream. Scandalously Delicious!

■ 2-Point Leading

Bananas Foster… A Brennan creation and now World Famous! Bananas sautéed in butter, brown sugar, cinnamon and banana liqueur, then flamed in rum. Served over vanilla ice cream. Scandalously Delicious!

■ 3-Point Leading

Bananas Foster… A Brennan creation and now World Famous! Bananas sautéed in butter, brown sugar, cinnamon and banana liqueur, then flamed in rum. Served over vanilla ice cream. Scandalously Delicious!

■ 4-Point Leading

Bananas Foster… A Brennan creation and now World Famous! Bananas sautéed in butter, brown sugar, cinnamon and banana liqueur, then flamed in rum. Served over vanilla ice cream. Scandalously Delicious!

■ 5-Point Leading

Bananas Foster… A Brennan creation and now World Famous! Bananas sautéed in butter, brown sugar, cinnamon and banana liqueur, then flamed in rum. Served over vanilla ice cream. Scandalously Delicious!

The color of the type is also important. The type on a menu should be dark, and the background should be light. A light blue-background with dark-blue type is often very attractive. When the type is white and the background is dark, this is called **reversed type**. Avoid reversed type on the inside of a menu. Reverse type however, is acceptable on the cover of the menu.

There are many variations of typefaces (Figs. 8-4, 8-5, and 8-6). These variations also include lowercase and uppercase letters. **Lowercase letters** are small letters, and **uppercase letters** are capital or large letters. Lowercase letters should be used in descriptive copy on the menu, and uppercase letters should be used for headings or subheadings on the menu.

Menu planners must also decide whether to use the italic version of the typeface. The **italic** version of the typeface is angled or slanted and makes the menu more difficult to read. This form of type should be used only for headings or subheadings and to highlight items on the menu.

## Color

THE colors selected for the paper and type on a menu should go together. A red background with yellow lettering, for instance, would clash horribly. Pink paper with black type would blend well. Professional printers or graphic artists can help the menu planner coordinate the colors of the paper and the type.

## Balance

A MENU is balanced when the number of offerings in each of the categories is proportionately balanced based on the restaurant's concept. A fine dinner restaurant offering 6 appetizers, 2 soups, 4 salads, 20 entrées, and 8 desserts is considered to be well balanced. A greater number of entrées is not only acceptable but also recommended, because entrées are the focus of the menu and are usually the most expensive food items as well.

The brunch menu seen in Figure 8-7 offers an excellent example of balance with 10 appetizers (including salads) and 22 entrées made up of soups, specials, and light entrées. The menu also has 12 extras/sides.

**Figure 8-4.  Cooper Black Typeface**

A B C D E F G H I J K L M
N O P Q R S T U V W X Y Z
a b c d e f g h i j k l m
n o p q r s t u v w x y z
1 2 3 4 5 6 7 8 9 0 $
1 2 3 4 5 6 7 8 9 0{ & ( )

7 Point Size:

9 Point Size:

10 Point Size:

12 Point Size:

14 Point Size:

16 Point Size:

18 Point Size:

20 Point Size:

24 Point Size:

28 Point Size:

30 Point Size:

36 Point Size:

42 Point Size:

48 Point Size:

54 Point Size:

60 Point Size:

**Figure 8-5. London Script Typeface**

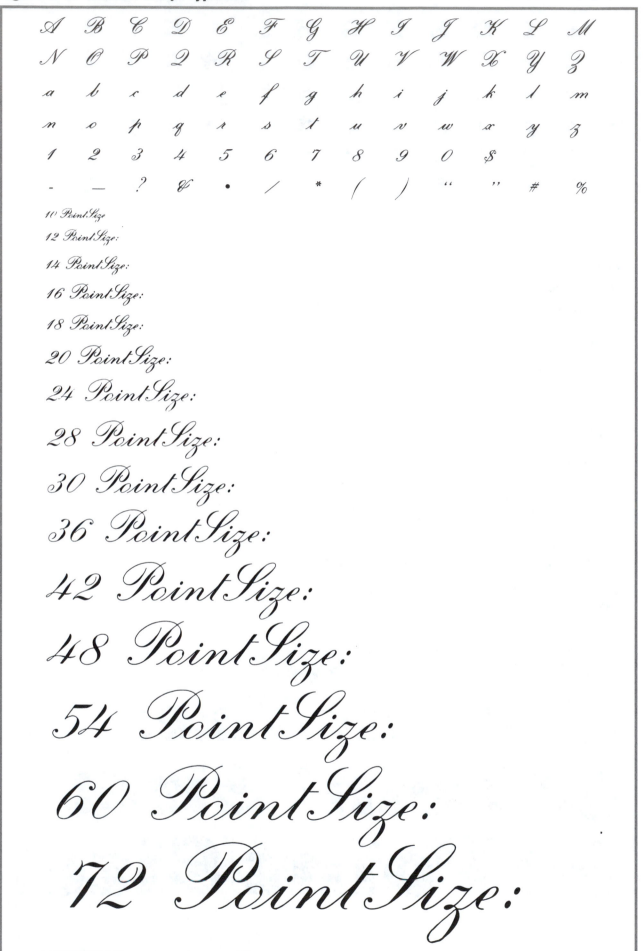

**Figure 8-6. Samples of Various Typefaces**

Eras Light
Eras Medium
**Eras Bold**
Eras Outline
**Eras Contour**
Fat Face
Fat Face Condensed
**Fortune Bold**
**Franklin Gothic**
Franklin Gothic Extra Cond
FRIEND
Friz Quadrata
**Friz Quadrata Bold**
**Futura Black**
**Futura Bold**
*Futura Bold Italic*
Futura Demibold
Futura Medium
*Futura Medium Italic*
GOLD RUSH
**Gorilla**
**Grizzly**
**Grotesque No. 9**

ACCENT
**Advertisers Gothic**
**AKI LINES**
**Amer. Typewriter Bold**
American Typewriter Bold Cond
Amer. Typewriter Medium
American Typewriter Med Cond
Arpad Light
Astur
**Avant Garde Bold**
Avant Garde Book
Avant Garde *Med.*
**Avant Garde Bold Condensed**
Avant Garde Medium Condensed
Bauhaus Medium
**Bauhaus Heavy**
Bauhaus Heavy Outline
**BLACKLINE**
**Blippo Black**
**Bolt Bold**
Bookman Bold
*Bookman Bold Italic*
**Bookman Contour**

**MACHINE**
MANDARIN
**Manhattan**
**Microgramma Bold Extended**
Microgramma Extended
MOORE COMPUTER
**NEON**
Newtext Book
**Newtext Demi**
Old English
Optima
*Palace Script*
**PEIGNOT Bold**
PEIGNOT LIGHT
PIONEER
**Playbill**
**PROFIL**
Ronda
RUSTIC
**SAPPHIRE**
**Serif Gothic Black**
Serif Gothic Bold
Serif Gothic Ex. Bold

## Variety

VARIETY refers to the diversity of food offerings within each category including product, food temperature (hot and cold), and cooking techniques (baked, broiled, sautéed, etc.).

**Figure 8-7. Brunch Menu**

# FRONTERA GRILL BRUNCH MENU

**Saturdays 10:30-2:30**

ENTREMESES PEQUEÑOS/small dishes

**Sopes Rancheros** - small corn masa boats with shredded beef, tomato-chile sauce and fresh Mexican cheese. 7.25

**Queso Fundido** - Amish handmade cheeses with garlicky roasted peppers, chorizo sausage and oregano. 7.25

**Tostaditas de Seviche** - crisp little tortillas piled with lime-marinated halibut, manzanilla olives, tomato, serrano and cilantro. 8.25

**Entremés Surtido** - appetizer platter of cheesy quesadillas, crispy chicken taquitos with sour cream, tangy seviche tostadas, crunchy jícama salad and guacamole; FOR TWO OR MORE ONLY. 6.95 per person

**Guacamole** - fresh and chunky, served with tortilla chips. 7.50

**Quesadillas Capitalinas** - Mexico City-style quesadillas (corn masa turnovers) stuffed with Amish handmade cheese and fresh epazote, with guacamole to daub. 6.95

**Panucho Yucateco** - traditional Yucatecan crispy tortilla filled with black beans and hardboiled egg, topped with shredded chicken in tangy escabeche . 7.50

**Tostaditas** - warm, crispy tortilla chips with two salsas: garlicky three-chile (cascabel, morita, guajillo) and roasted tomatillo with serrano and cilantro. 2.75

**Ensalada Frontera** - hearts of romaine and young greens with wood-grilled onions, radishes, fresh cheese and roasted-garlic dressing (balsamic vinegar, extra virgin olive oil). 7.50

**Ensalada de Jícama** -jícama salad with oranges, grapefruit and pineapple, tossed with orange-lime vinaigrette. 7.50

## ESPECIALIDADES

*We use only organically raised eggs*

**Jugo Natural** - fresh-squeezed juice of the day. 2.95

**Huevos Motuleños (Yucatan)** - two fried eggs on a crispy tostada with roasted tomatoes, country ham, peas, sweet fried plantains, queso fresco and black beans. 10.50

**Sapitos** - a trio of Xalapa-style gorditas (corn masa cakes) in chipotle-black bean sauce—each with its own topping: scrambled eggs, grilled chicken, chorizo and plantains; homemade crema and queso fresco. 9.95

**Huevos Fronterizos** - two eggs sunny-side up al ajillo (creamy, chipotle-scented roasted garlic sauce) with Yucatecan achiote sausage, atop homemade buttermilk biscuits; served with tangy baby greens. 10.50

**Huevos Estilo "El Bajjío"** - two poached eggs in crispy masa boats with black beans, creamy chile poblano sauce, Mexican greens and homemade chorizo. 10.50

**Chilaquiles del Día** - quick-simmered tortilla casserole with Mexican flavors-ask your server for details; served with tangy baby greens. 9.50
with one fried egg. 10.50
with grilled chicken breast. 11.50

**Hot Cakes Indígenas** - Iroquois white corn pancakes with whipped goat cheese, piloncillo-agave syrup, grilled chorizo and two eggs sunny-side up. 9.50

**Corona Azteca** - a crispy tortilla "crown" filled with scrambled eggs bathed in spicy tomato-guajillo sauce with avocado, sour cream and fresh Mexican cheese. 9.95

## Figure 8-7. Brunch Menu (Continued)

**Huevos a la Mexicana (de Lujo)** - eggs scrambled with fresh tomatoes, serranos, grilled green onions, cilantro and avocado; served with black beans and
salsa verde. 8.95
with chorizo. 9.95
with grilled Gulf shrimp. 10.75

**Pozole Rojo** - a big comforting bowl of Mexico's classic pork and hominy soup/stew—infused with rich red chile and topped with all the classic crunchy,

aromatic garnishes. 10.25

with one poached egg. 11.25

**Sopa de Tortilla** - a large earthenware bowl of rich tortilla soup with chicken, chile pasilla, avocado, queso fresco and homemade sour cream. 8.50

**Sopa de Frijoles Negros** - a large earthenware bowl of black bean soup with chorizo, queso añejo, cream and epazote. 8.50

**Pescado del Día** - fresh fish of the day. Market price.

## PLATILLOS FUERTES / light entrees

**Tacos al Carbón** - wood-grilled meat, poultry, fish or mushrooms sliced and served with roasted pepper rajas, two salsas, frijoles charros, guacamole, and homemade tortillas. 14.95
- Naturally raised skirt steak marinated with garlic and spices.
- Red chile-marinated pork (pastor style), with charcoaled pineapple, slab bacon and red onion (no rajas).
- Organic Gunthorp chicken breast marinated with fruit vinegar, spices and garlic.
- Tender portobello mushroom marinated with achiote and spices.
- Amish country duck marinated with red-chile adobo.
- Farm-raised catfish marinated with achiote and garlic.

**Papadzules Yucatecos** - classic Yucatecan "enchiladas" of homemade tortillas bathed with savory, smooth pumpkin-seed sauce, rolled around hardboiled egg, topped with habanero-sparked roasted tomato and pickled red onion; Frontera salad. 13.50

**Enchiladas de Mole** - homemade tortillas rolled around shredded chicken and doused with Oaxacan red mole. Black beans. 14.25

**Cazuela de Borrego** - earthenware casserole of charcoal-seared lamb simmered with rustic New Mexico chile sauce, white runner beans and grilled green beans; topped off with queso añejo and crispy onions and served with house salad and homemade tortillas for making soft tacos. 12.25

**Tamales de Frijol con Queso de Cabra** - black bean tamales filled with homemade goat cheese in "guisado" of wild and woodland mushrooms, organic roasted tomatoes, green chile and mint; watercress salad. 12.95

## EXTRAS / sides

**Sopa de Tortilla** - small tortilla soup with chicken and chile pasilla. 5.50

**Frijoles Refritos** - black beans fried with garlic, onion and epazote, topped with Mexican fresh cheese. 3.25

**Frijoles Charros** - pinto beans simmered with bacon, poblanos, tomato and cilantro. 3.25

**Arroz a la Mexicana** - traditional Mexican rice with a variety of flavors. Ask your server. 2.95

**Arroz y Frijoles** - black beans and Mexican rice. 4.25

**Puré de Papas** - rustic mashed potatoes. 4.25

**Ensaladita Frontera** - side salad with roasted garlic dressing. 4.25

**Cebollitas Asadas** - grilled green onions. 1.25

**Platanos con Crema** - sweet fried plantains with homemade sour cream and fresh cheese. 4.50

**Verduras en Escabeche** - homemade pickled jalapeños with carrots and cauliflower. 2.75

**Salsa Habanera** - all you can eat!—very spicy roasted habanero salsa with garlic and lime. 2.75

**Crema** - thick and rich cultured cream, a little sour, homemade. 2.25

Courtesy of Frontera Grill, Chicago, IL

**Figure 8-8. Tasting Menu**

### Commander's Tasting Menu
Seven Courses
A selection of Chef Carlos Guía's favorite
ingredients combined with varied culinary
techniques to create a complete "foodie" experience
*88.00*

## A la Carte

### Soups & Appetizers

**TURTLE SOUP AU SHERRY** 7.50
**GUMBO DU JOUR** 7.50
**SOUP DU JOUR** 7.00
**SOUPS 1-1-1**
*A demitasse portion of three soups:*
*Gumbo, Turtle and Soup du Jour 8.50*
**COMMANDER'S SALAD**
*Crisp greens, shaved Gruyère cheese, brioche croutons, housemade apple smoked*
*bacon and chopped egg ~ tossed in Commander's signature dressing 8.50*
**ARUGULA SALAD**
*Peppery arugula greens, Stilton cheese and candied pecans tossed in a*
*roasted pecan oil, cane vinegar and molasses vinaigrette 9.50*
**SHRIMP RÉMOULADE SALAD**
*Creole boiled Gulf shrimp, chilled and tossed with a spicy Louisiana*
*rémoulade sauce ~ served with butter lettuce, sun-dried tomatoes,*
*shaved onions and salted lemon zest 11.00*
**LOUISIANA ALLIGATOR "CORDON BLEU"**
*Crispy Creole seasoned alligator stuffed with housemade Creole mozzarella and*
*prosciutto di Parma ~ finished with a spicy filé cream 12.50*
**TABASCO "MASH" CURED AND SMOKED SALMON**
*Tabasco wood barrel house-smoked salmon layered with lemon verbena-chive*
*crème fraîche, marinated cucumbers and fennel pollen crisps*
*~ topped with Louisiana Choupique caviar 11.50*
**TASSO SHRIMP HENICAN**
*Flash fried and coated with Crystal hot sauce beurre blanc*
*~ served with five-pepper jelly and pickled okra 12.50*
**JUMBO LUMP CRAB CAKE**
*The ultimate in fresh Louisiana Blue Crabs: griddle seared jumbo lump crab cake*
*topped with truffled crabmeat salad and marinated crab claws 19.50*
**GULF OYSTER SHOOTER'S**
*Fresh Louisiana oysters topped with spicy housemade*
*Bloody Mary ~ spiked with Skyy vodka 12.50*

### Entrées

**PAN ROASTED FREE-RANGE CHICKEN**
*Amish country chicken breast served with a sauté of Farmer's Market*
*young vegetable "ratatouille" ~ finished with a fresh sorrel-toasted*
*pecan pesto and reduced natural jus 23.50*
**NEW ORLEANS SEAFOOD BARBECUE STEW**
*Jumbo Gulf shrimp, Louisiana P & J oysters and garlic crusted*
*fish sautéed with an Abita Amber beer, black pepper and rosemary*
*barbecue sauce ~ served with Louisiana popcorn rice 36.00*
**KUROBUTA PORK LOIN**
*Iron skillet seared Berkshire "black hog" served with fingerling*
*potato steak fries tossed with toasted garlic and buttermilk blue cheese,*
*cayenne ketchup emulsion and Creole mustard-bourbon sauce 34.00*
**LOUISIANA PECAN CRUSTED FISH**
*Creole seasoned and topped with a petit green salad and spiced pecans*
*~ finished with crushed corn cream and Creole meunière sauce 29.00*
**CREOLE SEASONED FILET MIGNON**
*Grilled and served over a warm Creole smashed new potato and andouille salad*
*~ with tobacco onions and housemade Worcestershire sauce 38.00*
**VEAL CHOP TCHOUPITOULAS**
*Roasted and served with goat cheese-thyme stone ground grits and*
*brandied wild mushroom demi-glace 39.00*
**GRILLED FISH OF THE DAY**
*Creole spiced and served with fire roasted corn maque choux*
*and smoked tomato emulsion 28.00*
**COMMANDER'S VEGETARIAN PLATE**
*Please inquire with your Captain for details 22.00*

**Courtesy of Commander's Palace, Las Vegas, NV**

Variety is crucial to a good menu. Variety is important not only in the number of selections offered within a category but also in the method of preparation. An appetizer category on a menu that includes Clams Casino, Crab Cakes, Portobello Mushrooms, Carpaccio, and Cantaloupe and Berries offers a good variety. Entrées can be steamed, broiled, sautéed, poached, braised, boiled, fried, roasted, or simmered. Customers appreciate variety on a menu. Variety also reflects a chef's creativity.

The dinner menu at Commander's Palace® in Las Vegas (Fig. 8-8) offers a large, diverse variety of items.

## Composition

THE composition of menu item groupings is important in planning a menu. The menu planner must evaluate how well certain accoutrements go with particular entrées. Sweet potatoes, for example, are excellent with ham, just as popovers are a good choice with roast beef. In general, when entrées have a lot of flavor, side dishes should have a less pronounced flavor. Beef Stroganoff might be served with peas or carrots, for example. Entrées that are less rich may come with, side dishes that have more flavor. Pairing an entrée of Baked Chicken with Zucchini Provençale (zucchini, tomatoes, bread crumbs, Parmesan cheese, garlic, and assorted spices) would work well.

Eye appeal is also very important in the composition of a menu item. A plate of Baked Haddock (white), steamed broccoli (green), and stewed tomatoes (ruby red), for example, would reflect good color and composition. Eye appeal enhances customer satisfaction as well.

The composition of menu items is well represented in the Figure 8-9 menu listing.

## Descriptive Copy

DESCRIPTIVE copy is an explanation of how an item is prepared and served. Descriptive copy helps to sell an item on the menu. Entrées should have the most elaborate descriptive copy, because they are the

**Figure 8-9. Luncheon Menu**

# NAHA
## lunch
### starters

Organic Camaroli **Risotto,** Roasted "Sweet Dumpling" Squash, Wood-Grilled Bulb Onions and Winter Savory *11*

**A Simple Salad** of Beautiful Greens, Bose Pears, Extra Virgin Olive Oil and *Saba* vinaigrette *8*

*Sea of Cortez "Mano de Leon"* **Sea Scallops**

with a "Hash" of Butternut Squash, Garnett Yams, Kurobuta Pork Belly and a Charred Leek vinaigrette *16*

**Today's Soup** *6*

NAHA *Mezze* of Hummus, Babaganoush, Pita Bread Crisps, Armenian String Cheese,

Kalamata Olives, Mediterranean *Greek* Salad, Feta Cheese Turnovers and Spiced Beef *16*

Salad of Organic Young **Beets,** Yellow Wax Beans and Mache, Candied Lemon Vinaigrette *8*

**Tartare** of *Yellowfin* **Tuna** with a Mosaic of Vegetables, Nicoise Garnishes, Aigrelette Sauce and Brioche Toast *18*

## From the Wood Burning Grill

NAHA Angus Beef **Burger** with Your Choice of Cheese,
"Red Hen" Brioche Toasted Bun, Caramelized Onions and Crisp Potato Fries *12*

Grilled **Skirt Steak** Brushed with Garlic, Sea Salt and Herbs, Young Garden Greens and Crisp Potato Fries *16*

"Heritage" **Pork** "T-Bone" with Caramelized Belgian Endive, Heirloom Apples, Toasted Hazelnuts and Rosemary *17*

"Armenian Style" **Lamb Skewers,** Mediterranean Chick Pea Salad, "Panisses" and Minted Sheep's Milk Yogurt *13*

## entrees, salads and sandwiches

Pan Roasted **Skate Wing,** Confit Fennel and Onions, Kalamata Olive Tapenade and Beurre Rouge *19*

**Lasagna** of Ratatouille Vegetables, Housemade Ricotta Cheese and Spinach Cream *13*

"Natural" British Columbia **Salmon,** Hot Smoked and Glazed with Mustard Seeds and Blossom Honey

with a Salad of Young Greens and French Lentils, English Thyme and Balsamic Syrup *15*

Open-Faced **Sandwich** of **Serrano Ham,** Winter Greens, Fried Farm **Egg** and **Manchego** *10*

"Southern Fried" **Chicken Salad,** Shaved Red Onions, Candied Pecans, Roasted Corn and Buttermilk Ranch Dressing *15*

Organic **Farm Egg Omelet** with Tender Leaf Spinach, Fennel, Goat Cheese and a Orange Scented Hollandaise *14*

Rustic **Chicken Caesar Salad** of Roasted Yukon Potatoes,
Olive Oil Cured tomatoes, Toasted Garlic Croutons and Shaved Parmesan *14*

Pissaladière-Traditional Riviera Style **Pizza**
of Caramelized Onions, Nicoise Olives, White Anchovies and Tomatoes, Small "Farmer's Market" Salad *10*

Salad "Lyonnaise"; Italian Frisee, Applewood Slab Bacon and Warm Poached Egg,
Sherry Wine-Dijon Mustard Vinaigrette *12*

Warm "Pulled" **Roasted Chicken Salad,** Italian Frisee,
Crimson Raisins, Winter Root Vegetables and Pine Nuts *13*

**An eighteen percent gratuity will be added to parties of six or more.**
**NAHA proudly supports Chicago's Green City Market.**

Courtesy of NAHA, Chicago, IL

most expensive items on the menu. One important rule that menu planners should remember when composing descriptive copy is to avoid the use of words that describe the killing process, such as *slaughtered* or *butchered*. In the United States, English should be used in the descriptive copy on ethnic menus.

Descriptive copy that is used by foodservice operations fits into one of three philosophies of profit management. The exclusive gourmet menu with a high check average uses a substantial amount of descriptive copy. This type of foodservice operation wants the customer to dine for a period of one and a half or two hours. More descriptive copy on a menu gives customers more information about the items on the menu, and it also keeps customers in the restaurant longer by giving them more to read.

The second philosophy of profit management requires little or no descriptive copy on the menu. This type of operation uses a short, limited menu and looks for a rapid turnover rate, expecting customers to stay only 15 to 20 minutes. The food selections are limited and simply stated along with the price, thus reducing the time the customer needs to decide what to order.

The third philosophy, the family-style foodservice operation, lists food items such as appetizers, desserts, and beverages, and merely limits the descriptive copy only for soups, salads, and entrées. This type of operation wants its customers to eat and enjoy themselves for approximately 45 minutes to one hour.

The Café 1401® menu (Fig. 8-10) at the Willard Intercontinental® in Washington, DC, has a number of breakfast items that are described in excellent detail.

# Truth-in-Menu

EACH and every item described on the menu must be accurately described. Truth-in-menu laws exist in several states to deter deceptive advertising on menus. Fines, court expenses, and negative publicity can result if a restaurant violates such laws. The National Restaurant Association published an "Accuracy in Menus" position paper to assist menu planners in preparing descriptions that accurately represent the items listed on a menu (see Appendix G).

**Figure 8-10. Breakfast Menu**

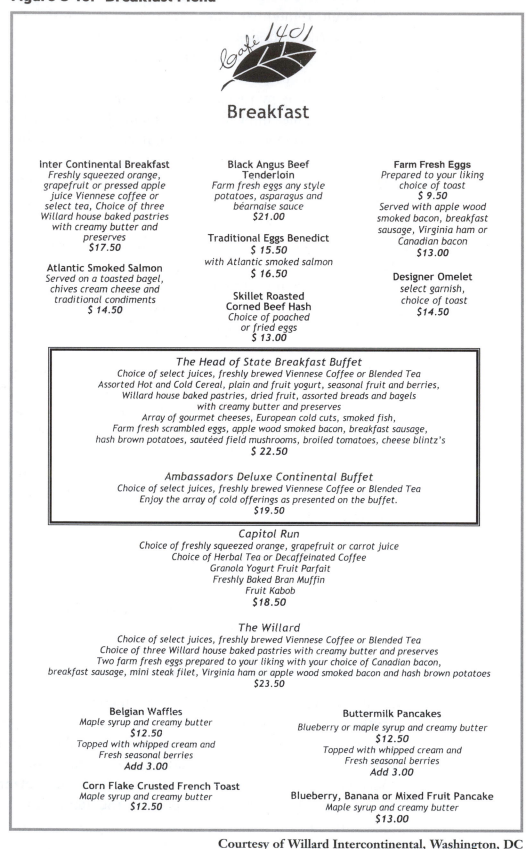

# Breakfast

**Inter Continental Breakfast**
*Freshly squeezed orange, grapefruit or pressed apple juice Viennese coffee or select tea, Choice of three Willard house baked pastries with creamy butter and preserves*
*$17.50*

**Atlantic Smoked Salmon**
*Served on a toasted bagel, chives cream cheese and traditional condiments*
*$ 14.50*

**Black Angus Beef Tenderloin**
*Farm fresh eggs any style potatoes, asparagus and béarnaise sauce*
*$21.00*

**Traditional Eggs Benedict**
*$ 15.50*
*with Atlantic smoked salmon*
*$ 16.50*

**Skillet Roasted Corned Beef Hash**
*Choice of poached or fried eggs*
*$ 13.00*

**Farm Fresh Eggs**
*Prepared to your liking choice of toast*
*$ 9.50*
*Served with apple wood smoked bacon, breakfast sausage, Virginia ham or Canadian bacon*
*$13.00*

**Designer Omelet**
*select garnish, choice of toast*
*$14.50*

**The Head of State Breakfast Buffet**
*Choice of select juices, freshly brewed Viennese Coffee or Blended Tea*
*Assorted Hot and Cold Cereal, plain and fruit yogurt, seasonal fruit and berries,*
*Willard house baked pastries, dried fruit, assorted breads and bagels*
*with creamy butter and preserves*
*Array of gourmet cheeses, European cold cuts, smoked fish,*
*Farm fresh scrambled eggs, apple wood smoked bacon, breakfast sausage,*
*hash brown potatoes, sautéed field mushrooms, broiled tomatoes, cheese blintz's*
*$ 22.50*

**Ambassadors Deluxe Continental Buffet**
*Choice of select juices, freshly brewed Viennese Coffee or Blended Tea*
*Enjoy the array of cold offerings as presented on the buffet.*
*$19.50*

**Capitol Run**
*Choice of freshly squeezed orange, grapefruit or carrot juice*
*Choice of Herbal Tea or Decaffeinated Coffee*
*Granola Yogurt Fruit Parfait*
*Freshly Baked Bran Muffin*
*Fruit Kabob*
*$18.50*

**The Willard**
*Choice of select juices, freshly brewed Viennese Coffee or Blended Tea*
*Choice of three Willard house baked pastries with creamy butter and preserves*
*Two farm fresh eggs prepared to your liking with your choice of Canadian bacon,*
*breakfast sausage, mini steak filet, Virginia ham or apple wood smoked bacon and hash brown potatoes*
*$23.50*

**Belgian Waffles**
*Maple syrup and creamy butter*
*$12.50*
*Topped with whipped cream and Fresh seasonal berries*
*Add 3.00*

**Corn Flake Crusted French Toast**
*Maple syrup and creamy butter*
*$12.50*

**Buttermilk Pancakes**
*Blueberry or maple syrup and creamy butter*
*$12.50*
*Topped with whipped cream and Fresh seasonal berries*
*Add 3.00*

**Blueberry, Banana or Mixed Fruit Pancake**
*Maple syrup and creamy butter*
*$13.00*

**Courtesy of Willard Intercontinental, Washington, DC**

# Menu Labeling

In 1990 Congress passed menu labeling regulations under the Nutritional Labeling and Education Act. Although the regulations were initially designed for the packaged foods industry to substantiate nutrient claims, they were revised in May 1994 to include claims made on placards, posters, and on signs in restaurants. By 1995 all restaurants had to comply with the menu labeling regulations. Beginning on May 2, 1997, the Food and Drug Administration (FDA) mandated that all nutrient and health claims on menus had to be scientifically substantiated as well. All segments of the foodservice industry including caterers, delicatessens, take-out establishments, restaurants, and institutional foodservice operations, were required to adhere to these regulations.

Once a restaurant makes a nutrient or health claim regarding a menu item, it must substantiate that claim. A **nutrient claim** makes a statement about the presence of a particular nutrient in a menu item. Words such as *cholesterol-free*, *fresh*, *healthy*, *natural*, *low in fat*, *light*, and *reduced* are terms that are commonly used. A **health claim** states that there is a relationship between a food item or meal and disease prevention, for example, fruits and vegetables in relation to cancer prevention.

The FDA recognizes recipes appearing in published cookbooks that have a nutritional analysis for each recipe, computer-generated databases, and menus endorsed by dietary or health professional organizations as acceptable sources of nutrient and health claims. Nutrient and health claims need not appear directly on the menu, but they must be available to patrons through a brochure, pamphlet, recipe file, notebook, bulletin board, or poster. Menus that do not make nutrient or health claims need not adhere to these regulations.

As of January 1, 2006, a new law called the Food Allergen Labeling and Consumer Protection Act was enacted. This law requires that Food manufacturers identify the eight major food allergens specified by the FDA.

The eight major allergens are:

1. **Egg**
2. **Fish**
3. **Milk**
4. **Peanuts**
5. **Shellfish (crab, crayfish, lobster, shrimp)**
6. **Soy**
7. **Tree nuts**
8. **Wheat**

This new law also extends to retail and foodservice operations that package and label food items that are served for human consumption. On the "Nutritional Facts" panel, food manufacturers must also specify the number of grams of trans fats found in the food item.

## Listing of Items

ITEMS should be presented on the menu in the order in which they are consumed. Most menus list appetizers, soups, salads, entrées and accompaniments, and then desserts. A French classical menu, however, lists the salads just before the desserts. The most profitable food items should be listed first and last in a particular category and the most popular and least profitable food items should be listed in the middle. When reading down a column of any list, the eye is trained to carefully look at the first few items, skim the middle section, and then study the last few items before looking at the next column. Very popular items are likely to be ordered regardless of their place on the menu, however.

The best location for the most profitable items is in the top half of quadrangle 2 on a single-fold menu (Fig. 8-11). When a customer opens a menu from right to left, the first page that the eyes see is page 2 (quadrangles 2 and 4). Thus, reading from left to right, customers will start reading at quadrangle 1 but will actually see quadrangle 2 first.

Entrées conveniently fall into place on the right after the list of appetizers, soups, and salads on the left. High-profit entrées, such as chicken and pasta, should be listed first under the entrée headings, and followed by lobster, sirloin, and veal.

**Figure 8-11. Diagram of a Single-Fold Menu**

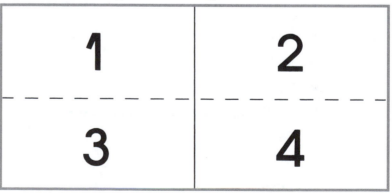

# Size of Menu

THE menu should be large enough to merchandise the food items without appearing crowded on the page. Too large a menu can be awkward to handle. The most popular menu size is $8\frac{1}{2}$ inches by 11 inches. Most menus consist of four pages. The cover forms pages 1 and 4, and the list of menu items inside makes up pages 2 and 3.

# Cover Design

THE front and back covers offer tremendous opportunities. The cover of a menu should reflect the décor and the theme of the operation. A specialty restaurant, for example, that features broiled steaks and uses red tablecloths and black napkins might want a red menu cover with black print.

The front cover should carry the name of the restaurant and a recognizable symbol or logo. The logo of a seafood restaurant called "The White Cap" might be an anchor or an embossed wave. The back cover of the menu might list the address and phone number of the restaurant or other information, such as the credit cards accepted at the establishment, then hours of operation, restaurant history, and available banquet or take-out service. Surprisingly enough, only 50 percent of restaurants use the back covers of their menus for merchandising purposes.

It is also important to remember that the menu cover should be durable, water-resistant, and stain-resistant, unless the menu changes daily and is disposable.

# Menu Design Software

TODAY many restaurant managers and chefs are purchasing software and creating in-house menus rather than using a professional printer, which can be expensive and time consuming. Menu design software offers a number of advantages.

- Creating a menu is easy because most software packages include pre-designed menu styles, an abundance of food illustrations, and built-in spell-checker designed to recognize culinary terms.
- Using the software eliminates the need to hire a graphic artist or a professional printer.
- Many software packages have built-in databases that store specials and seasonal items for repeated use.
- The foodservice manager or chef can print specials daily, allowing the restaurant to showcase signature dishes and high-profit items.
- The software allows for easy editing of the menu and changing offerings as needed.

Menu covers and table tent cards that are used to hold desktop-printed menus and specials are widely available from restaurant supply companies.

It is important to remember that when a menu is printed on a laser printer or a copy machine and inserted into a vinyl cover, the print may transfer to the vinyl. To prevent this from happening, the toner should be sealed to the menu page with a spray sealant, which is available from arts and crafts stores.

The computer on which the menu design software is run should have sufficient memory to support the software and to store graphics, illustrations, and photographs. A high-quality laser printer is recommended for more complex and sophisticated tasks, while a standard desktop printer suffices to print simple daily menus.

# For Review and Discussion

1. What are the factors that should be considered when selecting paper for a menu?
2. How and where on the menu is uppercase and lowercase type used?
3. What is "reversed type"?
4. How is type measured?
5. What is "leading"?
6. Explain "variety".
7. What are two aspects of composition?
8. In what order should items be listed on a menu?
9. What items might be listed on the back of a menu?
10. List five advantages of using menu design software.

# Chapter 9

# SALES HISTORY

In this chapter, we will discuss the use of sales history and the importance of menu engineering analysis. To plan for the future, it is wise to take a look at the past.

## Objectives

- ❏ To explain the importance of a sales history report
- ❏ To teach the student how to complete a sales history report
- ❏ To explain how menu engineering analysis works

# Sales History Background

THE **sales history**, also known as a **scatter sheet mix**, is a daily record of the menu items that have been sold. The sales history contains any information that can help to explain the sales volume for a particular day. The next list demonstrates the numerous uses of the sales history:

- **To forecast**
- **To keep a daily record of which food items were sold**
- **To keep a daily record of how many menu items were sold**
- **To predict sales volume**
- **To record information that will aid management in forecasting accurately**
- **To aid management in predicting a sales analysis**
- **To project the annual budget**
- **To aid management in determining the dollar amount that customers are willing to pay**

The purpose of a sales history is to help management accurately forecast the foodservice operation's needs. It is a difficult task for management to forecast the number of customers who will be dining at the foodservice operation in the future and the amount of supplies needed to accommodate those customers. If management purchases too many supplies, profits are lost, if it does not purchase enough supplies, customers are dissatisfied. Keeping a daily record of the number of actual menu items sold and the number of items sold helps management to forecast more accurately. By analyzing sales volumes past, it is possible to predict future sales volumes.

A seasonal foodservice operation in New England for example might open on weekends, and one or two days during the week out of season. After Memorial Day, sales volume slowly starts to increase week by week, because 90 percent of colleges have ended their academic year. In June, sales volume continues to grow as the elementary and secondary school year ends. During July, sales volume increases substantially, because this is when many people take vacations. In August and September, foodservice operations reach their peak season sales volume. August is a favorite month for family vacations, because children are out of school and the weather is at its warmest. In September, after Labor Day, the volume of families traveling is drastically reduced, because children are back in school. However, the foodservice operation does not yet close for the season. A considerable number of people prefer to vacation after Labor Day to avoid the extreme summer temperatures and the crowds. After September, the weekly sales volume decreases enough for a seasonal operation to close its doors.

When analyzing the sales history, compare the history of the same time periods; that is, Monday's business should compare with Monday's business. Monday's business should not be compared with that of another business day. Each day has its own unique characteristics. Monday is usually the slowest day of the week. On Mondays, customers have little disposable income left over from the weekend and most people are recuperating from weekend activities and are likely to relax at home when they return from work. In constrast, Saturday is the busiest day of the week, because people have disposable income to spend and more time to relax.

It is also important to compare the same meal periods (i.e., breakfast, lunch, dinner) on the same day of the week. Breakfast, lunch, and dinner have their own unique characteristics. Breakfast attracts a different type of customer, check average, and turnover rate than lunch and dinner. In actuality, these meals are three different types of businesses operating under one roof.

To accurately, forecast the number of customers for each meal period it is necessary to have pertinent information that influences sales on that particular day. Examples of such information include:

- **Day of the week**
- **Date**
- **Weather**
- **Time of day**
- **Meal period**
- **Special events within the community that will produce more sales (e.g., concerts, conventions, meetings, and bus tours)**
- **Employees who are absent from work that day**

Although it is difficult to be 100 percent accurate in forecasting each day's needs and to achieve maximum profit for that day using a sales history always proves beneficial. With experience, and a knowledge of the customers and of the surrounding community, forecasting can be a very accurate and exciting tool.

# Benefits of the Scatter Sheet

At the end of each meal period, the food items that are sold must be recorded onto the sales history ledger. This information is usually taken from the register slip or produced in a sales report from the point of sales computer register. Once this information has been recorded, the management team must analyze the results. This analysis should be done on a daily, weekly, and monthly basis. The management team should be looking for menu items that are not selling and whether the sales are in line with the annual sales projection.

If a restaurant is losing sales, the sales history record can be helpful in determining the problem. Most restaurants lose sales because customers do not like the approach that the restaurant is taking in one or more of these areas:

- **Sanitation**
- **Quality of the food**
- **Quality of the service**
- **Prices**
- **Atmosphere**
- **Location of the restaurant**

The sales history helps to determine the menu items that are selling and those that are not. (Management must determine why the food items are not selling and correct the problem.) The reason may be that price, portion size, food presentation, or any of several other possibilities. Once management knows the reason behind the poor sales of an item, it should promote the food item or take the item off the menu.

Management uses a scatter sheet to make an annual budgetary projection. Management needs to maintain a daily sales record of the amount of daily income. Weekly profits should be compared with annual profits and expense projections as well. If sales drop for three consecutive weeks, it is highly unlikely that the sales loss will be regained. Management cannot afford to wait until the beginning of the fourth quarter to check profits and expense projections. By then, it is too late to recover losses that have occurred earlier in the year.

It is helpful to determine the cost of foods on a menu and to eliminate items that are not selling. For example, when a restaurant sells 100 portions of prime rib at $8.95 per portion, this generates $895.00. If management increases the price of the prime rib to $11.95, and the number of portions sold decreases to 60 portions, there is a yield of only $717.00, reducing profit by $178.00. If management reduces the price to $10.95, and the number of portions sold increases to 90, the restaurant is now making $90.50 more in profit, and management has established the price that the market is willing to pay for the prime rib. The sales history keeps a record of how the prime rib is selling at the various price levels.

# How a Scatter Sheet Works

THE scatter sheet is composed of several elements (Fig. 9-1). Column 1 includes the week ending date, the menu item listings, a remarks area, and a meal period area. Column 2 includes the name of the restaurant and space for the weather and the days of the week. To find out how much of a particular item has been sold, management either:

1.  **Reviews the meal checks and counts the times that a particular item is sold, or**

2.  **Programs the cash register to keep a tally of each item on the menu so that a reading can be taken from the register tape.**

Column 3 shows the weekly total of the individual menu items that were sold. Column 4 shows the selling price of the individual item. Column 5 shows the item sales, which is calculated by multiplying column 3 by column 4. Column 6 shows the total of weekly sales, calculated by adding the totals of the individual items in column 5. Column 7 shows the percentage contribution to sales, indicating how much each individual menu item contributes to the total weekly sales of all of the menu items. This amount is calculated by dividing column 5 by column 6.

# Production Sheet

A **production sheet** is a schedule that provides employees with information:

*   **Who will be doing which task**
*   **When they will be doing the task**
*   **Where they will be doing the task**
*   **The equipment needed**
*   **The quantity of a product needed**

## Figure 9-1. Sales History Form: Scatter Sheet

| | Column 1 | Column 2 | | | | | | | Col. 3 | Col. 4 | Col. 5 | Col. 6 | Col. 7 |
|---|---|---|---|---|---|---|---|---|---|---|---|---|---|

| Menu Item | Mon | Tue | Wed | Thu | Fri | Sat | Sun | Weekly No. Sold | Selling Price | Item Sales | Total Weekly Sales | % Contribution to Sales |
|---|---|---|---|---|---|---|---|---|---|---|---|---|
| N.E. Chowder | 5 | 8 | 10 | 12 | 20 | 30 | 20 | 105 | $2.95 | $309.75 | $24,386.40 | .013 |
| French Onion | 7 | 7 | 12 | 11 | 25 | 23 | 29 | 114 | $3.25 | $370.50 | | .015 |
| Tossed Salad | 30 | 40 | 50 | 60 | 70 | 65 | 66 | 381 | $1.50 | $571.50 | | .023 |
| Greek Salad | 3 | 4 | 2 | 0 | 1 | 3 | 1 | 14 | $4.95 | $69.30 | | .003 |
| | | | | | | | | | | | | |
| Broiled Lobster | 15 | 20 | 30 | 31 | 32 | 35 | 50 | 213 | $24.95 | $5,314.35 | | .218 |
| Baked Stuff Lobster | 16 | 35 | 32 | 40 | 45 | 65 | 55 | 288 | $26.95 | $7,761.60 | | .319 |
| Fried Clams | 20 | 25 | 33 | 16 | 10 | 70 | 65 | 239 | $12.95 | $3,095.05 | | .127 |
| Broiled Scallops | 10 | 15 | 20 | 25 | 30 | 35 | 40 | 175 | $10.95 | $1,916.25 | | .079 |
| Sirloin Steak | 8 | 10 | 15 | 7 | 20 | 25 | 45 | 130 | $14.95 | $1,943.50 | | .080 |
| Tenderloin Strip | 19 | 18 | 17 | 12 | 11 | 13 | 15 | 105 | $13.50 | $1,417.50 | | .058 |
| Half Roast Duck | 7 | 6 | 4 | 3 | 2 | 0 | 8 | 30 | $14.95 | $448.50 | | .018 |
| | | | | | | | | | | | | |
| Baked Potato | 35 | 38 | 40 | 55 | 85 | 90 | 110 | 453 | $0.95 | $430.35 | | .018 |
| Mashed Potato | 20 | 19 | 35 | 20 | 15 | 12 | 20 | 141 | $0.75 | $105.75 | | .004 |
| Peas | 15 | 20 | 22 | 23 | 28 | 32 | 45 | 185 | $0.75 | $138.75 | | .006 |
| Corn | 20 | 25 | 31 | 38 | 39 | 41 | 46 | 240 | $0.75 | $180.00 | | .007 |
| Carrots | 35 | 39 | 40 | 41 | 42 | 43 | 45 | 285 | $0.75 | $213.75 | | .009 |
| | | | | | | | | | | | $24,386.40 | |
| Etc. | | | | | | | | | | | | |
| Etc. | | | | | | | | | | | | |

**MENU SCATTER SHEET: BRIAN'S RESTAURANT**

Week Ending: 6/16/07 Weather: clear, 80°F

TALLY

Remarks:

Meal Period: Dinner 6:00–10:00 P.M.

The sales history form is extremely helpful in assisting the chef in determining the quantity of food that the chefs need to prepare for production. The chef should refer to the sales history when making out the production sheet in order to see what was sold during the same time frame the week before. By reviewing the sales history, the chef knows how much to prepare.

# Menu Engineering

Menu engineering is a method of analyzing the popularity and contribution margin of each menu item. The menu engineering process was developed by Michael L. Kasavana and Donald I. Smith in their work *Menu Engineering: A Practical Guide to Menu Analysis*.

Menu engineering determines how much profit each item is contributing by determining each menu item's contribution margin and popularity. A *contribution margin* is the amount of money that contributes to paying the labor and operating expenses, and profit. The contribution margin is calculated by subtracting the menu item's food cost from the menu items selling price. For example, if a pizza is priced at $10.00 and the food cost is $2.00, the contribution margin for this menu item is $8.00 ($10.00 − $2.00 = $8.00). The $8.00 contributes to paying labor cost and operating cost, and for providing a profit.

Based on the sales of each menu item and their contribution margin, the menu items are placed in one of four performance classifications. If a contribution margin is above the mean average, then it is performing at a high level. If a menu item's contribution margin is below the mean average, it is performing at a low level.

## Menu Engineering's Four Classifications

| | |
|---|---|
| Stars | High-popularity, high-contribution margin items |
| Plowhorses | High-popularity, low-contribution margin items |
| Puzzles | Low-popularity, high-contribution margin items |
| Dogs | Low-popularity, low-contribution margin items |

All menu analysis programs that analyze which menu items are selling ask why certain other menu items are not selling and examine how sales of badly performing items can be increased. Is it that customers do not like the taste, portion size, color, texture, aroma, or price? Could it be that the item is hidden on the menu and that no real marketing has been done to promote it?

Menu items that are classified as stars are popular and have a high contribution/profit margin. Management needs to continue marketing efforts with these items and not let these menu items slip in sales.

Menu items that are classified as plowhorses include those that are popular but have a low contribution/profit margin. These menu items are good, steady-selling items but require a reduction in food cost to show a greater profit. The taste, texture, flavor, portion size, plate appearance, and price of these items must not be compromised to accomplish this goal, so management merely needs to purchase the ingredients at a lower price.

Menu items that are classified as puzzles are not popular and have low sales yet have a high contribution/profit margin. These items present puzzles that management must solve. Management merely needs to analyze why customers are not purchasing this product. Marketing is the key to increasing sales on these items. Special treatment, such as a colorful type or a different size font, placement in a primary space on the menu, selling by servers verbally, and providing free samples or orders of the item are a few recommendations to increase the sales of puzzles.

Menu items classified as dogs are those that are not popular and have a low contribution/profit margin. The reasons for their poor performance should be carefully examined, although they are usually obvious. It is prudent to investigate how the items are being marketed and if purchasing ingredients at a lower price might move items out of this classification.

## Software Programs Available

THESE software packages offer sales analysis information:

    ExecuChef Software: visit www.execuchef.com
    Tracrite and Optimum Control Restaurant Management Software:
       visit www.tracrite.net
    Johnson Technologies, Inc.: visit www.johnsontech.com
    info@restaurantexperts.com
    www.restaurantpitfallsandprofits.com

# For Review and Discussion

1.  Define **sales history**.

2.  Give five uses for a sales history.

3.  Why shouldn't a manager compare Monday's sales with Tuesday's sales?

4.  Which day of the week is usually the slowest for most foodservice operations, and why is this so?

5.  How can a sales history analysis be useful to management?

6.  Explain menu engineering.

# Chapter 10

# MERCHANDISING THE MENU

A MENU can be successful only if it is accurately costed and properly presented. The placement of menu items in an attractive and organized fashion with an effective description is integral to sales. This chapter examines the importance of marketing and merchandising the menu.

## Objectives

❏ To demonstrate how items can be effectively and appropriately merchandized on a menu

❏ To analyze and evaluate the merchandising power of an actual menu

**Merchandising** is the presentation of a product to the appropriate market at the right time in an organized and attractive display. A well-merchandised menu is a successful menu. When merchandising a menu it is important to list additional pertinent information, such as liquors and wines, appetizers, salads, steaks, seafood, sandwiches, desserts, take-out service, and specials.

## Displaying Additional Information on the Menu

ADDITIONAL information on a menu is practical knowledge that is provided to serve and accommodate customers better. Additional information might include a list of the credit cards accepted by the establishment; the hours of operation, the address, phone number, and e-mail address of the restaurant; professional association memberships; catering information, take-out service, and banquet accommodations. Mention of a gift shop and local tourist attractions; a listing of other restaurant locations, if the restaurant is part of a chain; and possibly a history of the property are also appropriate. Although many establishments do not include additional information on their menus, the back cover does allow for a great opportunity to merchandise (Fig. 10-1).

**Figure 10-1.  Web Site on Back Cover of Menu**

RELAIS &
CHATEAUX.
Relais Gourmands

**WWW.DANIELNYC.COM**

*Traditions
&
Qualité*

Courtesy of Restaurant Daniel, New York

## Listing Liquors

MOST restaurants do not list liquors on the menu. Waitstaff often take the drink order without offering customers a list. A separate liquor or wine list may be provided to call attention to the selections available and as a vehicle for increasing sales.

When listing liquors, the brand name should be given. Under vodka, for example, the recognizable brand names Smirnoff®, Grey Goose®, and Absolut® might be listed. Liquors should be presented in the order in which they are consumed at mealtime. "Before-dinner drinks," including scotches, whiskeys, bourbons, gins, vodkas, and rums, should lead the list. Beers may come next, followed by wines (red, white, sparkling, and Champagnes), with coffee drinks, brandies and liqueurs listed last. If a separate after-dinner drink menu is not used, drinks may be listed after desserts on a separate page (Fig. 10-2).

## Wine Lists

A LARGE wine selection should be presented on a separate wine list while a smaller wine selection can be included on the main menu, paired with entrées, a list may also appear on the liquor menu (Fig. 10-3).

It is always good merchandising to provide descriptive copy with wines. Who could resist a Chablis (Drouhin) from the burgundy class made from Chardonnay grapes, very dry, with a rich body?

## Appetizers

APPETIZERS should be listed before soups on the menu (Fig. 10-4). Good copy that is easy to read aids in selling appetizers. Six to ten appetizers on an average size à la carte menu provide a good balance. Variety is also important. The number of appetizer offerings should increase as the number of entrées increase.

**Figure 10-2. Excerpt from a Liquor Menu**

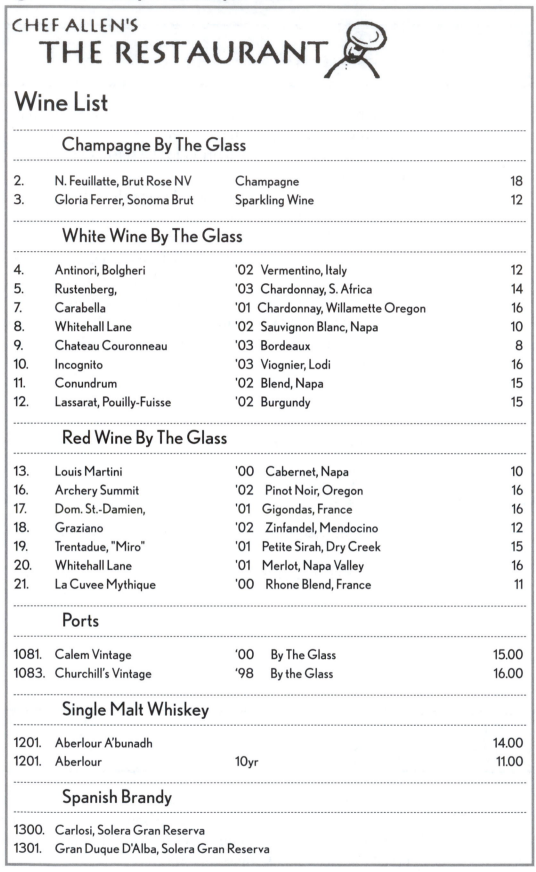

# CHEF ALLEN'S
# THE RESTAURANT

## Wine List

### Champagne By The Glass

| 2. | N. Feuillatte, Brut Rose NV | Champagne | 18 |
| 3. | Gloria Ferrer, Sonoma Brut | Sparkling Wine | 12 |

### White Wine By The Glass

| 4. | Antinori, Bolgheri | '02 Vermentino, Italy | 12 |
| 5. | Rustenberg, | '03 Chardonnay, S. Africa | 14 |
| 7. | Carabella | '01 Chardonnay, Willamette Oregon | 16 |
| 8. | Whitehall Lane | '02 Sauvignon Blanc, Napa | 10 |
| 9. | Chateau Couronneau | '03 Bordeaux | 8 |
| 10. | Incognito | '03 Viognier, Lodi | 16 |
| 11. | Conundrum | '02 Blend, Napa | 15 |
| 12. | Lassarat, Pouilly-Fuisse | '02 Burgundy | 15 |

### Red Wine By The Glass

| 13. | Louis Martini | '00 Cabernet, Napa | 10 |
| 16. | Archery Summit | '02 Pinot Noir, Oregon | 16 |
| 17. | Dom. St.-Damien, | '01 Gigondas, France | 16 |
| 18. | Graziano | '02 Zinfandel, Mendocino | 12 |
| 19. | Trentadue, "Miro" | '01 Petite Sirah, Dry Creek | 15 |
| 20. | Whitehall Lane | '01 Merlot, Napa Valley | 16 |
| 21. | La Cuvee Mythique | '00 Rhone Blend, France | 11 |

### Ports

| 1081. | Calem Vintage | '00 | By The Glass | 15.00 |
| 1083. | Churchill's Vintage | '98 | By the Glass | 16.00 |

### Single Malt Whiskey

| 1201. | Aberlour A'bunadh | | 14.00 |
| 1201. | Aberlour | 10yr | 11.00 |

### Spanish Brandy

| 1300. | Carlosi, Solera Gran Reserva |
| 1301. | Gran Duque D'Alba, Solera Gran Reserva |

*Courtesy of Chef Allen's, Aventura, FL*

**Figure 10-3. Wine List**

# Brennan's NEW ORLEANS

## *Les Vins*

## WHITE WINES

| | | Bottle |
|---|---|---|
| STAG'S LEAP WINE CELLARS CHARDONNAY . . . . . . . . . . . . . . . . . . . . . Vintage | 59.00 |
| Napa Valley | | |
| JORDAN CHARDONNAY . . . . . . . . . . . . . Vintage | 57.00 |
| Alexander Valley | | |
| ROBERT MONDAVI CHARDONNAY . . . Vintage | 47.00 |
| Napa Valley | | |
| BYRON CHARDONNAY . . . . . . . . . . . . . . . Vintage | 47.00 |
| Santa Maria Valley | | |
| POUILLY FUISSE, LOUIS JADOT . . . . . . . Vintage | 47.00 |
| Crisp, dry burgundy (Quel Vin!) | | |
| SONOMA CUTRER CHARDONNAY . . . . Vintage | 43.00 |
| Russian River Ranch | | |
| SEBASTIANI SONOMA CASK CHARDONNAY . . . . . . . . . . . . . . . . . . . . . Vintage | 32.00 |
| Sonoma County | | |
| KENDALL-JACKSON, VINTNER'S RESERVE CHARDONNAY . . . . . . . . . . . . . . . . . . . . . Vintage | 32.00 |
| California Vineyards | | |

| | | Bottle |
|---|---|---|
| MIRASSOU CHARDONNAY . . . . . . . . . . . Vintage | 30.00 |
| Monterey County | | |
| SAUVIGNON BLANC . . . . . . . . . . . . . . . . . Vintage | 30.00 |
| Crisp, medium body, clean finish | | |
| FUMÉ BLANC . . . . . . . . . . . . . . . . . . . . . . . Vintage | 29.00 |
| Crisp, dry, American | | |
| PIESPORTER . . . . . . . . . . . . . . . . . . . . . . . . Vintage | 29.00 |
| Fragrant, light Moselle | | |
| GEWURZTRAMINER . . . . . . . . . . . . . . . . . Vintage | 28.00 |
| Fragrant, spicy, fairly dry | | |
| MUSCADET . . . . . . . . . . . . . . . . . . . . . . . . . Vintage | 26.00 |
| Light, crisp, Loire Valley | | |
| CÔTES DU RHÔNE . . . . . . . . . . . . . . . . . . Vintage | 26.00 |
| Dry, well balanced from South France | | |
| RIESLING . . . . . . . . . . . . . . . . . . . . . . . . . . . Vintage | 25.00 |
| Delicate, floral aroma, fairly dry | | |
| DELOACH WHITE ZINFANDEL . . . . . . . . Vintage | 25.00 |
| California, Gold Medal Winner | | |

## RED WINES

| | | Bottle |
|---|---|---|
| STAGS' LEAP WINERY CABERNET SAUVIGNON . . . . . . . . . . . . Vintage | 77.00 |
| Full bodied, black fruit and cassis aromas are supported by ripe black fruit, raspberry and spicy vanilla flavors | | |
| STAG'S LEAP WINERY MERLOT . . . . . . . . . . . . . . . . . . . . . . . . . . . Vintage | 65.00 |
| Velvety-soft with expansive aromas and flavors of black fruit and spice | | |
| ROBERT MONDAVI WINERY, NAPA CABERNET SAUVIGNON . . . . . . . . . . . . Vintage | 55.00 |
| Medium bodied, aromas and flavors of berry and black currant with nuances of mocha, violets and spice | | |
| ST. EMILION . . . . . . . . . . . . . . . . . . . . . . . . Vintage | 48.00 |
| One of the fullest and heartiest of the French wines | | |
| MERLOT . . . . . . . . . . . . . . . . . . . . . . . . . . . . Vintage | 38.00 |
| Smooth, soft, round American wine | | |

| | | Bottle |
|---|---|---|
| ZINFANDEL . . . . . . . . . . . . . . . . . . . . . . . . . Vintage | 38.00 |
| Hearty American wine with jammy fruit and spicy finish | | |
| SEBASTIANI SONOMA CASK CABERNET SAUVIGNON . . . . . . . . . . . . Vintage | 38.00 |
| Robust American wine | | |
| ROBERT MONDAVI COASTAL PINOT NOIR . . . . . . . . . . . . . . . . . . . . . . . Vintage | 32.00 |
| Silky, soft, berry flavored American wine | | |
| CRU BEAUJOLAIS . . . . . . . . . . . . . . . . . . . Vintage | 29.00 |
| One of several villages allowed its own appellation due to quality and topography | | |
| CÔTES DU RHÔNE . . . . . . . . . . . . . . . . . . Vintage | 29.00 |
| Vigorous, robust wine from South France | | |

## SPARKLING WINES

| | | Bottle | | | Bottle |
|---|---|---|---|---|---|
| BILLECART-SALMON BRUT ROSÉ . . . . . . . N.V. | 85.00 | PIPER-HEIDSIECK BRUT . . . . . . . . . . . . . N.V. | 70.00 |
| VEUVE CLICQUOT "Yellow Label" BRUT . . N.V. | 80.00 | "J" JORDAN . . . . . . . . . . . . . . . . . . . . . . . Vintage | 65.00 |
| MOET & CHANDON, WHITE STAR . . . . . . N.V. | 75.00 | SCHRAMSBERG, ROSÉ . . . . . . . . . . . . . . . N.V. | 60.00 |

Entertaining Idea! Have a party in one of our lovely private rooms.

Courtesy of Brennan's, New Orleans, LA

**Figure 10-4. Appetizer Menu**

The Harraseeket Inn *Your Maine Vacation Begins here!*

BROAD ARROW TAVERN

## DINNER STARTERS

**WOOD OVEN ROASTED MAINE MUSSELS**
Roasted Hazelnut and Garlic Butter ... 9.95
(Huia Sauvignon Blanc, N.Z. Fragrant and Lush 9.00)

**STEAMED MAINE CLAMS**
Drawn Butter and Natural Broth ... 11.95
(Bridgeview Blue Moon Riesling. Fruity & Aromatic 9.00)

**WILD HARVESTED SHRIMP COCKTAIL**
Traditional Sauce and Lemon ... 13.00
(Brut D'Argent Jura Methode Champenpoise 6.00)

**REAL MAINE CRABCAKES**
Served with Salad Greens and
Dressed with Remoulade... 9.95
(Cambria Chardonnay, Napa 10.00)

**WOOD OVEN BAKED SPINACH & ASIAGO DIP**
Accompanied by Seasoned Pita Chips... 7.95
(Shipyard Export Ale, draft from Kennebunkport, Me. 3.75)

**CRISPY FRIED CHICKEN WINGS**
Accompanied by Spicy Sauce &
Bleu Cheese Dressing... 7.95
(Steele Sonoma Pinot Blanc. Dry & Floral 9.00)

**BROAD ARROW NACHOS**
Fresh Salsa Cruda, Sour Cream, Jalapenos
and a blend of Cheeses...8.95
(Bar Harbor Blueberry Ale, Bar Harbor, Me. 3.75)

**WILD IDEA BUFFALO CHILI**
Full of Flavor, Served with Chips and a Dollop
of Sour Cream cup...5.95 Bowl... 8.95
(Montevina Terra D'Oro Zinfandel 7.50)

**WOOD OVEN ROASTED BRUSCHETTA**
Prosciutto, Tomatoes, Sweet Onions, Chevre
and Aged Balsamic... 8.95

**FRIED TENDER CALAMARI**
Tossed with a Sweet Chili Sauce
and Pepperoncini 8.95

**Courtesy of Harraseeket Inn, Freeport, ME**

## Salads

SALADS are more commonly listed after the appetizers and the soups. Salads, like appetizers, should be set in readable type and should be given appropriate descriptive copy (Fig. 10-5). A chef's salad might be described as "a generous portion of romaine, iceberg, and Bibb lettuce, topped with Danish ham, Genoa salami, smoked turkey, sliced tomatoes, cucumbers, green peppers, and sliced hard-boiled eggs, served with a side of the house's own Thousand Island dressing. A complete meal in itself."

A description of the salad dressing itself can be important on the menu. An example might be: "a Thousand Island dressing made with rich mayonnaise,

**Figure 10-5.  Salad Menu**

# Salads

### Roasted Pepper Salad

Fresh field greens tossed with roasted sweet red peppers, tomatoes, roasted onion, pine nuts and Gorgonzola cheese, served with Balsamic vinaigrette.  $9.99

### Boaters Choice

Crisp romaine hearts and fresh field greens tossed with dried cranberries and candied walnuts. Topped with tomatoes, cucumbers, sweet red onion and the day's fresh catch, blackened, broiled or grilled. Served with ranch. $12.99

### Oriental Beef Salad

Tender Certified Angus beef steak, grilled, sliced and glazed with sweet and spicy Thai chili sauce. Served over crisp romaine hearts and fresh field greens. Tossed with scallions, pineapple, Mandarin oranges, snow peas and crispy lo mein noodles. Served with a sesame-ginger vinaigrette.  $14.99

### Blackened Chicken Caesar

A plump Eastern Shore boneless chicken breast, dusted with cajun seasoning, grilled, sliced and served over a traditional Caesar salad with Parmesan cheese.  $9.99

### Jerk Chicken Salad

Crisp romaine hearts and fresh field greens topped with jerk marinated chicken breast tenders, Mandarin oranges, pineapple, roasted sweet red peppers, tomatoes, and red wine vinegar marinated sweet onion. Served with poppy seed vinaigrette.  $11.99

### Buffalo Chicken Salad

Crisp romaine hearts and fresh field greens tossed with crumbled blue cheese and bacon, topped with tomatoes, celery, and golden brown spicy chicken breast tenders, served with blue cheese dressing.  $10.99

### Field of Greens

Fresh field greens, sweet red onion, cucumber, and tomatoes.
Served with your choice of dressing.
$3.99

Courtesy of Mack's Bayside Bar & Grill, Ocean City, MD

ketchup, Worcestershire sauce, relish, assorted spices, and just a touch of Tabasco sauce. A great dressing for any salad."

## Steaks

STEAKS require descriptive copy for better merchandising on a menu. There are many factors to consider when describing steaks: for example, the cut thickness, size, portion, and the manner in which it is prepared. Effective descriptive copy for a steak might read: "A 12-oz cut of filet broiled to perfection and topped with a creamy Hollandaise sauce with assorted spices" (Fig. 10-6).

Information that is provided to assist patrons in ordering a steak rare, medium rare, medium, or well done is also valuable. Steaks are one of the most expensive items on a menu and should be well described and placed on the right-hand side of the menu.

## Seafood

SEAFOOD, like steak, must be listed in large, easy-to-read type and should have adequate descriptive copy. Information concerning how the seafood is prepared and served is needed (Fig. 10-7). An example of descriptive copy for a seafood selection might read: "Scrod Bella Vista—a generous portion of baked scrod, topped with sliced onions, green peppers, and tomatoes, surrounded by a rich tomato sauce."

## Sandwiches

SANDWICHES should also have good descriptive copy in easy-to-read type. If sandwiches are a specialty item, they should be listed before the entrées. However, it is common practice to list only the most popular and profitable sandwiches after the entrées. Hot sandwiches on the menu can be given more extensive descriptive copy than cold sandwiches, if they are more profitable items (Fig. 10-8).

**Figure 10-6. Steak Menu**

# LEGENDARY STEAKS

*Our legendary steaks are cut from Midwestern corn-fed beef.
They're always fresh, never frozen, and cooked up just the way you like them.*

### FLO'S FILET™ *
Go with the Flo! Our signature tenderloin cooked to perfection.
Our most tender steak.  7 oz.  $16.99    9 oz.  $18.99

### BACON WRAPPED FILET*
Our fresh 9 oz. filet is wrapped
in thick-cut, peppered bacon and
then chargrilled over an open
flame.  $19.49

### BLEU CHEESE CRUSTED FILET*
A tender 9 oz. filet, cooked the way
you like, and topped with melted bleu
cheese. Served atop a marinated, grilled
portabella mushroom.  $19.49

**RIBEYE*** A favorite! Tender, juicy and flavorful, cut fresh from the rib loin.
12 oz.  $16.49    16 oz.  $18.49

**NEW YORK STRIP*** The steak lover's choice. Sink your teeth into hearty
flavor and robust taste.  11 oz.  $16.79    14 oz.  $18.49

**THE LONGHORN*** Our specialty. A giant USDA Choice porterhouse with a New
York strip and a large filet in one thick, delicious cut. Chargrilled over an open
flame.  20 oz.  $21.49

**FLO'S FILET* & GRILLED SHRIMP** Zesty grilled shrimp and Flo's Filet.
Served with rice and chipotle ranch sauce.  $20.49

**THE RENEGADE*** Hearty, USDA Choice top sirloin. Seasoned with our own
special Prairie Dust.  8 oz.  $12.79    12 oz.  $14.79

**CHOP STEAK*** Ground sirloin, seasoned, grilled and smothered with grilled
onions and mushrooms.  10 oz.  $10.99

**TEXAS T-BONE*** Every cowboy's dream. A New York strip and a filet in one
cut. Chargrilled over an open flame.  16 oz.  $19.49

**WILD MUSHROOM FILET TIPS*** Tender filet tips, grilled with red peppers,
onions and mushrooms, then smothered in wild mushroom sauce. Topped with a sliced
grilled portabella mushroom and served over mashed potatoes.  $14.79

**PRIME RIB*** USDA Choice prime rib, rubbed with our special spices and
slow roasted for tenderness. Sliced to order. Served with creamy horseradish
and au jus. If you're bold enough, ask for it with Cajun spices!
12 oz.  $16.49    16 oz.  $18.49

### GREAT STEAK ADDITIONS
Sautéed Mushrooms  $2.99   Grilled Onions  $1.49   A Plateful of Both!  $1.99
Half Rack of Ribs  $6.99   Skewer of Shrimp  $5.99

Legendary Steaks and Prime Rib are served with your choice of one side item
(unless one is specified), a Mixed Green or Caesar salad and hearth-baked bread.

Salad Dressings: House, Ranch, Fat-Free Ranch, Balsamic Vinaigrette,
Thousand Island, Chipotle Ranch, Bleu Cheese, Caesar, Italian,
Honey Mustard and Oil & Vinegar

*Consuming raw or undercooked meats, poultry, seafood, shellfish, or eggs may
increase your risk of foodborne illness, especially if you have certain medical conditions.

**Courtesy of Longhorn Steakhouse, Atlanta, GA**

**Figure 10-7. Seafood Selections Menu**

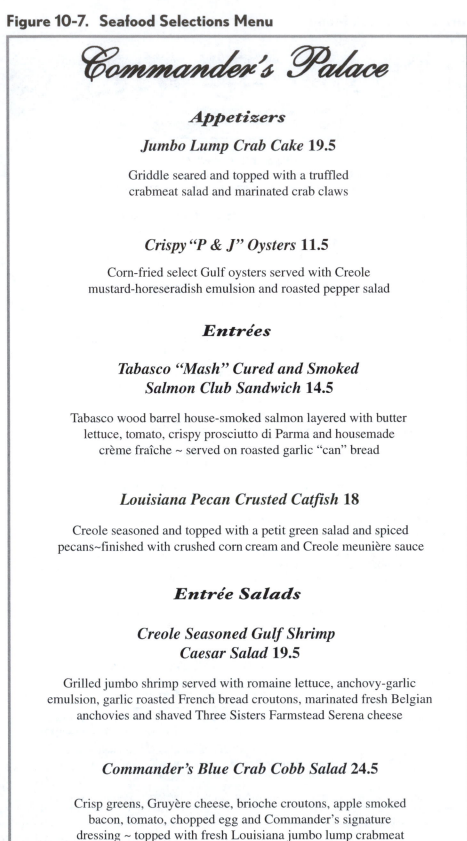

# Commander's Palace

### Appetizers

**Jumbo Lump Crab Cake 19.5**

Griddle seared and topped with a truffled
crabmeat salad and marinated crab claws

**Crispy "P & J" Oysters 11.5**

Corn-fried select Gulf oysters served with Creole
mustard-horeseradish emulsion and roasted pepper salad

### Entrées

**Tabasco "Mash" Cured and Smoked
Salmon Club Sandwich 14.5**

Tabasco wood barrel house-smoked salmon layered with butter
lettuce, tomato, crispy prosciutto di Parma and housemade
crème fraîche ~ served on roasted garlic "can" bread

**Louisiana Pecan Crusted Catfish 18**

Creole seasoned and topped with a petit green salad and spiced
pecans~finished with crushed corn cream and Creole meunière sauce

### Entrée Salads

**Creole Seasoned Gulf Shrimp
Caesar Salad 19.5**

Grilled jumbo shrimp served with romaine lettuce, anchovy-garlic
emulsion, garlic roasted French bread croutons, marinated fresh Belgian
anchovies and shaved Three Sisters Farmstead Serena cheese

**Commander's Blue Crab Cobb Salad 24.5**

Crisp greens, Gruyère cheese, brioche croutons, apple smoked
bacon, tomato, chopped egg and Commander's signature
dressing ~ topped with fresh Louisiana jumbo lump crabmeat

**Courtesy of Commander's Palace, Las Vegas, NV**

**Figure 10-8. Sandwich Menu**

## ~ BURGER & SANDWICH SUMMIT ~

*We serve our burgers medium, medium well or well. Turkey burgers can be substituted for any of our Bugaboo burgers.*
*All burgers and sandwiches are served with french fries.*

### Moosebreath Burger
A half-pound of fresh, seasoned USDA Choice ground beef, grilled to order, then generously topped with garlic-sauteed mushrooms and cheddar cheese. $7.29

### Cheesy Burger
A half-pound of fresh. seasoned USDA Choice ground beef, grilled to order, with your choice of cheddar, Monterey Jack or Swiss cheese. $6.49

### Bacon Cheeseburger
A half-pound of fresh, seasoned USDA Choice ground beef, grilled to order, topped with your choice of cheddar. Monterey Jack or Swiss cheese, and crispy bacon strips. $7.29

### Timberline Turkey Gobbler
A hot-off-the-grill turkey burger topped with cheddar cheese, crisp bacon strips and chipotle mayonnaise for a little extra kick. $6.49

### Lodge Chicken Club
A hearty sandwich piled high with marinated grilled chicken, crisp smoked bacon. lettuce, tomato. Monterey Jack cheese and herb-lemon mayonnaise. $7.79

**PRIME RIB SANDWICH**

### Prime Rib Sandwich (NEW)
A thick slice of slow-roasted, USDA Choice prime rib, cooked to order, topped with caramelized onions, then drizzled with whole-grain mustard hollandaise sauce and stacked between toasted onion Ciabatta points. Served with au jus and our seasoned french fries. $10.99

### Buffalo Chicken Sandwich
A hand-breaded chicken breast fried to a golden brown and basted with our signature Buffalo wing sauce. Served with lettuce, tomato, red onion and Bleu cheese dressing. $7.79

**TWIN PEAKS CHICKEN SANDWICH**

### Twin Peaks Chicken Sandwich
A boulder-pressed chicken sandwich, made with marinated grilled chicken, Monterey Jack and Swiss cheeses, pickles and spicy chipotle mayonnaise. Served hot off the griddle. $7.49

### Grizzly Peak BBQ Burger
A bear of a burger made with BBQ sauce, cheddar cheese and a jumbo, crispy onion ring. $7.49

### Rocky Ridge Roast Beef Sandwich
Thinly sliced prime rib sauteed with garlic-spiked gravy and grilled onions. Topped with melted Swiss cheese and served piping hot on a soft hoagie roll. $8.79

Add any of the following to your entree:
**Blackened Shrimp $4.49**   **Baby Back Ribs $6.99**   **Scallops $ /66**

**Courtesy of Bugaboo Creek Steak House, Atlanta, GA**

## Specials

THERE can be two types of specials on a menu. The first type is the one for which the restaurant is well known. The second type generates a high profit. To encourage customers to try the specials, use pictures on the menu, as many specialty establishments do, or place the specials inside a box or a graphic panel to attract attention (Fig. 10-9).

## Desserts

DESSERTS can be listed in two ways. The first method is to clearly list desserts with descriptive copy after entrées on the menu. The second method is to have a separate dessert menu that may also include after-dinner drinks and specialty coffees and teas (Fig. 10-10). The separate dessert menu offers a greater amount of space in which to describe dessert items elaborately, drawing greater attention to those items.

## Take-out Service

TAKE-OUT service requires proper merchandising. The best way to merchandise take-out service is to prepare a separate take-out menu. When listing take-out information, give proper descriptive copy in readable type, prices, portions, and packaging should be listed. A phone number should be provided, if delivery service is available. Advertising for take-out service can be placed on the back cover of the in-house menu as well.

## Evaluating the Sales Menu

THE special-occasion menu (Fig. 10-11) will be evaluated for print, balance, variety, composition, descriptive copy, listing of items, and color.

**Figure 10-9. Specialties Menu**

# The Marsh Tavern

## Tavern Specialties

### Grilled Chicken and Apple Salad
*Baby Spinach, Frisée, Tart Cherries and Almonds*
*With Honey Yogurt Dressing  $11*

### Equinox Turkey Salad
*Stonewood Farm Turkey, Applewood Smoked Bacon, Tomato, Cape Cod Blue Cheese*
*Alfalfa Sprouts and Green Goddess Dressing  $12*

### Crispy Fried Cod
*Buttermilk Onion Rings and Grilled Lime  $10*

### Yankee Chicken Pot Pie
*Traditional Chicken Pie with Cheddar Mashed Potatoes  $11*

### Tavern Angus Burger
*Served with Melted Vermont Cheddar*
*and Steak Fries  $11*

### Black Pepper Fettuccine with Roasted Vegetables
*Tomato Basil Sauce and Feta Cheese  $10*

*\*"Eating undercooked or raw foods may be hazardous to your health"*
*Applicable 9% Vermont State meals tax will be added to the above prices.*
*An 18% Gratuity will be added to parties of 6 or more*

*2/1/06*

## Specialty Beverages

### Sugar Maple Latte
*with Vermont Syrup  $5*

### Chocolate Buzz
*Espresso blended with Creamy Hot Cocoa  $5*

### Tavern Coffee
*Starbucks Coffee and Caramel*
*Topped with Whipped Cream  $5*

### Hot Apple Cider
*A Traditional Favorite  $5*

### Cappuccino  *$4*

### Latte  *$4*

In compliance with Vermont State Law, our Dining Rooms are smoke free.
Applicable 9% Vermont State meals tax will be added to the above prices.

*2/1/06*

Courtesy of Equinox Resort & Spa, Manchester, VT

**Figure 10-10.  Dessert Menu**

DANIEL

## FRUIT

**"Nougat Glacé aux Mendiants"**
Warm Waffle, Exotic Citrus Salad and Blood Orange Sorbet

Coconut **Chestnut Mont Blanc** "Gâteau Japonais"
Satsuma Clementine Nage with Lemongrass and Ginger Ice Cream

Caramel **Pear "Suzette"** with Grand Marnier Baba
Orange Blossom Mille Crêpe and Earl Grey Ice Cream

**Pineapple** Braised with Cardamom and Sarawack Pepper
Meyer Lemon Sorbet and a Cinnamon Sablé

Warm **Grapefruit** Tatin with Chilled Pomegranate-Green Tea Soup
Fromage Blanc Sorbet

| **Our Sommelier Suggests:** |
|---|
| Tokaji Aszǔ 5 Puttonyos 2000  $12  or  Château des Charmes 2000  $21 |

### SORBET

| Meyer Lemon | Berry |
|---|---|
| Green Apple | Blood Orange |

Assortment of Seasonal Fresh Fruits and Sorbets

## CHOCOLATE

Hot Chocolate Upside-Down **Soufflé** with Pistachio Ice Cream
**Chocolate-Mocha Tart** with Hazelnut Praline
Cinnamon Cappuccino and Java Coffee Ice Cream
**Sao Tomé Single Estate** Chocolate Fondant
Cocoa Nougatine, Chocolate Pot de Crème and Chocolate Ice Cream

Chocolate **Caramel** Millefeuille with Vanilla Confiture de Lait
"Fleur de Sel" Caramel Ice Cream

Warm **Griotte Black Forest** with Vanilla Sorbet
Whipped Cream and Bittersweet Chocolate

| **Our Sommelier Suggests:** |
|---|
| Vino Santo Castella Di Ama 1999 $16  **or**  Port Grahams 1977 $56 |

## ICE CREAM

| Vanilla | Ginger |
|---|---|
| Chocolate | Java Coffee |

WE ALSO OFFER A SELECTION OF CHEESES FROM OUR CHEESE TROLLEY
4 SELECTIONS - $21          6 SELECTIONS - $28

Courtesy of Restaurant Daniel, New York, NY

**Figure 10-11. Special Occasion Menu**

# THE INN at KEARSAGE

## GREAT BEGINNINGS

### Baked Brie
Brie baked in a flaky puff pastry and served with an assortment of fresh fruit

OR

### Maryland Crab Cakes
Crab cakes sautéed to a golden hue accompanied with salad greens and served with a rémoulade sauce

## SOUPS

### French Onion Soup
A slowly simmered onion soup topped with Swiss cheese and seasoned croutons

OR

### Potato and Leek Soup
A hearty soup of potatoes and leeks in a rich creamy base

## SALADS

### Mixed Green Salad
An assortment of green leaf, oak leaf, red leaf, and frisée
drizzled with a champagne vinaigrette

OR

### Waldorf Salad
A combination of tart apples, celery, walnuts, raisins, mayonnaise,
and fresh lemon juice presented on a base of mixed greens

## THE MAIN COURSE

### Roast Turkey with Dressing
Fresh Tom Turkey served with a chestnut
and sweet sausage dressing and cranberry sauce

OR

### Baked Ham
Slowly baked Virginia Ham covered with a rich honey glaze

## FROM THE GARDEN

### Acorn Squash
Fresh garden squash sprinkled with brown sugar,
butter, cinnamon, and a hint of nutmeg

OR

### Garlic Mashed Potatoes
Red Bliss potatoes blended with fresh garlic
and herbs, cream, and melted butter

## DESSERTS

### Pumpkin Crème Brulée
A rich pumpkin custard served with fresh berries

OR

### Apple Pie à la mode
Flaky pie crust filled with Golden Delicious and Granny Smith apples
topped with French vanilla ice cream

$27.95 per person

## Print

The print is clear and easy to read. The headings are printed in uppercase letters, and the descriptive copy is printed in lowercase roman typeface.

## Balance

The balance on this menu is poor because of the limited number of choices of entrées and vegetables. There should be a minimum of two vegetable choices and two potato choices. The entrées should include other selections, such as a broiled tenderloin with a bordelaise sauce or a baked swordfish with a horseradish crust.

## Variety

The variety offered on a special occasion menu is usually limited, because certain foods are traditional for that occasion, as seen on this Thanksgiving menu. Despite the limited selection of vegetables and entrées, the variety of the other food categories is good.

## Composition

The eye appeal and aesthetic value of the menu items are fairly good. To present a more colorful plate, a green vegetable such as broccoli or asparagus is recommended.

## Descriptive Copy

The descriptive copy is written in an interesting and appetizing fashion. The copy for each item is not too long or overly detailed. The food items are clearly and precisely described.

## Listing of Items

The food categories are listed in the proper serving sequence of appetizer, soups, salads, entrées, vegetables, desserts, and beverages. The prix-fixe menu includes the entire meal at a set price.

## Color

The colors used on Thanksgiving menus should include earth tones, such as browns, oranges, yellows, and greens. The graphics on the menu relate to the occasion being celebrated and include turkeys, pies, pumpkins, and other autumnal specialties.

# For Review and Discussion

1. Name five items of information that might be listed on the back cover of a menu.

2. List three very important things to remember when listing liquors.

3. How should wine selections be presented?

4. List 10 descriptive words that might be used on a menu to describe steaks.

5. Give 10 words that could be used to describe seafood items.

6. What are two important factors that affect the listing of sandwiches on a menu?

7. How can specials be highlighted on a menu?

8. Give two ways to list desserts.

9. What is the best way to market take-out service?

# Chapter 11

# FOODSERVICE EQUIPMENT ANALYSIS

EVERY foodservice operator needs the proper equipment to produce the food items listed on the menu. This chapter establishes guidelines for selecting and purchasing the most appropriate and practical equipment.

## Objectives

- ❏ To provide guidelines on how to purchase the most appropriate foodservice equipment for a particular operation

- ❏ To demonstrate how to complete a foodservice equipment analysis

# Guidelines for Selecting Equipment

To STAY within a budget, it is essential that foodservice operators are knowledgeable about the types and the volume of equipment that should be purchased. The following are guidelines to purchasing equipment.

## Justifying the Purchase of Equipment: If You Don't Need It, Don't Buy It!

After purchasing equipment, foodservice operators often find that, they have little or no use for it. How does one justify the purchase of equipment? Foodservice operators need to complete a foodservice equipment analysis before buying equipment. The purpose of the foodservice equipment analysis is to establish the type of equipment and the volume of equipment needed to produce the food products on the menu. Many foodservice operators rely totally on sales representatives to establish the type of equipment needed to produce the items on the menu. This dependence is weak, because sales representatives do not have a knowledge of the entire foodservice operation. Most foodservice equipment sales representatives do a good job recommending the type and number of pieces of equipment that are needed. They make recommendations on the needs and desires of the foodservice operators. Foodservice operators always must remember, however, that it is the sales representative's job to sell equipment, and it is the foodservice operator's job to know which equipment to purchase.

## When to Purchase New Equipment

When should new equipment be purchased? The foodservice operator should purchase new equipment when laws and building codes require the purchase and/or if customers will be viewing the equipment. Budget and the image the foodservice operation wishes to portray will play a role in decision making as well. New equipment is used primarily in the front of the foodservice operation.

To save money, consider purchasing used equipment. The National Restaurant Association reports that 80 percent of first-time foodservice operators in any given year fail due in part to the high cost of purchasing new equipment. The life span of a major piece of equipment, such as a broiler, fryer, or oven, is 10 years. Purchasing used equipment that has been liquidated can save 30 to 50 percent of the price of a new piece of equipment. One disadvantage of purchasing used equipment is that the equipment cannot be 100 percent depreciated by the second owner, if at all. The second owner may also lose the benefits of the dealership guarantee, or the manufacturer's warranty, and not know how well the used equipment has been maintained.

The best place to purchase used equipment is at a liquidation auction. To be successful at purchasing liquidated equipment, the foodservice operator should not be in a rush to furnish the operation. It takes time, energy, money, patience, and knowledge about the needed equipment. The foodservice operator should contact the nearest auction house or look in the newspaper to find out when an auction is being held.

It is always important to preview equipment to see if it operates. If it is damaged, is it repairable? Another important factor for the foodservice operation to establish is the amount of money he or she is willing to pay for each piece of equipment before the auction starts in order not to go over budget during the bidding process. During the preview time, the foodservice operator can find out about the procedures that the auction house uses and the types of payments it accepts. Most auction houses require that the equipment be moved from the hall immediately after the auction. As personal checks and credit cards require a reference check, most auction houses require that potential purchasers establish this before the auction begins.

Banks are another source for locating foodservice equipment sales sites. Banks hold auctions on the site of the foodservice operations on which they are foreclosing. Banks are also the first to know if a foodservice operation will be auctioned.

# Renting versus Leasing Foodservice Equipment

The term **leasing** means renting with an option to purchase the equipment. When renting equipment, there is no option to purchase the equipment. The main reasons for renting and/or leasing equipment follows.

- **If something goes wrong with the equipment, the foodservice operator does not have to pay for the service call.**

- **If the equipment breaks while in operation, the foodservice operator need not pay for the parts needed for repair.**

- **When a foodservice operation leases equipment, less operating capital is needed to open the foodservice operation. More money is needed to purchase equipment than to rent or lease equipment.**

- **As mentioned, 80 percent of people starting in the foodservice business fail during the first year. If this happens, it is better for the foodservice operator not to own the equipment, because he or she will not be able to retain the total value or return on investment. People who lease or rent equipment do not hold the title of ownership to that equipment; if the business fails their loss is not as great.**

## Equipment Design Considerations

Foodservice operators always should purchase equipment that reflects the image they wish to portray. As mentioned, an investment in new equipment is prudent for machinery that is visible to customers. Equipment that is hidden should be operationally sound but need not be new.

## Purchasing Automated Equipment

Time is money! Foodservice operators should purchase equipment that is efficient in performing the task to save time and money. Automatic devices, such as a timer on a Frialator™, allow the fry cook to cook while performing other tasks.

## Selecting Self-Cleaning or Easily Cleaned Equipment

Equipment that cleans itself is a miracle in disguise. A ventilation and exhaust hood system with steam lines within the ducts and an automatic timing device is an excellent example. The steam lines release steam into the ducts (passageways of air to travel) at a set time to clean off the built-up grease. Self-cleaning equipment saves energy and time. Easy-to-clean equipment, such as stainless steel tables, countertops, and shelves, are also assets.

## Selecting Equipment That Can Be Sanitized

Foodservice operators should purchase equipment that has been certified to withstand the harsh chemicals needed to sanitize the equipment. The National Sanitation Foundation (NSF) tests equipment to certify that the finish material can withstand abrasive chemicals during the cleaning process (certified equipment bears the NSF label). The Board of Health also examines foodservice equipment to see that it can be easily taken apart for efficient cleaning and sanitizing.

## Warranty versus Guarantee

A warranty and a guarantee both protect an investment for a certain period of time. A **warranty** is issued by the manufacturer and typically protects the major "heart" component(s) of the equipment for up to five years. Compressors, walk-in freezers, or coolers are excellent examples of equipment that usually carries warranties. If the compressor fails to operate under normal conditions, the warranty allows the owner to have it serviced or replaced without charge.

A **guarantee** is issued through the dealership where the equipment is purchased. It covers a time period of 30 days to two years, depending on the type of equipment. It protects the small parts of a piece of equipment. For example, if the door handle to a walk-in freezer or cooler falls off due to normal use, the owner can have it serviced without charge.

Guarantees and warranties vary greatly from manufacturer to manufacturer, so they should be read carefully, photocopied and filed separately from the originals.

## Selecting Standard Equipment and Building Specialized Equipment

Whenever possible, standard equipment should be selected. *Standard equipment* is equipment that has an established criterion in the foodservice industry. It is purchased from a company with a good reputation, is readily available, and does not cost a lot of money to replace.

*Specialized equipment* is designed and built to the foodservice operator's specifications. The equipment is designed to do a particular task in a foodservice operation. It is usually more costly to obtain and repair. Most operations purchase standard equipment, unless they need a customized piece of equipment for specialized tasks.

Advantages of purchasing standard equipment include:

- **Greater availability (the equipment is carried by most foodservice equipment dealers)**
- **A more affordable price**
- **Greater access to spare parts at a lower cost**

- A service history showing that the equipment is durable and has good production capabilities
- A warranty/or guarantee that extends for a longer period of time than those issued for specialized equipment

## Checking the Reputation of the Sales Dealership and Manufacturer

Because the equipment necessary to run a foodservice operation is costly, it is wise to research both the equipment itself and the reputation of the person or business from which the equipment will be purchased. Sources for information include the Better Business Bureau and current and former customers. Chefs, managers, and sales representatives also can serve as valuable information sources.

## Selecting Equipment with Advanced Technology

THE advanced technology found in equipment today allows the chef to save money on energy, to cook food faster, and to hold food longer. Equipment should be selected that can perform multiple cooking techniques or multiple noncooking technique tasks. Equipment such as the tilting skillet, the combination (combi) oven, and the flash-bake halo oven can perform a number of tasks. The tilting skillet, for example, allows for simmering, braising, stewing, boiling, steaming, grilling, sautéing, shallow frying, and griddling. The skillet also tilts for easy pouring and cleaning. The combination oven may be used for standard baking/roasting, convectional baking/roasting, steaming, slow cooking, and holding food long term. A flash-bake halo oven generates intense heat using a variety of levels of intense heating lights to brown foods in a short period of time.

For additional information on new technology used in foodservice equipment, log on to www.daubers.com.

# Foodservice Equipment Analysis

To SAVE money when purchasing equipment, foodservice operators should develop a list of equipment that is essential for producing the menu. Prior to shopping, they should establish equipment needs. Most people who shop without a list spend more money on equipment than necessary. Use of a foodservice equipment analysis is recommended to establish actual needs.

A foodservice equipment analysis is performed in this way. First the menu is established and meal items to be evaluated (Meal Item) are selected. Next, the number of portions to be prepared (Portion to Prepare) are calculated. This number is based on the foodservice operation's capacity, multiplied by the turnover rate, plus a 10 percent growth rate. For example, a 100-seat foodservice operation multiplied by a three-turnover rate per peak hour (three hours) equals 300 customers. A 10 percent growth rate is added to plan for the future capacity of the equipment, thus allowing for 330 customers to be served during the peak period.

**Portions to be prepared = [(operation's capacity × turnover rate) + 10% growth rate]**

$$= [(100 \times 3) + 10\%]$$

$$= 300 + 30$$

$$= 330$$

A **peak period** is an amount of time during which the foodservice operation is very busy. The peak period for breakfast lasts three hours, from 6:00 A.M. to 9:00 A.M.; the peak lunch period is from 11:00 A.M. to 2:00 P.M.; and peak dinner hours are from 6:00 P.M. to 9:00 P.M.

It is important to accurately forecast the number of customers that are being served on a busy night or during peak periods. When the number of customers is not forecasted accurately, food costs are high and profits are low due to overproduction or underproduction. Once the total customer count is established, the foodservice operator must estimate the number of product portions that will be sold. For example, he or she estimates the number of customers out of 330 who purchase the sirloin steak entrée. Factors that will influence the forecasted number include:

- **Total number of steaks offered**
- **Popularity of the food product**
- **Price of the food product**

- **Amount of advertising or marketing done to promote the item**
- **Quality of flavor (taste)**
- **Appearance/presentation**
- **Effort that the service staff makes to sell the item**
- **Order in which the menu items are listed**
- **Placement of the item on the menu**
- **Amount of time it takes to produce the item**

In the example in Figure 11-1, 120 portions are sold during a peak period from 6:00 P.M. to 9:00 P.M. on a Saturday night. Once the forecasted number of portions to be prepared has been calculated, each portion is given a weight in ounces or pounds or a volume measurement, such as cups, pints, quarts, or gallons (Weight or Volume per Portion). The portion size of the sirloin steak is 16 ounces (1 pound). To find the total amount produced, the number of portions that must be prepared is multiplied by the portion size:

$$120 \times 16 \text{ oz} = 1,920 \text{ oz} (120 \text{ lb}) \text{ (total amount produced)}$$

The total amount produced column can assist the chef or foodservice operator in deciding on the amount of food product to purchase. It is important to remember that the number in this column represents a 100 percent (edible) as-served quantity calculation of food items. A chef must purchase more than 120 pounds of sirloin steak to derive 120 portions.

The items per hour column (Items per Hour) indicates how many items must be produced during a one-hour period. To calculate this number, the number of peak hours is divided into the total amount produced column:

$$120 \div 3 = 40$$

Dividing 120 sirloin steak portions by 3 (hours) equals 40 sirloin steaks per hour.

Because most equipment, equipment catalogs, and company Web sites indicate the production capacity by the hour, this item-per-hour number is invaluable. A typical broiler catalog shows numerous models from which to choose. Foodservice operators make their selections based on their budget and on the production quantity they need to generate. In the example presented, 40 portions of sirloin steak per hour are needed. If the broiler was used only to broil steaks, which is highly unlikely, a broiler that would broil 40 (or as close to 40 as possible) sirloin steaks per hour would be selected.

The usage time column (Usage Time Range) indicates the amount of time needed to produce the food product. This time range includes the preparation and production time. In the sirloin steak example, the sirloin steaks will be cut from the sirloin strip and cooked to order. The time range

# Figure 11-1. Foodservice Equipment Analysis Sheet

Meal <u>Dinner</u>
Day <u>Saturday</u>
Peak Period <u>6:00 P.M. to 9:00 P.M.</u>

| Meal Item | Portion to Prepare | Weight or Volume per Portion | Total Amount Produced | Items per Hour | Usage Time Range | EQUIPMENT: Including Size and Number | | | |
|---|---|---|---|---|---|---|---|---|---|
| | | | | | | Preparation | Production | Holding | Service |
| Sirloin Steak | 120 | 16 oz | 120 lb | 40 | 5-9 P.M. | walk-in cooler table reach-in cooler | broiler | reach-in cooler | |
| | | | | | | | | | |
| | | | | | | | | | |
| | | | | | | | | | |
| | | | | | | | | | |
| | | | | | | | | | |
| | | | | | | | | | |
| | | | | | | | | | |
| | | | | | | | | | |
| | | | | | | | | | |
| | | | | | | | | | |
| | | | | | | | | | |
| | | | | | | | | | |

to prepare the steaks is from 5:00 P.M. to 6:00 P.M., and the cooked-to-order time range is the same as the peak period, 6:00 P.M. to 9:00 P.M. Indicating these four hours will assist the chef in producing a production schedule. A production schedule shows who will be cooking, when the food products are to be prepared and produced, and the equipment that is needed. The sirloin steaks will be produced from 5:00 P.M. to 6:00 P.M., cooked to order from 6:00 P.M. to 9:00 P.M., and cooked on a broiler.

The columns that remain on the Foodservice Equipment Analysis Sheet provide information concerning the actual equipment needed to prepare, produce, hold, and serve the food products. The preparation column (Preparation) indicates the equipment that is necessary to prepare the sirloin steaks. It is at this point in the process that the food product is taken from the storage area. In the example, the sirloin is fresh and stored in the walk-in cooler. From storage, the sirloin is placed on a table to be portioned. A knife and a tray or pan are also necessary. The portioned steaks are now returned to the walk-in cooler or to a reach-in cooler near the broiler. If it is used, the reach-in cooler should be included in the preparation column (Preparation), and the broiler should be listed in the production column (Production). The production equipment column indicates the major hot equipment needed during the production phase of the food item. Hot equipment usually refers to items like convection ovens, fryers, grills, steam equipment, and stoves.

The holding column (Holding) indicates where the food product is to be held during the peak period. Cook-to-order items are usually held in a dry or refrigerated state, while preprepared foods are held in a warm or hot state. The sirloins are held in a refrigerated state. Other holding equipment items include steam tables, food warmers, and ovens.

The last column to complete on the analysis sheet, the service column (Service), indicates the equipment required for serving the food product to the customer. No additional equipment is needed to serve the sirloin steaks if the style of service used is American. If the sirloins are prepared table-side, a *réchaud* and a *guéridon* or portable carving cart would be needed.

The last step in analyzing equipment needs is to determine the capacity of the equipment, based on the total quantity of food that must be produced by that individual piece of equipment. The broiler is the major piece of equipment that is needed to produce the sirloin steaks. What size broiler is needed? Calculate all of the food products that will go in the broiler during the peak period. If a menu lists broiled fish, chicken, or pork products, it is necessary to add these to the number of sirloin steaks. If 50 orders of broiled pork chops and 120 orders of sirloin steaks are needed, the total broiler production is 170 food items.

After equipment needs have been analyzed, the foodservice operator should research foodservice equipment catalogs or CDs (computer disks), equipment and company Web sites and talk to a salesperson to find out which broiler model will come close to producing 170 food products per hour. By carefully studying the menu, the operator can better evaluate the type of equipment that is needed to produce it. This exercise will save the operator money.

## Helpful Hints for Completing the Foodservice Equipment Analysis

- The foodservice equipment analysis is to be used only as a guideline.

- The purpose of the foodservice equipment analysis is to establish the type of foodservice equipment and the capacity of the equipment needed to produce the menu.

- The foodservice equipment analysis establishes a shopping list for the major, heavy-duty cooking equipment. Smaller pieces of equipment, such as plates, knives, and cups, should be placed on a separate list.

- Needs will vary greatly, depending on how the chef decides to purchase, prepare, store, produce, and serve food products.

- Not all columns on the equipment analysis form have to be used in the production of all products. A tossed salad does not need equipment in the production column.

- Soups, sauces, gravies, and other products with volume are usually made prior to the peak period and will not use the production column.

- Forecasting portions is a difficult task in the real job market. The use of a sales history will assist in achieving greater accuracy.

- The amount of money and floor space that the chef has greatly influences the type of equipment to be purchased.

- It is easier to use letters or numbers to represent a piece of equipment, such as the letter D to represent a mixer, than it is to write out the word *mixer* every time.

- Indicate the equipment when you use it in your planning. Some food products will use two or three pieces of equipment in the production column.

# Guidelines for Designing a Hot Cooking Line

THE cooking line is the heart of the kitchen. A **cooking line**, or **line**, is a grouping of the major pieces of equipment needed to cook the menu items. The layout of the line greatly contributes to the customers' dining experience.

An efficient layout allows the chef to produce menu items in an organized manner. Cooking in an organized manner allows the chef to cook items quickly, and to serve them hot.

These guidelines will assist in designing an efficient hot cooking line. The foodservice operator should:

- **Determine how many cooking stations there will be on the line. A cooking station is where a particular type of cooking technique takes place.**

- **Design the workstation for peak and slow production periods.**

- **Determine the maximum and minimum number of chefs needed to produce the menu items.**

- **Determine where the pickup station will be prior to laying out the line.**

## Figure 11-2. Straight-Line Flowchart

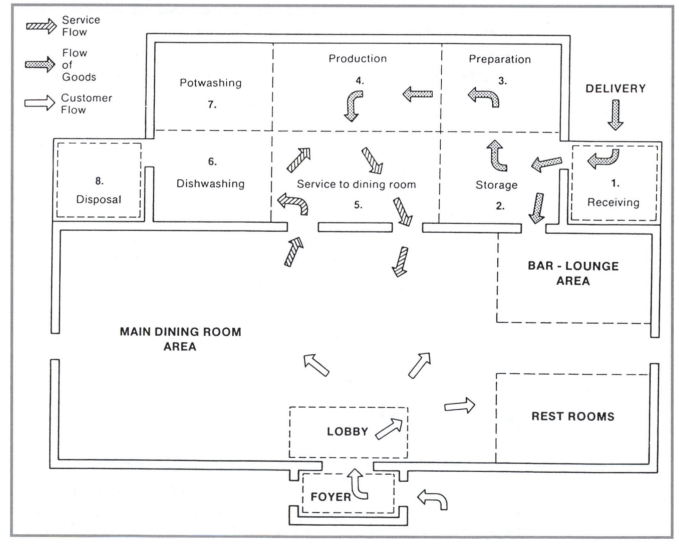

- **Analyze the percentage of work coming from each workstation. Determine how many menu items are being produced from the fry station as compared to those from other stations. If 70 percent of the menu items are being produced from the fry station, then design the fry station with adequate equipment to produce 70 percent of production.**

- **Provide good lighting. Working in one's own shadow can cause accidents.**

- **Provide excellent ventilation. Circulating fresh air and exhausting smoke, heat, and grease from the air keeps the chefs alert and healthy.**

- **Group similar and related tasks close together. When laying out a workstation, the foodservice operator should write out every step that the chef will go through to produce a menu item. Typically food flows through six steps: (1) receiving; (2) primary bulk storage (walk-in coolers or freezers) and/or secondary storage (reach-in refrigerators or freezers); (3) preparation (washing, peeling, cutting, chopping, etc.); (4) production (cooking the food), and holding the food for service; (5) service (serving the food to the customer); and (6) sanitation (which includes dishwashing, potwashing, and disposal). Grouping storage close to preparation or grouping preparation close to production eliminates wasted steps, motions, and time. See Figure 11-2 for a straight-line flow chart.**

- **When laying out the line, the front of each piece of equipment should be flush (even) with the one next to it. If necessary the back of the equipment can be uneven.**

Keeping these guidelines in mind when laying out the line will increase productivity.

# For Review and Discussion

1. List three items to keep in mind when selecting foodservice equipment.

2. Compare and contrast a warranty and a guarantee.

3. What is a foodservice equipment analysis?

4. Why is it important to do a foodservice equipment analysis before purchasing equipment for a foodservice operation?

5. When completing the foodservice equipment analysis, what are four factors that can influence the forecasted number of portions that are sold?

# DESCRIPTIVE COPY EXERCISE

From the list of menu items choose 25 and describe each selection, using four adjectives for each item. Once you have used an adjective, you cannot use it again.

## Breakfast Appetizers

Orange Juice     Mixed Fruit     Honeydew     Grapefruit

## Breakfast Entrées

Scrambled Eggs
Western Omelette
Denver Omelette
Mushroom Omelette
Eggs Benedict
Apple Pancakes with Syrup

French Toast with Syrup
Sirloin Steak with Choice of Eggs
Corned Beef Hash with Poached
    Eggs
Waffles with Syrup
Cheese Blintzes with Fruit

## Luncheon Appetizers

Buffolo Wings
Oysters on the Half Shell
Antipasto

Seasoned Onion Rings
Crab Cakes

## Luncheon Soups

Seafood Bisque with Sherry
French Onion Soup with Cheese
Seafood Gumbo

Broccoli and Cheese
Minestrone
Cream of Spinach

## Luncheon Salads

Chef Salad
Spinach Salad
Waldorf Salad

Crabmeat Salad
Cole Slaw

## Luncheon Entrées

Shrimp and Crabmeat au Gratin
Baked Stuffed Sole with
    Newburg Sauce
Shrimp Scampi
Sautéed Brook Trout
Filet Mignon with Onion Rings
Beef Stroganoff
Beef Stew with Biscuit
Chicken Divan

Chicken Cordon Bleu
Chicken Kiev
Veal Parmesan
Veal Marsala
Veal Gruyère
Herb Encrusted Baked
    Salmon
Kobe Beef Hamburger
Pan Roasted Tuna

## Luncheon Desserts

Pound Cake with Ice Cream
Blueberry Pie with Ice Cream
Pecan Pie with Whipped Cream
Boston Cream Pie
Lemon Meringue Pie

Strawberry Shortcake
Apple Crisp with Ice Cream
Chocolate Layer Cake
Chocolate Mousse Cake
Fruit Crisp

## Dinner Appetizers

Shrimp Cocktail
Clams on the Half Shell
Vegetarian Pizza
Stuffed Mushroom Caps

Spicy Calamari
Stuffed Portabella Mushrooms
Spring Rolls with an Assortment
    of Dipping Sauces

## Dinner Soups

Clam Chowder
Cream of Asparagus
Gazpacho

Vichyssoise
Sweet and Sour

## Dinner Salads

Caeser Salad
Tossed Greens

Field greens with Raspberry
   Vinaigrette
Boston Bibb with Crabmeat

## Dinner Entrées

Fettucini Alfredo
Veal Dijonnaise
Veal Picatta
Veal à la Holstein
Roast Beef with Popovers
Chateaubriand
Broiled Lamp Chops with
   Mint Jelly
Broiled Swordfish
Baked Stuffed Shrimp
Braised Beef Short Ribs

Pistachio Encrusted Rack of Lamb
Baked Stuffed Lobster
Roast Duckling with Cherry
   Sauce
Lobster Thermidor
Shrimp Teriyaki
Sole Rockefeller
Seafood Brochette
Roast Chicken
Baked Lasagna with a Bolognese
   Sauce

## Dinner Desserts

Banana Cream Pie
Black Forest Cake
Lemon Chiffon Pie
Cherry Pie with Ice Cream
Apple Tart with Brandy
   Whipped Cream

Tiramisu
Chocolate Soufflé
Indian Pudding with Whipped
   Cream
Carrot Cake
Amaretto Cheese Cake

# DESCRIPTIVE TERMS FOR MENUS

Artfully seasoned

As you prefer it

Assortment of

At its delightful perfection

Baked golden brown

Blazed in cognac

Blended with a distinctive
  sauce

Choice center cut

Cooked in an artfully
  seasoned sherry sauce

Craftily marinated

Delicately boiled and served
  with savory herbs

Delicate wine sauce

Deliciously seasoned

Delightfully different

Extraordinary ingredients

Fluffy tenderness

Fragrant mixture of

Generous portion

Gourmet's delight

In an intriguing blend of

In a traditional manner

Nappé with a piquante sauce

Nationally famous

Prepared according to the authentic
  version

Prepared to your epicurean taste

Roasted to a turn

Sauce enlivened with onions and herbs

Served in a distinctive sauce

Served steaming in a casserole

Served with a lavish hand from a bowl
  and tossed well to your taste

Simmered in its own juice

Taste-enriched with a perky piquant
  sauce

Tender, bited-size flakes

Tender flakes

Tender sweet

Tenderly sautéed in butter

Thick, generous portion

Thick, generous treat

This classic French sauce

To make a meal a feast

Truly delightful

With a natural flavor

# WORDS FREQUENTLY MISSPELLED ON STUDENTS' MENUS

accompaniment
avocado
bacon
banquet
barbecue sauce
béarnaise
blueberries
broccoli
burgundy
cantaloupe
cinnamon
cocktail
combination
croutons
delicate
delicious
diner
dining

fettuccini, fettucine
filet mignon
flambéed, flambé
fried
hollandaise
hors d'oeuvre
iceberg lettuce
lasagna
linguine
manicotti
Maître d'hôtel
mayonnaise
mozzarella
occasion
omelette, omelet
Parmesan
parsley
pimiento (pimento)

potato
prosciutto
provolone
purveyor
raisins
restaurant
ricotta
romaine
Romano
Roquefort
sprig
syrup
Tabasco
vinaigrette
vinegar
Worcestershire sauce
zucchini

# CULINARY TERMS

**à la Creole**   In the style of Louisiana cookery; with onions, tomatoes, green peppers, and sometimes okra.

**à la Florentine**   Foods that have a spinach base, such as cream soup with spinach.

**à la King**   A white cream sauce with green peppers, pimiento, and mushrooms.

**à la Mode**   With ice cream.

**à la Parisienne**   Garnish for chicken or fish consisting of mushroom, asparagus, truffles, with a white wine sauce.

**Aglio e Olio**   A sauce made with garlic and oil served over pasta.

**al dente**   To the bite.

**Amandine** or **Almandine**   With almonds.

**Antipasto**   A cold appetizer consisting of meats, cheese, olives, and vegetables.

**Arugula**   A bitter salad green.

**au Gratin**   Topped with bread crumbs and cheese, and browned.

**au Jus**   Served in its own juice.

**Baba**   Spongy yeast cake soaked in rum.

**Baguette**   A narrow crisp French bread.

**Baklava**   A layered sweet dessert popular in Greece.

**Béarnaise**   An egg butter sauce to which tarragon, chervil, shallots, and meat juices have been added. Sometimes served with tenderloin.

**Beaujolais**   A region in the southern part of Bourgogne, France, known for its red wines.

**Béchamel**   A white cream sauce made with butter, flour, and milk.

**Beurre Blanc**   A white French sauce of butter, vinegar, wine, and shallots served with fish and poultry.

**Biscotti**   A crunchy Italian cookie usually served with coffee.

**Bisque**   A creamy soup made with shellfish—usually shrimp and lobster.

**Bok Choy**   Referred to as Chinese white cabbage.

**Bolognese**   A hearty dish made of meat and vegetables often served with pasta. Cream is often added to this dish for flavor.

**Bordeaux**   The most important area in France for the production of wine.

**Bordelaise**   A brown sauce that contains shallots, red wine, tarragon, thyme, and sometimes bone marrow.

**Bortsch** or **Borscht**   A vegetable soup that contains cabbage and red beets or a beef base. Originated in Russia.

**Bouillabaisse**   A seafood stew containing crab, mussels, sea bass, onions, tomatoes, saffron, garlic, and assorted herbs with white wine, and Cognac.

**Bouillon**   Originally referred to as plain white stock. In today's restaurants, it is a clear soup made from fish, meat, or vegetables.

**Bouquet Garni**   An assortment of herbs to flavor soups, stews, or sauces.

**Boursin**   Cream cheese flavored with herbs and garlic. This cheese is factory made.

**Brie**   French cheese characterized by its white rind and rich, creamy, yellow color.

**Brochette**   Foods that are grilled on a skewer, for example, beef or chicken with onions, green peppers, tomatoes, and mushrooms.

**Bruschetta**   Italian garlic bread.

**Burrito**   A tortilla filled with meat, cheese, or refried beans. Served with lettuce, tomato, guacamole, and sour cream.

**Calvados**   An apple brandy from Normandy.

**Camembert**   A mild, creamy cheese from France.

**Canapé**   A small piece of bread, plain or toasted, and topped with seafood, meats, and sometimes eggs.

**Cannelloni**   Pasta stuffed with cheese and meat.

**Cannoli**   A deep fried dessert filled with ricotta cheese.

**Caper**   The bud of a plant that grows in southern California and the Mediterranean Sea area, pickled and used in sauces, butter, and salads.

**Cappuccino**   Espresso with steamed milk.

**Carpaccio**  Raw beef finely sliced and served with lemon juice, olive oil, and seasonings, Sometimes served with onions and capers.

**Cassoulet**  A rich dish made of duck, goose, pork, sausages, and white beans.

**Caviar**  The eggs of sturgeon, salmon, whitefish, and lumpfish, usually salted. The best caviar comes from Russia and Iran.

**Chablis**  One of the most famous dry, white wines from France.

**Chanterelles**  Wild mushrooms often used in sauce.

**Chantilly**  A salad dressing consisting of whipped cream and mayonnaise, flavored with liqueur or vanilla.

**Chasseur**  A garnish containing shallots, white wine, and sliced mushrooms.

**Chateaubriand**  A double cut of tenderloin served to two people. Served with a variety of vegetables and a border of duchesse potatoes.

**Cherries Jubilee**  A dessert of vanilla ice cream covered with flaming Bing cherries.

**Chive**  A plant that has a distinctive onion flavor and is used in salads, soups, and sour cream.

**Cilantro**  Referred to as Chinese parsley.

**Clairet**  A light red wine made in Bordeaux and Bourgogne.

**Cointreau**  An orange-flavored liqueur.

**Compote**  Stewed fruits, usually served cold.

**Confit**  Preserved duck, goose, or pork.

**Consommé**  A clear soup, usually beef, poultry, or game, garnished with an assortment of vegetables and herbs.

**Cordon Bleu**  Chicken or veal filled with ham and Swiss cheese then breaded and sautéed or deep-fried. Usually served with a Supreme sauce.

**Coquille Saint Jacques**  A shell or shell-shaped dish that contains seafood, often with a cream sauce, topped with bread crumbs, grated cheese, and then browned.

**Couscous**  Cooked cracked wheat served in salads or as an accompaniment.

**Crêpe**  A thin pancake stuffed with fruits or various meats.

**Crème Fraîche**  A thickened cream used in sauces.

**Croissant**  A crescent-shaped pastry usually served at breakfast.

**Croquettes**  A small often oblong-shaped mass of chopped fish or meat that has been mixed with a white sauce, breaded, and deep fried.

**Crouton**  A cube of dried bread flavored with an array of herbs and spices. Served in salads or soups.

**Demi-Glace**   A rich brown sauce that has been reduced.

**Demitasse**   A small cup of black coffee.

**Drawn Butter**   Seasoned melted butter, usually served with fish.

**Duchesse Potatoes**   Mashed potatoes seasoned with nutmeg, butter, and egg yolk. Shaped and piped onto a buttered sheet pan.

**Éclair**   An oblong pastry filled with custard for dessert or with creamed food for an entrée.

**Eggs Benedict**   Poached eggs with hollandaise sauce and ham or bacon, served on an English muffin.

**Enchiladas** Soft corn tortillas filled with either chicken, meat, refried beans, or cheese and then topped with a sauce.

**Escalope**   A thinly sliced piece of veal sautéed in fortified butter.

**Espagnole**   A brown sauce.

**Espresso**   A strong coffee served with a twist of lemon.

**Fajitas**   Marinated meat that is grilled and served with tortillas, onions, peppers, tomatoes, guacamole, cheese, and sour cream.

**Fines Herbes**   An assortment of chopped herbs, consisting of parsley, chives, chervil, and tarragon.

**Fricassee**   Diced veal or chicken in a white sauce.

**Galantine**   A dish of forcemeat, for example, galantine of duck.

**Gazpacho**   A cold vegetable soup garnished with croutons, chopped vegetables, fresh chives, and hard boiled eggs. Sour cream or crème fraîche may also be added.

**Gelato**   Italian ice cream.

**Goulash**   A rich beef stew that contains paprika and onions.

**Guacamole**   Avocado with vegetables, cilantro, lime juice, and seasonings. Served as a dip or accompaniment.

**Hoisin**   A rich brown sauce used in Chinese cooking.

**Hollandaise**   A sauce consisting of egg yolks, butter, lemon juice, white wine, and paprika.

**Hors d'oeuvre**   A French word for *appetizer*.

**Huevos Rancheros**   Corn tortillas covered with fried eggs and salsa. Garnished with fresh chives and sour cream.

**Jícama**   A sweet potato from Mexico.

**Julienne**   Any vegetable that is cut in a matchlike fashion, such as julienne of carrots.

**Kimchee**   A spicy condiment made from fermented vegetables. Used in Korean cooking.

**Kirsch**   A liqueur that is distilled from fermented cherries. Used in desserts for extra flavor.

**Lasagna**   An Italian dish made with pasta, tomato sauce, and various cheeses.

**Linguica**   A spicy Portuguese sausage.

**London Broil**   Marinated flank steak that is cut across the grain.

**Lyonnaise**   Sautéed, sliced potatoes with onions.

**Macédoine**   A mixture of various fruits or vegetables.

**Maître d'Hôtel**   Butter that contains lemon juice, white wine, parsley, and Worcestershire sauce.

**Marmite**   A clear broth served in an earthenware pot that usually has beef and vegetables in it.

**Medaillon** or **Medallion**   Small cut of pork tenderloin or beef.

**Milanaise**   In the style of Milan cookery. A dish that is dipped in egg, bread crumbs, and cheese, and then fried.

**Minestrone**   A rich Italian vegetable and pasta soup.

**Mirepoix**   A combination of onion, carrots, and celery. Used as a basis for sauces.

**Mornay**   A white cream sauce to which cheese has been added.

**Mousseline**   Hollandaise sauce to which whipped cream has been added.

**Napoleon**   A rectangular puff pastry filled with cream.

**Newburg**   A cream sauce to which egg yolk and sherry have been added.

**Normande**   A sauce made from white wine and cream, served with fish.

**O'Brien Potatoes**   Potatoes that are diced and cooked, then sautéed with green peppers, pimientos, and bacon.

**Osso Buco**   Braised veal shank served with risotto.

**Panko**   Japanese bread crumbs used for fried foods.

**Pâté**   A mixture of meat, usually pork, fish, or game. Baked in an earthenware dish or in a pastry case, usually served cold.

**Pesto**   A sauce consisting of pine nuts, garlic, basil, olive oil, and cheese. Originated in Italy.

**Petit Four**   A small cake or pastry.

**Pierogi**   Polish dumplings filled with pork, cabbage, potatoes, onions, and seasonings.

**Primavera**   Fresh vegetables usually served with pasta.

**Prosciutto**   Literally means ham in Italian. Often served with melon and figs as an appetizer.

**Provençale**   Cooking style of the southern province of France, consisting of tomato sauce, garlic, herbs, and olives.

**Quesadilla**   A tortilla filled with vegetables, meat, refried beans, or cheese.

**Quiche**   A pie filled with eggs, cream, vegetables, or meat.

**Radicchio**   Referred to as Italian chicory. Used mostly in salads.

**Ragout**   Brown or white stew usually with a small amount of red sauce.

**Ragu**   A hearty meat sauce consisting of vegetables, white wine, and various seasonings. Often served with pasta.

**Ravioli**   An Italian pasta dish filled with meat, vegatables, or cheese.

**Rémoulade**   A cold sauce made with mayonnaise, mustard, gherkins, capers, and sometimes anchovies.

**Robert**   A sauce made with onions, mustard, white wine, and vinegar. Often served with roast pork.

**Roulade**   Rolled meat or fish stuffed with vegetables.

**Salsa**   A sauce consisting of green chiles, green tomatoes, onions, and cilantro. Used as a dip and in cooked dishes.

**Serviche**   Marinated fish served raw.

**Shallot**   A member of the onion family.

**Shish Kabob** or **Shish Kebab**   Beef, lamb, chicken, or fish roasted on a skewer, served with tomatoes, green peppers, onions, and mushrooms.

**Smitane**   A sauce made of white wine and sour cream.

**Sole**   A flat, delicate-tasting fish. The true sole, English Dover sole, is found only in Europe.

**Spumoni**   Ice cream that is flavored with fruit. Originated in Italy.

**Steak Tartare**   Tenderloin that has been minced, seasoned, and reshaped. It is often served with raw onions, capers, and egg yolk. The meat is served raw.

**Tabbouleh**   Bulghur wheat combined with onions, tomatoes, parsley, mint, lemon juice, olive oil, and various seasonings.

**Tapenade**   A condiment consisting of anchovies, olives, lemon juice, olive oil, and seasonings.

**Tiramisu**   Lady fingers or sponge cake soaked in Marsala wine and coffee. Layered with mascarpone cheese and shaved chocolate.

**Tomatillo**   A green tomato from Mexico.

**Torte**   A rich cake layered with cream.

**Tortilla**   A flat bread made from wheat or corn flour. Used for tacos and burritos.

**Tostada**   A fried tortilla topped with either beef, chicken, or cheese. Also served with tomato, lettuce, guacamole, and sour cream.

**Tournedos**   A small filet from the thickest part of the tenderloin.

**Truffe** or **Truffle**   A black fungus similar to a mushroom that grows underground. It is used as a garnish, for the most part, because of its high price.

**Turbot**   A flat fish that is similar to halibut.

**Vacherin**   A dessert that has meringue and whipped cream on a pastry.

**Velouté**   A creamy white sauce that is made from white stock.

**Vermicelli**   A thin pasta used in consommé.

**Vichyssoise**   A soup from France made of potatoes or leeks.

**Vinaigrette**   A cold dressing made of oil and vinegar, herbs, spices, and lemon juice.

**Vol-au-Vent**   A puff pastry filled with an array of creamed foods.

**Wiener Schnitzel**   Breaded veal cutlets garnished with anchovies, capers, lemon slices, and hard boiled eggs.

**Yorkshire Pudding**   Popover pastry usually served with roast beef. Originated in England.

# MEASUREMENTS

## General Equivalents

| | |
|---|---|
| 16 tablespoons | = 1 cup |
| 1 cup (standard measure) | = ½ pint (8 fluid ounces) |
| 2 cups | = 1 pint |
| 16 ounces | = 1 pound |
| 3 quarts (dry) | = 1 peck |
| 4 pecks | = 1 bushel |
| 32 ounces | = 1 fluid quart |
| 128 ounces = 8 pounds | = 1 fluid gallon |
| 1 No. 10 can | = 13 cups |
| 1 pound margarine | = 2 cups |
| 1 pound flour | = 4 cups |

## Decimal Equivalents of Fractions Used in Cooking

¼ = 0.25    ⅔ = 0.66

⅓ = 0.33    ¾ = 0.75

½ = 0.5

The abbreviation beside the fraction tells what unit of measure to use.

# A PRACTICAL GUIDE
# TO THE NUTRITION LABELING LAWS
# FOR THE RESTAURANT INDUSTRY

## *Foodservice Operations: Making Nutrient Content Claims*

ALTHOUGH restaurant food is generally exempted from nutrition labeling requirements, nutrient claims made by restaurateurs are regulated under NLEA (The Nutrition Labeling and Education Act of 1990). A nutrient content claim is a word or phrase used to describe the level of a nutrient in a particular food or dish. There are three types of claims described in the following section. If you make one of these types of claims in advertising, on promotional materials or on a menu, that food item must meet the specific FDA definition.

## Absolute Claims

An absolute claim is a statement made about the exact amount or range of a nutrient in a food. "Low fat" and "calorie free" are examples of absolute claims. Definitions of these terms are not required to appear in print, in the ad, on the menu or promotional materials, but the food must meet the specific criteria.

---

This guide was prepared as a member service by Donna Shields, MS, RD, for the National Restaurant Association.

# Relative or Comparative Claims

A relative or comparative claim is a statement that compares the amount of a nutrient in a food with the amount of that nutrient in a reference food. Claims such as "light," "reduced," and "less" are examples of relative claims.

A reference food may be the restaurant's regular product, or another restaurant's product, that has been offered for sale to the public on a regular basis for a substantial period of time. Nutrient values for a reference food may also be derived from a valid database, an average of top national or regional brands, or a market basket norm. A "reduced" claim may only be used to compare individual foods that are similar. "More" or "less" claims, however, may be used to compare any foods within the same product category (e.g., potato chips and pretzels).

Definitions of relative claims are not required to appear in print, in the ad, on the menu or promotional materials, but the food must meet the specific criteria. The criteria include a comparison of the two foods, the percentage of reduction and the actual nutrient content of both foods.

# Implied Claims

An implied claim is a statement made that implies that a nutrient is present or absent in a food. Such claims often use an ingredient name that implies the inclusion or absence of a nutrient. "High in oat bran" implies the food is high in fiber, which means the food must meet the criteria for a "high-fiber" claim. There is a fair amount of gray area relating to implied claims, and FDA has determined it will review questions that arise on a case-by-case basis. The context in which a statement is made can alter its meaning. You must use good judgment when writing menu or advertising copy. For example, consider the claim "Made with whole wheat flour." Are you implying that the fiber content of this dish is higher because of the whole wheat flour or are you simply stating an ingredient? This question is open to interpretation.

# Statements that are Not Nutrient Claims

FDA does not consider all statements that describe the content of a food to be nutrient content claims. FDA will examine the context in which the statement appears to determine if a nutrient content claim is implied. For example, if promotional materials highlighted a restaurant's oat bran muffins and the display bore a bright banner with "oat bran" in large, bright letters, the emphasis on "oat bran" probably would cause FDA to view the materials as making an implied "good source" claim for fiber. The rules in this area, however, leave room for interpretation. People, therefore, may reasonably disagree as to whether a particular statement constitutes a nutrient content claim.

Generally, statements that pertain to the inclusion or absence of ingredients having a perceived value are not considered nutrient content claims. For example:

- **Contains no MSG**
- **Contains no milk or milk fat**
- **Made with whole fruit and honey**

Statements in which an ingredient is part of the identity of the food are not considered nutrient content claims. For example:

- **Whole wheat pasta**
- **Multigrain bread**

If you identify such items with a symbol, to denote some nutritional benefit or make other claims, however, you may be making an implied claim and must explain it and meet the appropriate criteria.

# Nutrient Content Claims

All nutrient content claims are based on Reference Amounts of food. Reference Amounts are standardized serving sizes, as determined by FDA, that must be used as the basis for nutrient content claims, as well as health claims. These amounts represent the average and customary amount of a given food typically consumed at one time. The Reference Amounts for foods, main dishes and meals appear in Table F-1, and F-2 (p. 213–220).

You will need to refer to the Reference Amount chart to interpret the following nutrient content claim terms. Working with Reference Amounts means becoming familiar with gram weights of food products, but gram weights are easy to determine with an electronic digital scale. Substantiation for any nutrient content claims must be available, in written form, for customers, upon request.

The following is a list of terms, established by FDA, to be used when making nutrient content claims. The description accompanying each term defines the criteria that a food must meet in order to use the term. As you will see, this is where Reference Amounts come into play. Under wording options, alternatives for some of the terms are also given. Remember: terms that are not defined by FDA may not be used to characterize the level of nutrient content in a food.

## Table F-1. Reference Amounts Customarily Consumed Per Eating Occasion

**BAKERY PRODUCTS:**

Biscuits, croissants, bagels, tortillas, soft bread sticks,
  soft pretzels, corn bread, hush puppiess . . . . . . . . . . . . . . . . . . . . . . . . . . . . . . . . . . . . . .55 g

Breads (excluding sweet quick type), rolls . . . . . . . . . . . . . . . . . . . . . . . . . . . . . . . . . . . . .50 g

Bread sticks—see crackers

Toaster pastries—see coffee cakes

Brownies . . . . . . . . . . . . . . . . . . . . . . . . . . . . . . . . . . . . . . . . . . . . . . . . . . . . . . . . . . . . . . . . .40 g

Cakes; heavy weight (cheese cake; pineapple upside-down cake;
  fruit, nut, and vegetable cakes with more than or equal to 35
  percent of the finished weight as fruit, nuts, or vegetables)[1] . . . . . . . . . . . . . . . .125 g

Cakes, medium weight (chemically leavened cake with or
  without icing or filling except those classified as light
  weight cake; fruit, nut, and vegetable cake with less than
  35 percent of the finished weight as fruit, nuts, or vegetables;
  light weight cake with icing; Boston cream pie; cupcake;
  eclair; cream puff)[2] . . . . . . . . . . . . . . . . . . . . . . . . . . . . . . . . . . . . . . . . . . . . . . . . . . . . .80 g

Cakes, light weight (angel food, chiffon, or sponge cake
  without icing or filling)[3] . . . . . . . . . . . . . . . . . . . . . . . . . . . . . . . . . . . . . . . . . . . . . . . .55 g

Coffee cakes, crumb cakes, doughnuts, Danish, sweet rolls,
  sweet quick type breads, muffins, toaster pastries . . . . . . . . . . . . . . . . . . . . . . . . . . .55 g

Cookies . . . . . . . . . . . . . . . . . . . . . . . . . . . . . . . . . . . . . . . . . . . . . . . . . . . . . . . . . . . . . . . . . .30 g

Crackers that are usually not used as snack, melba toast,
  hard bread sticks, ice cream cones[4] . . . . . . . . . . . . . . . . . . . . . . . . . . . . . . . . . . . . . . .15 g

Crackers that are usually used as snacks . . . . . . . . . . . . . . . . . . . . . . . . . . . . . . . . . . . . . .30 g

Croutons . . . . . . . . . . . . . . . . . . . . . . . . . . . . . . . . . . . . . . . . . . . . . . . . . . . . . . . . . . . . . . . . . .7 g

French toast, pancakes, variety mixes . . . . . . . . . . . . . . . . . . . . . . . .110 g prepared for french
                                                                              toast and pancakes; 40 g
                                                                              dry mix for variety mixes

Grain-based bars with or without filling or coating, e.g.,
  breakfast bars, granola bars, rice cereal bars . . . . . . . . . . . . . . . . . . . . . . . . . . . . . . . .40 g

Ice cream cones—see crackers

Pies, cobblers, fruit crisps, turnovers, other pastries . . . . . . . . . . . . . . . . . . . . . . . . . .125 g

Pie crust . . . . . . . . . . . . . . . . . . . . . . . . . . . . . . . . . . . . . . . . . . . . . .1/6 of 8 inch crust;
                                                                              1/8 of 9 inch crust

Pizza crust . . . . . . . . . . . . . . . . . . . . . . . . . . . . . . . . . . . . . . . . . . . . . . . . . . . . . . . . . . . . . . .55 g

Taco shells, hard . . . . . . . . . . . . . . . . . . . . . . . . . . . . . . . . . . . . . . . . . . . . . . . . . . . . . . . . . .30 g

Waffles . . . . . . . . . . . . . . . . . . . . . . . . . . . . . . . . . . . . . . . . . . . . . . . . . . . . . . . . . . . . . . . . . . .85 g

**BEVERAGES:**

Carbonated and noncarbonated beverages, wine coolers, water . . . . . . . . . . . . . . . . . . . .240 mL

Coffee or tea, flavored and sweetened . . . . . . . . . . . . . . . . . . . . . . . . . . . . . . .240 mL prepared

*(Continues)*

**Table F-1.    Reference Amounts Customarily Consumed Per Eating Occasion (Continued)**

## CEREALS AND OTHER GRAIN PRODUCTS:

Breakfast cereals (hot cereal type), hominy grits . . . . . . . . . . . . . . . . . .1 cup prepared; 40 g plain dry cereal; 55 g flavored, sweetened cereal

Breakfast cereals, ready-to-eat, weighing less than 20 g per cup,
e.g., plain puffed cereal grains . . . . . . . . . . . . . . . . . . . . . . . . . . . . . . . . .15 g

Breakfast cereals, ready-to-eat weighing 20 g or more but less
than 43 g per cup; high fiber cereals containing 28 g or
more of fiber per 100 g . . . . . . . . . . . . . . . . . . . . . . . . . . . . . . . . . . . . . . .30 g

Breakfast cereals, ready-to-eat, weighing 43 g or more per
cup; biscuit types . . . . . . . . . . . . . . . . . . . . . . . . . . . . . . . . . . . . . . . . . . . .55 g

Bran or wheat germ . . . . . . . . . . . . . . . . . . . . . . . . . . . . . . . . . . . . . . . . . . . . . .15 g

Flours or corn meal . . . . . . . . . . . . . . . . . . . . . . . . . . . . . . . . . . . . . . . . . . . . . .30 g

Grains, e.g., rice, barley, plain . . . . . . . . . . . . . . . . . . . . . . .140 g prepared; 45 g dry

Pastas, plain . . . . . . . . . . . . . . . . . . . . . . . . . . . . . . . . . . . . . . .140 g prepared; 55 g dry

Pastas, dry, ready-to-eat, e.g., fried canned chow mein noodles . . . . . . . . . . . . .25 g

Starches, e.g., cornstarch, potato starch, tapioca, etc. . . . . . . . . . . . . . . . . . . . .10 g

Stuffing . . . . . . . . . . . . . . . . . . . . . . . . . . . . . . . . . . . . . . . . . . . . . . . . . . . . . . . .100 g

## DAIRY PRODUCTS AND SUBSTITUTES:

Cheese, cottage . . . . . . . . . . . . . . . . . . . . . . . . . . . . . . . . . . . . . . . . . . . . . . . . .110 g

Cheese use primarily as ingredient, e.g., dry cottage cheese, ricotta cheese . . . . . . . . . . . . . . . . . . .55 g

Cheese, grated hard, e.g., Parmesan, Romano . . . . . . . . . . . . . . . . . . . . . . . . . . .5 g

Cheese, all others except those listed as separate categories—
includes cream cheese and cheese spread . . . . . . . . . . . . . . . . . . . . . . . . . . .30 g

Cheese sauce—see sauce category
Cream or cream substitute, fluid . . . . . . . . . . . . . . . . . . . . . . . . . . . . . . . . . . .15 mL

Cream or cream substitutes, powder . . . . . . . . . . . . . . . . . . . . . . . . . . . . . . . . . .2 g

Cream, half & half . . . . . . . . . . . . . . . . . . . . . . . . . . . . . . . . . . . . . . . . . . . . . .30 mL

Eggnog . . . . . . . . . . . . . . . . . . . . . . . . . . . . . . . . . . . . . . . . . . . . . . . . . . . . . .120 mL

Milk, condensed, undiluted . . . . . . . . . . . . . . . . . . . . . . . . . . . . . . . . . . . . . . .30 mL

Milk, evaporated, undiluted . . . . . . . . . . . . . . . . . . . . . . . . . . . . . . . . . . . . . . .30 mL

Milk, milk-based drinks, e.g., instant breakfast, meal replacement, cocoa . . . . . . . . . . . . .240 mL

Shakes or shake substitutes, e.g., dairy shake mixes, fruit frost mixes . . . . . . . . . . . . . . . .240 mL

Sour cream . . . . . . . . . . . . . . . . . . . . . . . . . . . . . . . . . . . . . . . . . . . . . . . . . . . . .30 g

Yogurt . . . . . . . . . . . . . . . . . . . . . . . . . . . . . . . . . . . . . . . . . . . . . . . . . . . . . . . .225 g

## DESSERTS:

Ice cream, ice milk, frozen yogurt, sherbet:
all types, bulk and novelties

(e.g. bars, sandwiches, cones) . . . . . . . . . . . . . . . . . . . . . . . . . . . . . .1/2 cup includes the volume
for coatings and wafers for
the novelty type varieties

Frozen flavored and sweetened ice and pops, frozen fruit
    juices: all types, bulk and novelties (e.g., bars, cups) . . . . . . . . . . . . . . . . . . . . .85 g

Sundae . . . . . . . . . . . . . . . . . . . . . . . . . . . . . . . . . . . . . . . . . . . . . . . . . . . . .1 cup

Custards, gelatin or pudding . . . . . . . . . . . . . . . . . . . . . . . . . . . . . . . . . . . .1/2 cup

## DESSERT TOPPINGS AND FILLINGS:

Cake frostings or icings . . . . . . . . . . . . . . . . . . . . . . . . . . . . . . . . . . . . . . . .35 g

Other dessert toppings, e.g, fruits, syrups, spreads, marshmallow
    cream, nuts, dairy and nondairy whipped toppings . . . . . . . . . . . . . . . . . . . . .2 tbsp.

Pie fillings . . . . . . . . . . . . . . . . . . . . . . . . . . . . . . . . . . . . . . . . . . . . . . . . . .85 g

## EGG AND EGG SUBSTITUTES:

Egg mixtures, e.g., egg foo young, scrambled eggs, omelets . . . . . . . . . . . . . . . . .110 g

Eggs (all sizes)[4] . . . . . . . . . . . . . . . . . . . . . . . . . . . . . . . . . . . . . . . . . . . .50 g

Egg substitutes . . . . . . . . . . . . . . . . . . . . . . . . . . . . . . .An amount to make 1 large
(50 g) egg

## FATS AND OILS:

Butter, margarine, oil, shortening . . . . . . . . . . . . . . . . . . . . . . . . . . . . . . . . .1 tbsp.

Butter replacement, powder . . . . . . . . . . . . . . . . . . . . . . . . . . . . . . . . . . . . .2 g

Dressings for salads . . . . . . . . . . . . . . . . . . . . . . . . . . . . . . . . . . . . . . . . . . .30 g

Mayonnaise, sandwich spreads, mayonnaise-type dressings . . . . . . . . . . . . . . . . . .15 g

Spray types . . . . . . . . . . . . . . . . . . . . . . . . . . . . . . . . . . . . . . . . . . . . . . . . .0.25 g

## FISH, SHELLFISH, GAME MEATS[5], AND MEAT OR POULTRY SUBSTITUTES:

Bacon substitutes, canned anchovies,[6] anchovy pastes, caviar . . . . . . . . . . . . . . . . .15 g

Dried, e.g., jerky . . . . . . . . . . . . . . . . . . . . . . . . . . . . . . . . . . . . . . . . . . . . .30 g

Entrees with sauce, e.g., fish with cream sauce,
    shrimp with lobster sauce . . . . . . . . . . . . . . . . . . . . . . . . . . . . . . . . .140 g cooked

Entrees without sauce, e.g., plain or fried fish and
    shellfish, fish and shellfish cake . . . . . . . . . . . . . . . . . . . .85 g cooked; 110 g uncooked[7]

Fish, shellfish or game meat,[5] canned[6] . . . . . . . . . . . . . . . . . . . . . . . . . . . . . .55 g

Substitute for luncheon meat, meat spreads, Canadian bacon,
    sausages and frankfurters . . . . . . . . . . . . . . . . . . . . . . . . . . . . . . . . . . . .55 g

Smoked or pickled fish,[6] shellfish, or game meat,[5] fish or shellfish spread . . . . . . . . . . . . . . .55 g

Substitutes for bacon bits—see Miscellaneous Category

## FRUITS AND FRUIT JUICES:

Candied or pickled[6] . . . . . . . . . . . . . . . . . . . . . . . . . . . . . . . . . . . . . . . . . . .30 g

Dehydrated fruits—see Snacks Category

*(Continues)*

**Table F-1.    Reference Amounts Customarily Consumed Per Eating Occasion (Continued)**

Dried . . . . . . . . . . . . . . . . . . . . . . . . . . . . . . . . . . . . . . . . . . . . . . . . . . . .40 g

Fruits for garnish or flavor, e.g., maraschino cherries[6] . . . . . . . . . . . . . . . . . . . . .4 g

Fruit relishes, e.g., cranberry sauce, cranberry relish . . . . . . . . . . . . . . . . . . . .70 g

Fruits used primarily as ingredients, avocado[8] . . . . . . . . . . . . . . . . . . . . . . . . .30 g

Fruits used primarily as ingredients, others (cranberries, lemon, lime)[8] . . . . . . . . . . .55 g

Watermelon . . . . . . . . . . . . . . . . . . . . . . . . . . . . . . . . . . . . . . . . . . . . . .280 g

All other fruits (except those listed as separate categories), fresh, canned, or frozen[8] . . . . . .140 g

Juices, nectars, fruit drinks . . . . . . . . . . . . . . . . . . . . . . . . . . . . . . . . . . . .240 mL

Juices used as ingredients, e.g., lemon juice, lime juice . . . . . . . . . . . . . . . . . . .5 mL

## LEGUMES:

Bean cake (tofu),[6] tempeh . . . . . . . . . . . . . . . . . . . . . . . . . . . . . . . . . . . .85 g

Beans, plain or in sauce . . . . . . . . . . . . . . . . . . . . . . . . . . .130 g for beans in sauce or
canned in liquid

## MISCELLANEOUS CATEGORY:

Baking powder, baking soda, pectin . . . . . . . . . . . . . . . . . . . . . . . . . . . . . . . . .1 g

Baking decorations, e.g., colored sugars and sprinkles for cookies,
cake decorations . . . . . . . . . . . . . . . . . . . . . . .1/4 tsp or 4 g if not measurable by teaspoon

Batter mixes, bread crumbs . . . . . . . . . . . . . . . . . . . . . . . . . . . . . . . . . . . .30 g

Cooking wine . . . . . . . . . . . . . . . . . . . . . . . . . . . . . . . . . . . . . . . . . . . .30 mL

Drink mixers (without alcohol) . . . . . . . . . . . . . . . . . . . . . . . .Amount to make 240 mL
drink (without ice)

Chewing gum[4] . . . . . . . . . . . . . . . . . . . . . . . . . . . . . . . . . . . . . . . . . . . .3 g

Meat, poultry and fish coating mixes, dry; seasoning
mixes, dry, e.g., chili seasoning mixes, pasta salad seasoning mixes . . . . . . .Amount to make one
Reference Amount of
final dish

Salad and potato toppers, e.g., salad crunchies, salad crispins,
substitutes for bacon bits . . . . . . . . . . . . . . . . . . . . . . . . . . . . . . . . . . . . .7 g

Salt, salt substitutes, seasoning salts (e.g., garlic salt) . . . . . . . . . . . . . . . . . . . . .1 g

Spices, herbs (other than dietary substitutes) . . . . . . . . . . . . . . . . . .1/4 tsp. or 0.5 g if not
measurable by teaspoon

## MIXED DISHES:

Measurable with cup, e.g., casseroles, hash, macaroni and cheese,
pot pies, spaghetti with sauce, stews, etc. . . . . . . . . . . . . . . . . . . . . . . . . . . . .1 cup

Not measurable with cup, e.g., burritos, egg rolls, enchiladas,
pizza, pizza rolls, quiche, all types of sandwiches . . . . . . . . . . . . . . .140 g, add 55 g for products with gravy or sauce
topping, e.g., enchilada
with cheese sauce, crepe
with white sauce[9]

## NUTS AND SEEDS:

Nuts, seeds, and mixtures, all types: sliced, chopped, slivered,
and whole . . . . . . . . . . . . . . . . . . . . . . . . . . . . . . . . . . . . . . . . . . . . . .30 g

Nut and seed butters, pastes, or creams . . . . . . . . . . . . . . . . . . . . . . . . .2 tbsp.

Coconut, nut and seed flours . . . . . . . . . . . . . . . . . . . . . . . . . . . . . . . .15 g

## POTATOES AND SWEET POTATOES/YAMS:

French fries, hash browns, skins, or pancakes . . . . . . . . . . . . . . . . . . . . .70 g prepared, 85 g for
frozen unprepared
french fries

Mashed, candied, stuffed, or with sauce . . . . . . . . . . . . . . . . . . . . . . . . . . . .140 g

Plain, fresh, canned, or frozen . . . . . . . . . . . . . . . . . . . . . . . . . . . . .110 g for fresh or frozen;
160 g for canned in liquid

## SALADS:

Gelatin Salad . . . . . . . . . . . . . . . . . . . . . . . . . . . . . . . . . . . . . . . . . . .120 g

Pasta or potato salad . . . . . . . . . . . . . . . . . . . . . . . . . . . . . . . . . . . . . .140 g

All other salads, e.g., egg, fish, shellfish, bean, fruit, or
vegetable salads . . . . . . . . . . . . . . . . . . . . . . . . . . . . . . . . . . . . . . . . .100 g

## SAUCES, DIPS, GRAVIES, AND CONDIMENTS:

Barbecue sauce, hollandaise sauce, tartar sauce, other sauces for
dipping (e.g., mustard sauce, sweet and sour sauce), all dips
(e.g., bean dips, dairy-based dips, salsa) . . . . . . . . . . . . . . . . . . . . . . . . .2 tbsp

Major main entree sauces e.g., spaghetti sauce . . . . . . . . . . . . . . . . . . . . . .125 g

Minor main entree sauces, (e.g., pizza sauce, pesto sauce), other
sauces used as toppings (e.g., gravy, white sauce, cheese sauce),
cocktail sauce . . . . . . . . . . . . . . . . . . . . . . . . . . . . . . . . . . . . . . . . . .1/4 cup

Major condiments, e.g., catsup, steak sauce, soy sauce, vinegar,
teriyaki sauce, marinades . . . . . . . . . . . . . . . . . . . . . . . . . . . . . . . . . .1 tbsp

Minor condiments, e.g.; horseradish, hot sauces, mustards,
Worcestershire sauce . . . . . . . . . . . . . . . . . . . . . . . . . . . . . . . . . . . . .1 tsp

## SNACKS:

All varieties, chips, pretzels, popcorns, extruded snacks, fruit-based
snacks (e.g., fruit chips), grain-based snack mixes . . . . . . . . . . . . . . . . . . .30 g

## SOUPS:

All varieties . . . . . . . . . . . . . . . . . . . . . . . . . . . . . . . . . . . . . . . . . . . .245 g

## SUGARS AND SWEETS:

Baking candies (e.g., chips) . . . . . . . . . . . . . . . . . . . . . . . . . . . . . . . . .15 g

Hard candies, breath mints . . . . . . . . . . . . . . . . . . . . . . . . . . . . . . . . . .2 g

*(Continues)*

### Table F-1.  Reference Amounts Customarily Consumed Per Eating Occasion (Continued)

Hard candies, roll-type, mini-size in dispenser packages . . . . . . . . . . . . . . . . . . . . . . . . . .5 g

Hard candies, others . . . . . . . . . . . . . . . . . . . . . . . . . . . . . . . . . . . . . . . . . . . . . . . . . . . . . .15 g

Sugar substitutes . . . . . . . . . . . . . . . . . . . . . . . . . . . . . . . . . . . . . . . . .An amount equivalent
to one reference
amount for sugar in
sweetness

Syrups . . . . . . . . . . . . . . . . . . . . . . . . . . . . . . . . . . . . . . . . . .30 mL for syrups used
primarily as an ingredient
(e.g., light or dark corn
syrup); 60 mL for all others

## VEGETABLES:

Vegetables primarily used for garnish or flavor, e.g., pimento, parsley . . . . . . . . . . . . . . . . . .15 g

Chili pepper, green onion . . . . . . . . . . . . . . . . . . . . . . . . . . . . . . . . . . . . . . . . . . . . . . . .30 g

All other vegetables without sauce: fresh, canned,
or frozen . . . . . . . . . . . . . . . . . . . . . . . . . . . . . . . . . . . . .85 g for fresh or frozen;
95 g for vacuum canned;
130 g for canned in liquid,
cream-style corn, canned or
stewed tomatoes, pumpkin
or winter squash

All other vegetables with sauce: fresh, canned, or frozen . . . . . . . . . . . . . . . . . . . . . . . . . . .110 g

Vegetable juice . . . . . . . . . . . . . . . . . . . . . . . . . . . . . . . . . . . . . . . . . . . . . . . . . . . . .240 mL

Olives[6] . . . . . . . . . . . . . . . . . . . . . . . . . . . . . . . . . . . . . . . . . . . . . . . . . . . . . . . . . . . . .15 g

Pickles, all types[6] . . . . . . . . . . . . . . . . . . . . . . . . . . . . . . . . . . . . . . . . . . . . . . . . . . . . . .30 g

Pickle relishes . . . . . . . . . . . . . . . . . . . . . . . . . . . . . . . . . . . . . . . . . . . . . . . . . . . . . . . .15 g

Vegetable pastes, e.g., tomato paste . . . . . . . . . . . . . . . . . . . . . . . . . . . . . . . . . . . . . . . . . .30 g

Vegetable sauces or purees, e.g., tomato sauce, tomato puree . . . . . . . . . . . . . . . . . . . . . . . .60 g

---

[1] Includes cakes that weigh 10 g or more per cubic inch. [2] Includes cakes that weigh 4 g or more per cubic inch but less than 10 g per cubic inch. [3] Includes cakes that weigh less than 4 g per cubic inch. [4] Label serving size for ice cream cones and eggs of all sizes will be one unit. Label serving size of all chewing gums that weigh more than the reference amount that can reasonably be consumed at a single-eating occasion will be one unit. [5] Animal products not covered under the Federal Meat Inspection Act or the Poultry Products Inspection Act, such as flesh products from deer, bison, rabbit, quail, wild turkey, geese, ostrich, etc. [6] If packed or canned in liquid, the reference amount is for the drained solids, except for products in which both the solids and liquids are customarily consumed (e.g., canned chopped clam in juice.) [7] The reference amount for the uncooked form does not apply to raw fish in $101.45 or to single-ingredient products that consist of fish or game meat as provided for in $101.9(b)(11). [8] For raw fruit, vegetables, and fish, manufacturers should follow the label statement for the serving size specified in Appendices A and B to the regulation entitled "Food Labeling: Guidelines for Voluntary Nutrition Labeling and the Identification of the 20 Most Frequently Consumed Raw Fruits, Vegetables, and Fish; Definition of Substantial Compliance; Correction" (56 FR 60880 as amended 57 FR 8174, March 6, 1992). [9] Pizza sauce is part of the pizza and is not considered to be sauce topping.

## Table F-2. Reference Amount Criteria for Main Dish and Meals

| MAIN DISH | MEALS |
|---|---|
| • Weighs at least 6 oz. per serving | • Weighs at least 10 oz. per serving |
| • Contains no less than 40 grams each of at least 2 different foods from at least 2 specified food groups | • Contains no less than 40 grams each of at least 3 different foods from at least 2 specified food groups |
| • Represented as a main dish | • Represented as a breakfast, lunch, dinner or meal |

### SPECIFIED FOOD GROUPS INCLUDE:

1) bread, cereal, rice and pasta group

2) fruit and vegetable group

3) milk, yogurt, and cheese group

4) meat, poultry, fish, dry beans, eggs and nuts group

Gravies, condiments, pickles and similar foods do not qualify as food group requirements. Sauces may meet a requirement if they are from one of the food groups, i.e., a fruit sauce that provides at least 40 grams of fruit per serving.

### DAILY VALUES

The amount of nutrients recommended for a 2000 calorie diet.

| Nutrient | Daily Value |
|---|---|
| **Total Fat** | .65 grams (g) |
| **Saturated Fat** | .20 g |
| **Cholesterol** | .300 milligrams (mg) |
| **Sodium** | .2400 mg |
| Potassium | .3500 mg |
| **Total Carbohydrate** | .300 g |
| **Dietary Fiber** | .25 g |
| **Protein** | .50 g |
| **Vitamin A** | .5000 International Units (IU) |
| **Vitamin C** | .60 mg |
| **Calcium** | .1000 mg |
| **Iron** | .18 mg |
| Vitamin D | .400 IU |
| Vitamin E | .30 IU |
| Thiamin | .1.5 mg |
| Riboflavin | .1.7 mg |
| Niacin | .20 mg |
| Vitamin B6 | .2 mg |
| Folate | .4 micrograms (mcg) |

*(Continues)*

**Table F-2. Reference Amount Criteria for Main Dish and Meals (Continued)**

Biotin . . . . . . . . . . . . . . . . . . . . . . . . . . . . . . . . . . . . . . . . . . . . . . . . . . .3 mg
Pantothenic Acid . . . . . . . . . . . . . . . . . . . . . . . . . . . . . . . . . . . . . . . . . .10 mg
Phosphorous . . . . . . . . . . . . . . . . . . . . . . . . . . . . . . . . . . . . . . . . . . .1000 mg
Iodine . . . . . . . . . . . . . . . . . . . . . . . . . . . . . . . . . . . . . . . . . . . . . . . .150 mcg
Magnesium . . . . . . . . . . . . . . . . . . . . . . . . . . . . . . . . . . . . . . . . . . . .400 mg
Zinc . . . . . . . . . . . . . . . . . . . . . . . . . . . . . . . . . . . . . . . . . . . . . . . . . . .15 mg
Copper . . . . . . . . . . . . . . . . . . . . . . . . . . . . . . . . . . . . . . . . . . . . . . . . .2 mg

Mandatory nutrients for nutrition labeling are those noted in **boldface**.

# Calories

*Free*   Less than 5 calories per Reference Amount.

**Wording Options:**
Free of Calories
No Calories
Zero Calories
Without Calories
Trivial Source of Calories

*Low*   40 calories or less per Reference Amount when Reference Amount is 30 grams or more, or more than 2 tablespoons.

Food with Reference Amounts of 30 grams or less or 2 tablespoons or less, such as olives, croutons, grated cheese, can be called "low calorie" only if they contain 40 calories or less per 50 grams. This prevents a "low-calorie" claim being based on a small amount of food.

For main-dish items and meals, 120 calories or less per 100 grams. (See Table F-2, pp. 219–220)

**Wording Options:**
Low in Calories
Low Source of Calories
Few Calories
Contains a Small Amount of Calories

*Reduced*   Minimum of 25 percent fewer calories per Reference Amount.

For main-dish items and meals, minimum of 25 percent fewer calories per 100 grams.

This claim may not be made if the food to which comparison is being made meets the criteria for "low calorie."

*Example:* Reduced calorie blueberry coffee cake, with 25 percent fewer calories than a standard blueberry coffee cake recipe. Calorie content has been reduced from 200 to 150 calories per serving.

**Wording Options:**
Lower Calorie
Fewer Calories
Calorie Reduced

**Light/Lite**    If food derives less than 50 percent of its calories from fat, one-third fewer calories or 50 percent less fat per Reference Amount. If food derives greater than 50 percent or more of its calories from fat, 50 percent less fat per Reference Amount.

*Example:* Our lite rice pudding has 100 calories per serving compared to a standard rice pudding recipe with 150 calories.

For main-dish items and meals, meet the requirements for low calorie or low fat and identify nature of the claim.

*Example:* A lite chicken stir fry with brown rice, a low calorie meal. (See definition of low calorie meal.)

The words "light" or "lite" may be used for other descriptions, such as "Lite Bites" referring to smaller portion sizes. If so, explanation must appear with, or in close proximity to, the statement.

**Alternative Usage:**
Light in Color
Light in Texture
Lightly Flavored
Light Bites (smaller portion sizes)
Light Corn Syrup (statement of identity)

# Fat

**Free**    Less than 0.5 grams of fat per Reference Amount and per serving.

For main-dish items and meals, less than 0.5 grams of fat per serving size.

Consistent with FDA's labeling requirements for packaged foods, restaurateurs should be prepared to identify on request any ingredient that adds a trivial amount of fat to the food, main dish, or meal that is the subject of the claim.

**Wording Options:**
Free of Fat
Nonfat
No Fat
Zero Fat
Without Fat
Trivial Source of Fat
Negligible Source of Fat

*Low*  3 grams of fat or less per Reference Amount when Reference Amount is greater than 30 grams, or more than 2 tablespoons.

Foods with Reference Amounts of 30 grams or less or 2 tablespoons or less, such as olives, croutons, grated cheese, can be called "low fat" only if they contain 3 grams of fat or less per Reference Amount and per 50 grams. This prevents "low fat" claims from being based on a small amount of food.

For main-dish items and meals, must contain 3 grams of fat or less per 100 grams and not more than 30 percent of calories from fat.

**Wording Options:**
Low in Fat
Little Fat
Low Source of Fat
Contains a Small Amount of Fat

*Reduced*  Minimum of 25 percent less fat per Reference Amount.

For main-dish items and meals, minimum of 25 percent less fat per 100 grams.

This claim may not be made if the food to which it is being compared meets the criteria for "low fat."

*Example:* Reduced fat chocolate cake has 30 percent less fat than a standard chocolate cake recipe. Fat content has been reduced from 10 grams to 7 grams.

**Wording Options:**
Lower in Fat
Lower Fat
Less Fat

Fat Reduced
Reduced in Fat

**Light/Lite**  If food derives greater than 50 percent or more of its calories from fat, 50 percent less fat per Reference Amount. If the food derives less than 50 percent of its calories from fat, 50 percent less fat or one-third fewer calories per Reference Amount.

*Example:* This lite blue cheese dressing has 50 percent less fat than a standard blue cheese dressing recipe. Fat has been reduced from 10 grams to 5 grams per serving.

# Saturated Fat

**Free**  Less than 0.5 grams of saturated fat and less than 0.5 grams trans fatty acid per Reference Amount and per serving.

For main-dish items and meals, less than 0.5 grams of saturated fat and less than 0.5 grams trans fatty acid per serving.

Consistent with FDA's labeling requirements for packaged foods, restaurateurs should be prepared to identify on request any ingredient that adds a trivial amount of saturated fat to the food, main dish, or meal that is the subject of the claim.

**Wording Options:**
No Saturated Fat
Zero Saturated Fat
Without Saturated Fat
Free of Saturated Fat

**Low**  1 gram of saturated fat or less per Reference Amount and no more than 15 percent of calories from saturated fat.

For main-dish items and meals, must contain 1 gram of saturated fat or less per 100 grams and less than 10 percent of calories from saturated fat.

**Wording Options:**
Low in Saturated Fat
Low Source of Saturated Fat
A Little Saturated Fat
Contains a Small Amount of Saturated Fat

**Reduced**  Minimum of 25 percent less saturated fat per Reference Amount.

For main-dish items and meals, minimum of 25 percent less saturated fat per 100 grams.

This claim may not be made if the food to which it is being compared meets the definition of "low saturated fat."

*Example:* This Garden Omelet is lower in saturated fat than a standard vegetable omelet receipe. Saturated fat has been reduced 50 percent from 6 grams to 3 grams.

**Wording Options:**
Less Saturated Fat
Lowered Saturated Fat
Reduced in Saturated Fat
Lowered in Saturated Fat

# Cholesterol

**Free**  Less than 2 milligrams of cholesterol per Reference Amount and per serving and 2 grams or less of saturated fat per Reference Amount.

For main-dish items and meals, contains less than 2 milligrams of cholesterol and 2 grams or less of saturated fat per serving.

If the total fat content of a food, main dish, or meal exceeds the following levels when making a cholesterol-free claim, you must declare the total amount of fat next to the claim.

Per Reference Amount

Food = more than 13 grams per serving
Main dish = more than 19.5 grams
Meal = more than 26 grams

Consistent with FDA's labeling requirements for packaged foods, restaurateurs should be prepared to identify on request any ingredients that add a trivial amount of cholesterol to the food, main dish, or meal that is the subject of the claim.

*Example:* Cholesterol-free French fries. Contains _____ grams of fat per serving. (If potatoes are fried in a vegetable oil, they are still a fairly high fat food. If your particular finished product contains more than 13 grams of fat per Reference Amount, you must declare the fat content in grams.) This type of regulation guards against customers being misled into thinking "cholesterol free" is synonymous with low fat.

**Wording Options:**
Zero Cholesterol
No Cholesterol
Free of Cholesterol
Without Cholesterol
Trivial Source of Cholesterol

**Low**    20 milligrams or less of cholesterol and 2 grams or less of saturated fat per Reference Amount. Must also contain 13 grams or less of total fat per Reference Amount.

Foods with Reference Amounts less than 30 grams or less than 2 table-spoons, such as croutons or grated cheese, can be called "low cholesterol" only if they meet the above criteria based on the Reference Amount and on a 50 gram basis. This prevents a "low-cholesterol" claim from being based on the small amount of food.

For main-dish items, must contain 20 milligrams of cholesterol or less and 2 grams of saturated fat or less per 100 grams and 19.5 grams or less of total fat per serving.

For meals, must contain 20 milligrams or less of cholesterol and 2 grams or less of saturated fat per 100 grams and 26 grams or less of total fat per serving.

When fat content exceeds the listed criteria, the total fat content in grams must be declared.

*Example:* Low-cholesterol pound cake. This pound cake contains 15 grams of fat per serving. (If a recipe has replaced butter and eggs with vegetable oil, lowering cholesterol but maintaining a fat content higher than 13 grams, then the fat content declaration must be made).

**Wording Options:**
Low in Cholesterol
Little Cholesterol
Contains a Small Amount of Cholesterol

**Reduced**    Minimum of 25 percent less cholesterol and 2 grams or less of saturated fat per Reference Amount and 13 grams or less of total fat per Reference Amount and per serving (and per 50 grams if the Reference Amount is 30 grams or less or 2 tablespoons or less).

For main-dish items, minimum of 25 percent less cholesterol and 2 grams or less of saturated fat per 100 grams and 19.5 grams of total fat or less per serving.

For meals, minimum of 25 percent less cholesterol and 2 grams or less of saturated fat per 100 grams and 26 grams of total fat or less per serving.

When fat exceeds listed criteria, fat content in grams must be declared.

*Example:* This cholesterol-reduced seafood Newburg has 30 percent less cholesterol than a standard seafood Newburg recipe. Cholesterol has been reduced from 80 mg to 55 mg of cholesterol per serving.

**Wording Options:**
Less Cholesterol
Lower Cholesterol
Reduced in Cholesterol
Lower in Cholesterol

# Sodium

**Free**    Less than 5 milligrams of sodium per Reference Amount and per serving.

For main-dish items and meals, must contain less than 5 milligrams of sodium per serving.

Consistent with FDA's labeling requirements for packaged foods, restaurateurs should be prepared to identify on request any ingredients that add a trivial amount of sodium to the food, main dish, or meal that is the subject of the claim.

**Wording Options:**
No Sodium
Zero Sodium
Without Sodium
Free of Sodium
Trivial Source of Sodium

**Low**    140 milligrams or less of sodium per Reference Amount when Reference Amount is 30 grams or more, or more than 2 tablespoons. When Reference Amount is 30 grams or less or 2 tablespoons or less, use same criteria based on Reference Amount and 50 grams.

For main-dish items and meals, must contain 140 milligrams or less of sodium per 100 grams.

*Very Low*    35 milligrams or less of sodium based on above criteria.
**Wording Options:**
Very Low in Sodium

*Reduced*    Minimum of 25 percent less sodium per Reference Amount.

For main-dish items and meals, minimum of 25 percent less sodium per 100 grams.

This claim may not be made if the food to which it is compared meets the requirements for "low sodium."

*Example:* Made with a reduced-sodium soy sauce–50 percent less sodium than regular soy sauce. Sodium content has been reduced from 700 mg to 350 mg per serving.

**Wording Options:**
Reduced in Sodium
Less Sodium
Lower Sodium
Lower in Sodium

*Light in Sodium/Lite in Sodium*    Minimum of 50 percent less sodium per Reference Amount.

For main-dish items and meals, must meet the criteria for low sodium.

*Salt Free*    Meet criteria for sodium free.

*Unsalted No Salt Added Without Added Salt*    These terms are allowed if:

- there is no salt added during preparation
- the food it resembles is normally prepared with salt

If the food does not meet the criteria for a sodium-free food, a declaration statement "not a sodium free food" or "not for the control of sodium in the diet" appears near the claim.

*Lightly Salted*    Minimum of 50 percent less sodium added than is normally used in preparation. If a food does not meet the criteria for a "low-sodium" food, a declaration statement "not a low-sodium food," must appear near the claim.

Remember, salt and sodium are not the same and you cannot use these words interchangeably. *Salt* refers to sodium chloride, which is composed of 40 percent sodium. It is the sodium content of a food that is the basis for nutrient content claims.

---

# Sugar

**Free**    Less than 0.5 grams of sugar per Reference Amount and per serving.

For main-dish items and meals, must have 0.5 grams or less of sugar per serving.

If the food is not labeled "low calorie" or "reduced calorie," a declaration statement "not a low-calorie food" or "not a reduced-calorie food," must appear near the claim.

Consistent with FDA's labeling requirements for packaged foods, restaurateurs should be prepared to identify on request any ingredients that add a trivial amount of sugar to the food, main dish, or meal that is the subject of the claim.

**Wording Options:**
Free of Sugar
Sugarless
No Sugar
Zero Sugar
Without Sugar
Trivial Source of Sugar

**Low**    Cannot be used as a claim.

**Reduced**    Minimum of 25 percent less sugar per Reference Amount.

For main-dish items and meals, minimum of 25 percent less sugar per 100 grams.

*Example:* Our reduced-sugar lemonade has 25 percent less sugar than a standard lemonade recipe. Sugar content has been reduced from 8 to 6 grams per serving.

**Wording Options:**
Reduced in Sugar
Less Sugar

Lower Sugar
Sugar Reduced
Lower in Sugar

**No Added Sugar No Sugar Added Without Added Sugar**    These terms are allowed if:

- no sugar or ingredient that contains added sugar, such as jam, jelly, or concentrated fruit juice has been added during preparation
- the food it resembles normally uses sugar in the preparation

If the food does not meet the criteria for a low-calorie or reduced-calorie food, a declaration statement, "not a low-calorie food" or "not a reduced-calorie food" must appear near the claim.

## Other Nutrient Content Claim Terms You Need To Know

Provides
Contains
Good
Source    To use these terms, the food must contain 10 to 19 percent of the Daily value per Reference Amount. These terms cannot be used to make a total carbohydrate claim. Refer to the Daily Value chart in (Table F-2, p. 219–220) for information concerning the Daily Values for specific nutrients.

If using these terms to describe a main dish or meal, identify the food component that is the subject of the claim.

*Example:* The black-eyed peas in this meal provide fiber.

High
Excellent
Source of
Rich in    To use these terms, the food must contain 20 percent or more of the Daily Value per Reference Amount. Refer to (Table F-2, p. 219–220) for information concerning the Daily Values for specific nutrients.

If using these terms to describe a main dish or meal, identify the food component that is the subject of the claim.

*Example:* The fruit compote in our breakfast special is an excellent source of vitamin C.

| | |
|---|---|
| More<br>Added<br>Enriched<br>Fortified | To use these terms, the food must contain at least 10 percent more of the Daily Value for protein, vitamins, minerals, fiber, or potassium per Reference Amount compared to the reference food. |

*Example:* These apple bran muffins contain 25 percent more fiber than our regular apple muffins. Fiber content of an apple muffin is 3 grams per serving; apple bran muffin is 4 grams per serving.

If using these terms to describe a main dish or meal, use the above criteria based on 100 grams of product.

"Fortified" and "enriched" cannot be used to describe single-ingredient meat or poultry products.

Fiber — To make any fiber claim, the food must meet the criteria for either "good source" or "high." If the food is not "low fat," you must declare the fat content per serving.

Lean — To use this term for meat, poultry, seafood, and game, food must have less than 10 grams of fat, less than 4 grams of saturated fat, and less than 95 milligrams per Reference Amount and 100 grams.

If using this term to describe a main dish or meal, use the above criteria based on 100 grams and serving size.

Extra Lean — To use this term for meat, poultry, seafood, and game, food must have less than 5 grams of fat, less than 2 grams of saturated fat, and less than 95 milligrams of cholesterol per Reference Amount and 100 grams.

If using this term to describe a main dish or meal, use the above criteria based on 100 grams and serving size.

Fresh — When "fresh" is used in a manner that implies that the product is unprocessed, the food must be in its raw state and not have undergone freezing, thermal treatment, or any other form of preservation. Apart from this restriction, terms such as *fresh*, *freshly prepared*, and *freshly baked* should be used in a truthful and non-misleading manner. The use of these terms will be reviewed on a case-by-case basis.

Natural    There is no set definition or regulation governing the use of this word. Current FDA policy, however, treats a claim of "natural" as meaning that nothing artificial or synthetic has been included in the food that would not normally be expected to be in the food.

Healthy    To use this term, a food must be low fat, low in saturated fat, contain 480 milligrams or less of sodium per serving, and provide at least 10 percent of the Daily Value per Reference Amount for protein, fiber, iron, calcium, vitamins A or C. Seafood or game meats must have 5 grams or less of fat and 2 grams or less of saturated fat per Reference Amount and 100 grams, and 95 milligrams or less of cholesterol per 100 grams. The sodium and other nutrient criteria are the same.

Raw fruits or vegetables are exempted from the requirement that "healthy" foods provide at least 10 percent of the Daily Value per Reference Amount for the above-referenced nutrients.

If using this term to describe meals or main dishes, they must be low fat, low in saturated fat, and have 600 milligrams or less of sodium and 90 milligrams or less of cholesterol per serving. A main dish must contain 10 percent of the Daily Value for 2 nutrients, and, for meals, 3 nutrients.

For additional information visit the companion Web-site at www.wiley.com/college/mcvety.

# NATIONAL RESTAURANT ASSOCIATION'S ACCURACY IN MENUS

Accuracy in Menus offers foodservice operators specific guidelines for the proper representation of products served. Truthful representation involves more than just item description. Photographs, graphic illustrations, printed advertisements and verbal depiction by employees must also be accurately presented. This guide outlines some common misrepresentations which can be easily avoided by clarification of terms.

Customer satisfaction and prevention of government intervention depends on accuracy in menu offerings. Care should be taken that all written or spoken words are substantiated with product, invoice or label.

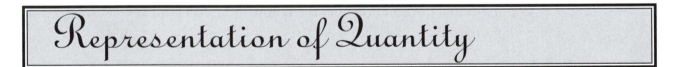

## Representation of Quantity

PROPER operational procedures should preclude any misinterpretations regarding size or quantity.

Steaks are often merchandised by weight. It is generally assumed that declared weight is that prior to cooking and can be safely listed as such. "Jumbo" eggs should mean exactly that, since Jumbo is a recognized egg standard (30 ounces). Similarly, "Petite" and "Super Colossal" are official size descriptions for olives. Check with your suppliers for official standards or purchase a copy of *Specs, The Comprehensive Foodservice Purchasing and Specification Manual*, published by CBI Publishing Company, Inc., Boston, MA.

Although double martinis are obviously twice the size of the normal drink, the use of terms such as "extra-large drink" should be verified. Also, remember the implied meaning of words: a bowl of soup contains more than a cup of soup.

# Representation of Quality

FEDERAL and state standards of quality grades exist for many restaurant products, including meat, poultry, eggs, dairy products, fruits and vegetables. Terminology used to describe grades include Prime, Grade A, Good, No. 1, Choice, Fancy, Grade AA and Extra Standard.

Menu descriptions which use these words may imply certain quality and must be accurate. An item appearing as "Choice sirloin of beef" connotes the use of USDA Choice Grade sirloin of beef. The term "prime rib" is an exception to this rule; prime rib is a long established, accepted description for a cut of beef (the "prime" ribs, the sixth to twelfth ribs) and does not represent the grade quality unless USDA is used in conjunction.

The USDA definition of ground beef is just what the name implies. No extra fat, water, extenders or binders are permitted. The fat limit is 30 percent. Seasonings may be added as long as they are identified. These requirements identify only product ground and packaged in federal- or state-inspected plants.

# Representation of Price

IF YOUR pricing structure includes a cover charge, service charge or gratuity, these must be appropriately brought to your customers' attention. If extra charges are made for requests, such as "all-white meat" or "no-ice drinks," these should also be stated at the time of ordering.

Any coupon or premium promotion restrictions must be clearly defined.

If a price promotion involves a multi-unit company, clearly indicate which units are participating.

# Representation of Brand Names

ANY brand name product that is advertised must be the one served. A registered or copywritten trademark or brand name must not be used generically to refer to a product. Several examples of brand name restaurant products are:

Armour Bacon, Sanka, Log Cabin Syrup, Coca-Cola, Seven-Up, Swift Premium Ham, Pepsi-Cola, Starkist Tuna, Ry-Krisp, Jell-O, Heinz Catsup, Maxwell House Coffee, Folgers Coffee, Kraft Cheese, Tabasco Sauce, Ritz Crackers, Seven and Seven and Miracle Whip.

Your own house brand of a product may be so labeled, even when prepared by an outside source if its manufacturing was to your specification.

# Representation of Product Identification

SUBSTITUTING one food item for another is common. These substitutions may be due to nondelivery, availability, merchandising considerations or price. Menus must accurately specify all subsitutions that are made. Common examples are:

Maple syrup and maple-flavored syrup
Boiled ham and baked ham
Chopped and shaped veal pattie and veal cutlet
Standard ice cream and French-style ice cream
Cod and haddock
Noodles and egg noodles
Light-meat tuna and white-meat tuna
Milk and skim milk
Pure jams and pectin jams
Whipped topping and whipped cream
Turkey and chicken
Hereford beef and Black Angus beef
Peanut oil and corn oil
Beef liver and calves' liver
Ice milk and ice cream
Powdered eggs and fresh eggs
Picnic-style pork shoulder and ham
Ground beef and ground sirloin of beef
Capon and chicken
Cream and half & half
Margarine and butter
Nondairy creamers or whiteners and cream

Pollack and haddock
Flounder and sole
Cheese food and processed cheese
Cream sauce and nondairy cream sauce
Bonito and tuna fish
Roquefort cheese and bleu cheese
Tenderloin tips and diced beef
Mayonnaise and salad dressing

# Representation of Points of Origin

PRODUCTS identified by their points of origin must be authentic. Claims may be substantiated by packaging labels, invoices or other documentation provided by the product's supplier. Mistakes are possible, as sources of supply change and availability of product shifts. The following are common assertions of points of origin:

Lake Superior whitefish
Idaho potatoes
Maine lobster
Imported Swiss cheese
Puget Sound sockeye salmon
Bay scallops
Gulf shrimp
Florida orange juice
Smithfield ham
Wisconsin cheese

Danish bleu cheese
Louisiana frog legs
Florida stone crabs
Chesapeake Bay oysters
Colorado brook trout
Alaskan king crab
Imported ham
Long Island duckling
Colorado beef

There is widespread use of geographic names used in a generic sense to describe methods of preparation or service. Such terminology is commonly understood and accepted by the customer and need not be restricted. Examples are:

Russian dressing
French toast
New England clam chowder
Country fried steak
Irish stew
Danish pastries
German potato salad

Denver sandwich
Country ham
French dip
French fries
Swiss steak
English muffins
Manhattan clam chowder

Russian service                    Swiss cheese
French service

## Representation of Merchandising Terms

EXAGGERATIONS in advertising are acceptable if they do not mislead. "We serve the best gumbo in town" is understood by consumers for what it is—boasting for advertising's sake. However, "We use only the finest beef" implies that USDA Prime beef is used since a standard exists for this product. Similarly, a customer who orders a "mile-high pie" would expect it to be heaped with a fluffy topping. However, to advertise a "foot-long hotdog" and then serve something less would be in error.

Mistakes are possible in properly identifying steak cuts. The National Association of Meat Purveyors' *Meat Buyer's Guide* lists industry standards which should be used.

Since most foodservice sanitation ordinances prohibit the preparation of foods in home facilities, the term "homemade" should not be used when describing menu offerings. "Homestyle," "homemade style," or "our own" are suggested alternatives.

Use of the following terms should be verifiable:

Fresh daily                    Corn-fed porkers
Fresh roasted                  Slept in Chesapeake Bay
Flown in daily                 Finest quality
Kosher meat                    Center-cut ham
Black Angus beef               Own special sauce
Aged steaks                    Low calorie
Milk-fed chicken

## Representation of Means of Preservation

MENUS often list foods which have been canned, chilled, bottled, frozen or dehydrated. If these terms are used to describe menu selections, they must be accurate. Frozen orange juice is not fresh, canned peas are not frozen and bottled applesauce is not canned.

# Representation of Food Preparation

THE means of food preparation is often the determining factor in the customer's selection of a menu entrée. Absolute accuracy is a must. Readily understood terms include:

| | |
|---|---|
| Charcoal-broiled | Roasted |
| Stir-fried | Poached |
| Sautéed | Fried in butter |
| Deep-fried | Mesquite-grilled |
| Baked | Grilled |
| Smoked | Steamed |
| Broiled | Rotisseried |
| Prepared from scratch | Barbecued |

# Representation of Verbal and Visual Presentation

MENUS, wall placards or other advertising which contains a pictorial representation of a meal or platter must not be misleading. Examples of visual misrepresentation include:

- mushroom caps pictured in a sauce when mushroom pieces are actually used

- whole strawberries pictured on a shortcake when sliced strawberries are actually used

- single thick slice of meat pictured when numerous thin slices are actually used

- six shrimp pictured when five shrimp are actually used

- vegetables or other extras pictured with a meal when they are not actually included

- a sesame seed–topped bun pictured when a plain bun is actually used

Servers must also provide accurate descriptions of products. Examples of verbal misrepresentations include:

- the question "Would you like sour cream or butter with your potatoes?" when in fact an imitation sour cream or margarine is served
- the statement "The pies are baked in our kitchen" when in fact the pies were baked elsewhere

# MENU MARKETING CHARACTERISTICS

| MARKETING CHARACTERISTICS | GOOD MENUS | COMMON MISTAKES |
|---|---|---|
| Size | Large enough to read; small enough to handle | Too small; too large |
| Descriptive copy | For each item | Not enough descriptive copy |
| Printing | *No reverse type;* large enough to read; uppercase for headings and subheadings | Headings and subheadings not in uppercase; too small; too much type; too crowded |
| Listing | Items listed in order eaten; profitable items first and last in a column | Clip-ons cover other specials; omission of liquor or desserts; in wrong order; listing entrées on left; low-profit items listed first |
| Cover | Fits décor | Back cover not used |

# MENU-MAKING PRINCIPLES

Before a menu is made, the foodservice operator should analyze:

| | |
|---|---|
| Type of customer | Adequacy of equipment |
| Location | Sales volume |
| Hours of service | Markets |
| Type of operation | Competition |
| Capacity and condition of kitchen | Season |
| Skill and capability of kitchen crew | Occasion |
| Skill and experience of foodservice crew | Cost and profits |

The foodservice operator should know foods and be acquainted with grades, varieties, and differences in these following classifications:

Meats—fresh and processed
Poultry—fresh and frozen
Vegetables—canned, fresh, and frozen
Fruits—fresh, preserved, frozen, and canned
Dairy products—pasteurized and graded
Condiments and relishes
Flour—cereals and mixes
Beverages—coffee, tea, and cocoa
Groceries—spices and seasonings

To satisfy guests, the menu planner must consider:

| | |
|---|---|
| Turnover | Texture |
| Leftovers | Color |
| On-hand supplies | Arrangement |

Variety                    Speed of service
Balance                    Merchandising
Temperature                Weather
Season

The foodservice operator should know how the kitchen operates and be familiar with the personnel and the equipment, and the function of each.

Chef = manager
Sous chef = principal assistant
Saucier = sauce chef
Garde manger = cold chef
Poissonier = seafood chef
Rotisseur = roasting chef
Entremetier = vegetable chef
Boucher = butcher
Potager = soup chef

The foodservice operator must understand the task that each of these individuals performs and not plan a menu that will overwork any one station.

# Bibliography

"A Road Map for 2000," *Restaurant Institution*, 1 January 2000, 66–74.

American Culinary Federation. "Food Pyramid Gets Personal," *National Culinary Review* (June 2005): 8.

American Diabetes Association, www.diabetes.org/home.jsp.

Marion Bennion and Barbara Scheule, *Introductory Foods*, 12th ed. (Upper Saddle River, NJ: Prentice-Hall, 2000).

John Birchfield, *Design and Layout of Foodservice Facilities*, 3rd ed. (John Wiley & Sons, 2003).

Klaus Boehm, Brian Chadwick, and Fay Sharman, *The Taste of France*, (Boston: Houghton Mifflin, 1982).

Paul R. Dittmer and J. Desmond Keefe, *Principles of Food, Beverage, and Labor Cost Controls*, 8th ed. (New York: John Wiley & Sons, 2006).

Karen Eich Drummond, *Nutrition for the Foodservice Professional*, 3rd ed. (Hoboken, NJ: John Wiley & Sons, 2001).

John A. Drysdale and Jennifer Aldrich, *Profitable Menu Planning*, 3rd ed. (Upper Saddle River, NJ: Prentice-Hall, 2003).

Mary Anne Eaton and Janet Rouslin, *Nutrition: A Culinary Approach*. (Dubuque, IA: Kendall/Hunt Publishing Co., 2003).

Felice J. Freyer, "New Food-Labeling Law Could Save Lives," *Providence Journal*, December 29, 2005.

"Food Allergies: New food-labeling requirements" 3 January 2006. www.mayoclinic.com/health/food-allergies.

Wayne Gisslen, *Professional Cooking*, 4th ed. (New York: John Wiley & Sons, 1999).

Mary B. Grosvenor and Lori A. Smolin, *Nutrition Science and Application*, 2nd ed. (Fort Worth, TX: Saunders College Publishing, 1994).

Health and Human Services and the Department of Agriculture. "Dietary Guidelines for Americans 2005" (12 January 2005). www.healthierus.gov/dietaryguidelines or www.mypyramid.gov.

Sharon Tyler Herbst, *Food Lover's Companion*, 3rd ed. (Hauppauge, NY: Barron's Educational Series, 2001).

Sandy Kapoor, *Professional Healthy Cooking*, (New York: John Wiley & Sons, 1995).

Costas Katsigris and Chris Thomas, *Design and Equipment for Restaurants and Foodservice: a Management View*, 2nd ed. (Hobokon, NJ: John Wiley & Sons, 2006).

Edward A. Kazarian, *Food Service Facilities Planning*, 3rd ed. (New York: John Wiley & Sons, 1989).

Lothar A. Kreck, *Menus: Analysis and Planning*, 2nd ed. (New York: Van Nostrand Reinhold, 1984).

Lendal H. Kotschevar and Margaret E. Terrell, *Food Service Planning: Layout and Equipment*, 2nd ed. (New York: John Wiley & Sons, 1985).

Lendal H. Kotschevar and Marcel R. Escoffier, *Management by Menu*, 3rd ed. (Chicago, IL: Educational Foundation of the National Restaurant Association, 1994).

Sarah R. Labensky and Alan M. Hause, *On Cooking Techniques from Expert Chefs*, (Englewood Cliffs, NJ: Prentice-Hall, 1995).

Donald E. Lundberg, *The Restaurant: From Concept to Operation*, 2nd ed. (New York: John Wiley & Sons, 2001).

Paul McVety, Sue Marshall, and Bradley J. Ware, *The Menu and the Cycle of Cost Control*, 3rd ed. (Dubuque, IA: Kendall/Hunt Publishing Co., 2005).

Jack E. Miller and David V. Pavesic, *Menu Pricing and Strategy*, 4th ed. (New York: John Wiley & Sons, 1996).

Jack E. Miller, Lea R. Dopson, David K. Hayes, *Food and Beverage Cost Control*, 3rd ed. ( Hoboken, NJ: John Wiley & Sons, 2005).

Clement Ojugo, *Practical Food and Beverage Cost Control.* (Albany, NY: Delmar, 1999).

Nancy Scanlon, *Marketing by Menu*, 3rd ed. (New York: John Wiley & Sons, 1999).

Arno Schmidt, *Chef's Book of Formulas, Yields, and Sizes*, (New York: John Wiley & Sons, 1990).

Carl Scriven and James Stevens, *Food Equipment Facts*, (New York: John Wiley & Sons, 1982).

Albin G. Seaberg, *Menu Design Merchandising and Marketing*, 4th ed. (New York: John Wiley & Sons, 1991).

Donna Shields, "A Practical Guide to the Nutrition Labeling Laws for the Restaurant Industry, " National Restaurant Association, 1996.

Frances Sizer and Eleanor Whitney, *Nutrition Concepts and Controversies*, 9th ed. (Belmont, CA: Wadsworth, 2000).

*The Sourcebook of Zip Code Demographics*, 10th ed. (New York: CACI Marketing Systems, 1995).

*Tableservice Restaurant Trends*, (Chicago: The National Restaurant Association Research Department 1988).

United States Department of Agriculture and the Oldways Preservation and Exchange Trust, "Food Pyramid" (2005). http://foxnews.webmd.com/content/tools/1/slide_food_pyramid.htm.

Peter E. VanKleek and Hubert E. Visick, *Menu Planning: A Blueprint for Profit* (New York: McGraw-Hill, 1974).

Rande L. Wallace, *Introduction to Professional Foodservice*, (New York: John Wiley & Sons, 1996).

# Index